Events That Changed America in the Twentieth Century

Events That Changed America in the Twentieth Century

edited by
John E. Findling
&
Frank W. Thackeray

THE GREENWOOD PRESS
"EVENTS THAT CHANGED AMERICA" SERIES

GREENWOOD PRESS
Westport, Connecticut • London

Library of Congress Cataloging-in-Publication Data

Events that changed America in the twentieth century / edited by John
    E. Findling & Frank W. Thackeray.
        p.   cm.—(Greenwood Press "Events that changed America"
    series)
    Includes bibliographical references and index.
    ISBN 0–313–29080–6 (alk. paper)
    1.   United States—History—20th century.   I.   Findling, John E.
II.   Thackeray, Frank W.   III.   Series.
E742.E84   1996
973.9—dc20   95–40032

British Library Cataloguing in Publication Data is available.

Library of Congress Catalog Card Number: 95–40032
ISBN: 0–313–29080–6

First published in 1996

Greenwood Press, 88 Post Road West, Westport, CT 06881
An imprint of Greenwood Publishing Group, Inc.

Printed in the United States of America

The paper used in this book complies with the
Permanent Paper Standard issued by the National
Information Standards Organization (Z39.48–1984).

10 9 8 7 6 5 4 3 2

Contents

Illustrations

Preface

This volume, which describes and evaluates the significance of ten of the most important events in the United States during the twentieth century, is the first in a multivolume series intended to acquaint readers with the seminal events of American history. Future volumes will cover the most important events of earlier centuries. A companion series of volumes addresses the global experience, "Events That Changed the World."

Our collective classroom experience provided the inspiration for this project. Having encountered literally thousands of entry-level college students whose knowledge of the history of their country was sadly deficient, we determined to prepare a series of books that would concentrate on the most important events affecting those students (and advanced high school students as well) in the hope that they would better understand their country and how it came to be. Furthermore, we hope these books will stimulate the reader to delve further into the events covered in each volume and to take a greater interest in history in general.

The current volume is designed to serve two purposes. First, the editors have provided an introduction that presents factual material about each event in a clear, concise, chronological order. Second, each introduction is followed by a longer, interpretive essay by a specialist exploring the ramifications of the event under consideration. Each essay concludes with an annotated bibliography of the most important works about the event. The ten chapters are followed by three appendices that provide additional information useful to the reader. Appendix A is a glossary of names, events, organizations, and terms mentioned but not fully explained in the introductions and essays. Appendix B is a timeline of twentieth-century events, and Appendix C is a listing of presidents, vice presidents, and secretaries of state in the twentieth century.

The events covered in this volume were selected on the basis of our combined teaching and research activities. Colleagues and contributors made suggestions as well, and for this we thank them. Of course, another pair of editors might have arrived at a somewhat different list than we did; but we believe that we have assembled a group of events that truly changed America in the twentieth century.

As with all published works, numerous people behind the scenes deserve much of the credit for the final product. Barbara Rader, our editor at Greenwood Publishing Group, has encouraged us from the very beginning. Our student research assistant, Bob Marshall, was helpful at many stages of the project. We are especially grateful to Brigette Colligan, who was always ready to type or retype whatever we asked her to. Various staff members of the Indiana University Southeast (IUS) computer center cheerfully unscrambled disks and turned mysterious word-processing programs into something we could work with. We benefited from funds that IUS provided to hire student research assistants and pay for other costs associated with the project. Special thanks go to Roger and Amy Baylor and Kate O'Connell for making their establishment available to us, enabling us to confer about this project and discuss its many facets with our colleagues and former students in a congenial atmosphere. Among those who helped us make this a better book are John Newman, Sam Sloss, Sheila Anderson, Kimberly Pelle, Rick Kennedy, Jo Ann Waterbury, Brook Dutko, Andrew Trout, and Kathy Nichols. We also wish to thank Lewis L. Gould and Robert A. Divine of the University of Texas and Nicholas Cullather of Indiana University for their assistance in locating authors for some of the essays. And, most important, we thank our authors, whose essays were well-conceived and thoughtful and whose patience when the project seemed to lag was much appreciated.

Finally, we wish to express our appreciation to our spouses, Carol Findling and Kathy Thackeray, and to our children, Jamey Findling and

Alex and Max Thackeray, whose interest in our work and forbearance during its long gestation made it all worthwhile.

John E. Findling
Frank W. Thackeray

Many progressives supported the woman suffrage campaign, but not all Americans shared their feelings. (Reproduced from the Collections of the Library of Congress)

1

Progressivism, 1901–1914

INTRODUCTION

The political movement known as progressivism first entered national politics around 1900 and remained a dominant force until the onset of World War I in Europe in 1914. By 1901, the Progressive platform generally stressed political reform to bring about a greater degree of democracy and citizen participation (including woman suffrage) in government. In addition, Progressives believed that government should control more closely the activities of big business and revise the tax structure by reducing the high tariff rates and imposing an income tax. Some Progressives adopted a social agenda, demanding measures that would improve the quality of life; abolition of child labor and prohibition of alcohol were important issues.

Progressivism sprang from a variety of roots. Much of its ideology came from populism, a rural-dominated movement, which by 1900 was no longer a factor in national politics. The leadership of the Progressive movement, however, came out of an urban reform drive that had flowered in a number of midwestern and eastern cities during the 1890s. Progressive mayors, such as Tom Johnson of Cleveland and Sam "Golden Rule" Jones of Toledo, Ohio, won national acclaim for their successful efforts to divest city government of the corruption of political machines and special interests. Others achieved success at the state level, notably Robert LaFollette of Wisconsin, who later became a U.S. Senator and the leader of a national Progressive movement. Much Progressive publicity came from the pens and typewriters of a group of writers who, by the early 1900s, were publishing articles and books exposing the evils of everything from child labor abuses to corporate monopolism. These writers, whom Theodore Roosevelt came to call "muckrakers," included Lincoln Steffens, whose articles stripped away the secret corruption of city governments, Ida Tarbell, who exposed the ruthless corporate tactics of Standard Oil, and Upton Sinclair, whose popular novels laid bare the horrors of American factory life.

When Theodore Roosevelt became president in 1901 upon the assassination of William McKinley, the nation had, for the first time, a president sympathetic to many of the reform impulses of the previous fifteen years. Roosevelt's record as a New York state legislator, member of the U.S. Civil Service Commission, superintendent of the New York City police, and, finally, governor of New York, reflected his reform-mindedness; and while the loyal Republican never thought of himself as a Progressive while in the White House, he was responsive to the increasing public demand for reform.

In 1902, Roosevelt surprised everyone by ordering his attorney general to enforce the Sherman Anti-Trust Act by filing suit against the Northern Securities Company, a railroad trust by which the banker J. P. Morgan and others attempted to create a monopoly of all the railroads serving the American Northwest. The case eventually reached the Supreme Court, which ruled Northern Securities to be in violation of the Sherman Act and ordered it dissolved. The decision had a great psychological effect on the country, led to the filing of other suits, and gave Roosevelt the nickname "trustbuster."

President Roosevelt extended government regulation over business in other ways as well. For the first time, labor fell under government protection when Roosevelt intervened in the anthracite coal strike (1902) after management refused to negotiate. The president's threat to take over the mines brought both sides to the arbitration table. In 1903, the Elkins Act was passed, strengthening the Interstate Commerce Act (1887), which had ineffectually tried to regulate railroads. The Elkins Act prohibited railroads from charging anything other than their published rates, and the Hepburn Act (1906) significantly increased the authority of the Interstate Commerce Commission, created in the original act, to investigate railroad practices and bring action against those in violation of the law.

In 1906, Congress passed two acts that further increased the government's role in the economy. The Pure Food and Drug Act, a product of public concern with patent medicines of dubious quality, banned the interstate sale of any misbranded or adulterated food or medicine, although it did not deal with the frequently outrageous advertising of these goods. The Meat Inspection Act, a direct result of Upton Sinclair's muckraking novel, *The Jungle,* prohibited the interstate sale of unhealthful meat or meat products and set up a system for inspecting meat and meat-packing plants.

William Howard Taft, Roosevelt's secretary of war and his hand-picked choice to carry on his reform program, easily won the presidential election of 1908. Although lacking Roosevelt's immense energy and public appeal, Taft was successful in continuing Roosevelt's policies in some areas. Taft's attorney general filed twice as many antitrust suits against American businesses as had Roosevelt's. Under Taft, Congress further strengthened the Interstate Commerce Commission and passed the Sixteenth Amendment to the Constitution, legalizing an income tax, and the Seventeenth Amendment, calling for the direct election of U.S. senators (who previously had been chosen by state legislatures). By 1912, both these amendments had been ratified by the necessary number of states.

In other areas, however, Taft sorely disappointed Roosevelt. Although most Progressives favored a lower tariff, Taft's effort in this area, the Payne-Aldrich Tariff (1909), was manipulated by pro-business forces in Congress, so that, in the end, tariff rates were actually raised. A nasty dispute in the Department of the Interior between Richard Ballinger, the secretary of the interior and a Taft appointee, and Gifford Pinchot, the chief forester and a Roosevelt man, ended with Taft's siding with Ballinger and firing Pinchot, a move that Roosevelt interpreted as a sellout to the large timber and mining interests, who, with Ballinger's support, wanted to exploit the resources of protected national forest reserves.

By 1910, Roosevelt was openly criticizing Taft and his policies, which contributed to a deepening rift in the Republican party between Taft and the conservatives on one side, and the Progressives, led initially by LaFollette, on the other. In early 1912, Roosevelt announced that he would seek the Republican nomination for president that year, directly challenging Taft, the incumbent. When the Republican convention, controlled by forces loyal to Taft, renominated him, Roosevelt left the party and formed his own, which he formally called the Progressive party. (More popularly it was known as the Bull Moose party, after the animal Roosevelt chose as its symbol.) The Democrats, having no nationally prominent individual to nominate, waited until the 46th convention ballot to choose Woodrow Wilson, the progressive but little-known governor of New Jersey.

The campaign of 1912 revolved around which kind of progressivism should prevail in the United States. Taft, whose administration had been thoroughly discredited by Roosevelt and whose party was in disarray, campaigned on his conservative record, but few listened. Roosevelt espoused a program that he called the New Nationalism, in which the federal government would play a strong and dynamic role in national life through the continuous exercise of regulatory powers. Wilson's program, termed the New Freedom, was more Jeffersonian in outlook. Under the New Freedom, the federal government would have the potential to exercise great power, but it would utilize that power only when needed to destroy inequities in the system or to restore free and open competition in the marketplace.

Wilson and the Democrats won the election over Roosevelt (and Taft) due partly to the fact that the Democrats were unified and the Republicans were not and also because party loyalty kept many Republicans from voting for Roosevelt, who personally was much more popular than either of the other two candidates. With this election, the mantle of progressivism passed from the Republican to the Democratic party and the political career of Theodore Roosevelt came to an end.

Wilson's first year and a half in office marked the high point of progressivism. Before the onset of World War I took national attention away from domestic reform, Wilson persuaded Congress to pass four major pieces of legislation which, to his way of thinking, completed the Progressive agenda.

The first of these was the Underwood Tariff (1913), an effort to end the high protective tariff that had existed since the Civil War. Wilson urged passage of this act to convince business of the necessity of efficiency, and his careful cultivation of influential committee chairmen and calls for party loyalty overcame the lobbying efforts of the business community, which predicted an economic disaster if the bill passed. It did pass, brought no significant long-term economic decline, and included the first U.S. income tax, which was seen as a means to replace the federal income lost through the lowering of tariff rates.

The second of Wilson's great Progressive measures was the Federal

Reserve Act (1913). A short, but sharp, economic panic in 1907 and a subsequent congressional investigation had revealed the need for major banking and currency reform, and the Federal Reserve Act provided just that. Passed after another round of diligent politicking on Wilson's part, the act established a network of twelve district banks under the control of a new federal regulatory agency, the Federal Reserve Board. These banks were so-called "banker's banks," with which only other banks could do business. Since the Federal Reserve Board had substantial authority over the setting of interest rates and the issuance of currency, its control over the banking industry was significant.

The third and fourth Progressive measures on Wilson's agenda both dealt with the antitrust question. The Federal Trade Commission Act (1914) established a regulatory agency, the Federal Trade Commission, to investigate and supervise the activities of business, much as the Interstate Commerce Commission could do for railroads and the Federal Reserve Board, for banks. The Clayton Anti-Trust Act (1914) amended and strengthened the Sherman Anti-Trust Act and made more consistent the enforcement authority given to each of the three regulatory agencies. Significantly, too, it exempted labor and agricultural organizations from antitrust laws.

Following the passage of these two acts in 1914, Wilson felt that his mission of domestic reform was accomplished. He believed that business was now adequately checked under the umbrella of reform, and he stepped away from the issue by turning down a bill to allow banks to give long-term credit to farmers and another outlawing child labor. Only in 1916, when his reelection was on the line and he needed the support of Progressive strongholds in the Midwest and West, did Wilson don the Progressive mantle again. He appointed Louis Brandeis, a liberal jurist (and the first Jew) to the Supreme Court, supported a rail worker's bill providing for an eight-hour working day, an agricultural credit bill, and a measure limiting child labor. His rebirth as a Progressive in 1916 probably helped him in his successful reelection bid, but with World War I dominating his second term, further efforts to advance Progressive causes did not come from the White House.

The war itself did help propel a couple of Progressive social issues into reality. Although the suffrage movement had been very active in the years before the war, and many states had passed legislation allowing women to vote on state and local matters, Congress did not pass the nineteenth Amendment to the Constitution until 1919. Many historians point to the highly useful service women provided the country during the war as the crucial factor in the congressional vote. By the presidential election of 1920, enough states had ratified the amendment to make it part of the Constitution, and women voted nationally for the first time.

Anti-German agitation during the war helped bring about Prohibition, which found constitutional legitimacy as the eighteenth Amendment upon ratification in 1920. This measure set a limit of one-half of one percent on the alcoholic content of any beverage commercially produced and sold, although farmers could still legally make and drink their own liquor at home. Urban drinkers, however, were out of luck, and the "Noble Experiment," as it has been called, led to widespread scoffing at the law by ordinary Americans and large-scale racketeering and violence by organized mobsters in the 1920s. Although it did reduce drinking in America by about one-third, few considered Prohibition a success, and it was repealed by the twenty-first Amendment in 1933.

INTERPRETIVE ESSAY
Laura Hague

In the decades preceding the opening of the twentieth century, rapid changes in the economy and demography of the United States challenged the American dream. The widespread and divergent responses to these changes mark the time historians call the Progressive era. Few periods in American history have provoked as many differences in interpretation. When did the Progressive era begin? When did it end? What were the origins of progressivism? Who were the Progressives? What did they believe? What is their legacy? Seemingly, every facet of the Progressive era is debated. Despite the diversity of interpretation, there is consensus that, especially after 1900, what is called the Progressive era was an urban-based reform movement of unprecedented scope aimed primarily at making adjustments to the political, social and economic by-products of industrialization.

Three major trends stemming from industrialization provided the stimulus for progressive reform. First, inept and corrupt governance became a pressing concern as government on all levels expanded its role from insuring public order to providing public services. Second, both economic expansion and centralization occurred simultaneously, in part from government action on behalf of business but mostly because of new ways of organizing business. The increasing disruption of society as a booming population fed the unregulated development of big business was the final incitement to this new age of reformism.

After the Civil War, the United States turned away from reform to concentrate on economic expansion. The bloodiness of the conflict and the failure of abolitionists' naive expectations of civil peace in the South prompted the disillusioned nation to indulge itself in what historians later called "the Great Barbecue." Personal enrichment through government corruption, or what was then seen as business sleight-of-hand, gave a prosperous cast to a time of increasing social unrest.

No single instance of misuse of government power and money stands out from the rest. At the federal level, the Credit Mobilier scandal, which involved fraud in the construction of the first transcontinental railroad, made the Grant administration the premier example of Washington corruption until the 1920s. Machine politics so dominated state government that in many states, both North and South, the two-party system existed only in theory. And in city after city, as well as in many rural counties, the "boss system" controlled both local government and the dispensation of services until long after the turn of the century.

A good part of the rampant governmental corruption stemmed from the necessarily close relationship between business and politics. The Civil War had enlarged the federal government's responsibility for meeting desirable public goals, such as an efficient and thorough transportation system linking the East and West coasts. Accomplishing such a goal meant that the government needed either to build and operate railroads itself or to provide subsidies in the form of land, and routes to private enterprise. Government personnel were the first to know who would be the recipient of federal largesse, the size of the grant, and the location. Thus, businesses dependent on that information were willing to pay for prior knowledge of decisions, and knowledgeable government insiders were well-situated to make their own business deals. Similar relationships between business and government emerged on the local level when municipalities contracted with private enterprise for public works or the provision of basic services.

New methods of doing business incited charges of corruption and unfairness. The late nineteenth century witnessed the birth of big business, which emerged in forms substantially different from prior business arrangements. Earlier, even a prosperous business, perhaps an iron furnace, did one thing only and operated with roughly the same profit margin as smaller businesses. After producing pig iron, the furnace would sell its product to another business, such as a forge, for processing into finished products, and that business would sell its inventory to a wholesaler for further distribution to retailers. When giant corporations, like U.S. Steel, emerged, they handled all elements of production up through wholesaling their own finished products. Because of this vertical integration of all aspects of production, the new corporations were able to operate at a substantially lower profit margin and offer lower wholesale prices. Unable to compete, thousands of small businesses were forced to close, with their skilled employees left to seek unskilled positions in the new big businesses. Understandably, the displaced owners and workers, as well as those who feared they might suffer the same fate, suspected the "robber barons" like Andrew Carnegie, J.P. Morgan, and John D. Rockefeller, of unfair and corrupt business practices.

Improved transportation and efficient business practices helped stimulate rapid industrialization. Production of manufactured goods soared. Already a world leader in the steel industry in 1880, the United States saw its steel production soar from fewer than three million tons to over 30 million by 1914. However, this industrialization would not have been possible without two important demographic changes in the American population.

At the close of the Civil War, the American population stood at less than 40 million; by 1900 the population was more than 75 million. Part of the surge in numbers can be found in a postwar baby boom. The other source was from immigration. The United States had always experienced high rates of immigration, but now contemporary observers noticed a troubling new trend that grew even stronger after 1900. Native whites saw the newcomers as not only overwhelmingly poor but also different from earlier immigrants. The new immigrants tended to be Catholics and Jews from southern and eastern Europe with the "unwholesome" habit of settling in cities. Native-born Protestants fled to the suburbs and then looked back aghast at the urban spectacle: impoverished people with bizarre religious beliefs and customs, speaking odd languages, dancing and drinking, had replaced the sober, upright American citizen. The foreigners lived in tenements, wore rags, and died from disease and hunger. The sober, upright American citizen was shocked. All that drinking and dancing would simply have to go. Throughout the 1880s and 1890s, reformers sought to eliminate the corruption of the cities, first through exhorting the poor to adopt middle-class values and then by attempting to legislate morality. In fact, the first of the major Progressive reform efforts, prohibition of alcohol, focused on making it impossible for the poor to engage in such an unhealthy habit.

While the initial reaction of many middle-class Americans to poverty in the cities was to blame it on the customs of the foreign immigrants, closer observers realized that another demographic change belied such simplistic analysis. The employment opportunities of the cities attracted even larger numbers of native-born rural Americans than foreign immigrants. These native newcomers shared with the foreigners the same harsh living conditions, yet held the same values as the prosperous inhabitants of the suburbs. Reformers began to understand that if the teetotaling farmer's son from Maine was as poor as the beer-drinking Slovak, personal habits were not necessarily the cause of poverty.

Though industrialization generated overall increases in income and living standards, it also invoked a terrible cycle of economic boom and bust. Employing all available hands during good times, businesses thought little of firing many workers during lean times and reducing the wages of those remaining. Because few laborers, even during prosperity cycles, were paid enough to support a family, most families relied on the combined income of parents and children to survive. The prospect of an entire family being thrown onto the reduced wages of one or two family members for a year or more every decade contributed to the creation of an urban tinderbox that flamed repeatedly from the 1870s to about 1920.

Incidents of civil unrest captured public attention throughout the last decades of the nineteenth century. Though much, if not most, of the violence was at the hands of police or an employer's security force, the Haymarket Riot (1886) in Chicago, the Homestead Strike (1892) in Pennsylvania, and the Pullman Strike (1894) were among the many protests that raised the prospect of imminent class warfare and inspired many middle-class activists and concerned employers to look for ways to change the situation.

The fear of an insurrection by the laboring classes deepened when populism appeared on the national scene in the 1890s. The Populists' concrete proposals for restructuring the entire American financial system and their critique of the centralization of economic and political power in the United States affirmed the arguments of advocates for the urban poor. This time, the criticisms could not be shrugged off, as they had been before, as the un-American ravings of foreigners. The radical voice of the Populists was raised by native-born farmers in such unlikely lo-

cales as Texas, Georgia, and Kansas. Their political popularity throughout the South and Midwest forced the two major parties to reevaluate
their response to the issues of the day.

While the size of the problems in politics, economics, and society demanded a response, trends within the middle and upper classes fash-
ioned the shape of that response. The same economy that created so
much disruption also provided a prosperity that both expanded and
changed the middle class. The impact of the philosophy of positivism
on education led to a belief that all questions could be answered through
the diligent application of scientific method. Large numbers of women
were coming of age with an education but without prospects of employing their knowledge in the professions. Finally, the rise of social gospel
admonished prosperous Christians against ignoring the plight of their
less fortunate neighbors.

From 1860 to 1900, national wealth grew from $16 billion to $88 billion.
This economic expansion, driven by industrialization, fueled the growth
of the middle class by increasing demand for the services of professionals
and, more significantly, by adding a new component to the middle class.
In the nineteenth century, the middle class was significantly different
from what is presently considered middle class. The most important
characteristic of its members was that they did not work with their
hands. Doctors, lawyers, professors, clergymen, merchants, and owners
of other small businesses comprised the occupational makeup of the middle class in the Victorian Era. With the increase in overall national prosperity, an important change in the composition of the middle class was
occurring—the addition of white collar workers. Whereas the older professions were at least nominally independent, the white-collar worker
was an employee. Paid to manage some aspect of a large corporation,
the white-collar worker was only slowly accepted by the older members
of the middle class. Standing in the community was another defining
aspect of the middle class, whether traditional or not. Throughout the
country, middle-class households were not the average but the most
prosperous in their local communities. Under stress from competition
with big business and loss of status as an economically independent
class, many middle-class men and women sought to retain community
leadership by spearheading reform in a moderate direction.

Education was extremely important to the middle class. Without it,
there could be little hope of entering the professions. With parents ever
more able to afford greater degrees of schooling for their children, the
middle-class family was able to take advantage of the expansion of

higher education. New colleges sprang up across the nation. With the encouragement of middle-class voters, government too undertook to expand higher education through land grants and direct appropriation. Many of the new colleges were public universities, dedicated to educating the widest possible sector of the public by keeping tuition reasonably low and locations central.

In the colleges, increasing numbers of students learned to employ scientific method in their examinations of social questions. Concurrently, the philosophy of pragmatism was calling into question ancient verities. As put into practice by educator John Dewey, pragmatism emphasized the importance of the environment surrounding an individual on his or her behavior and values. These two understandings, pragmatism and scientific method, undergirded the Progressive reform spirit. Where once reformers had focused on changing individuals in order to solve social problems, now they worked to change the environmental conditions that caused problems for individuals. And, armed with the methodology of science, the Progressives were certain they could pinpoint exactly which environmental conditions were problems and how they could be efficiently solved. Educated and knowledgeable, the Progressives proceeded to professionalize the world of social reform.

One unforeseen consequence of expanded education was the involvement of middle-class women in the public domain. The Victorian age had produced distinct spheres of activity based on gender. Men were to be responsible for public matters—government, business, and the like. Women were to be the nurturers of children and moral support of men. Simply put, men took care of all things outside the home and women were restricted to domestic matters indoors. While the separate spheres model was never universally or perfectly practiced, its hold on the middle and upper classes was strong. Poor women of all races, especially while unmarried, often had to work outside of their homes, though generally in "feminine" occupations like spinning, domestic work, and canning; and they largely considered education past basic literacy to be an unmarketable frivolity. The uselessness of education for women seemed evident; the middle-class female college graduate promptly found that she had been overeducated for the one career really open to her, being a wife and mother. Rather than give in to this frustrating situation, however, the educated woman increasingly took advantage of two possibilities. She hired servants to take over the upkeep of the household, freeing her to contribute publicly through the reform activities of women's clubs, or she chose to remain single and make a career of social reform. Whatever her choice, the middle-class woman of the Progressive era provided the bulk of talent and time at the grass-roots level of reform.

While new trends in education and wider access to it provided the intellectual framework for progressivism, and college-educated young women provided much of its energetic workforce, the basis of Progressive reform was spiritual. The original reform response to the problems brought about through industrialization and economic expansion, as noted above, was one of moral chastisement. Further, in many countries that have industrialized during the twentieth century, the response to the resulting social problems has been an authoritarian crackdown on the poorest members of society. That the response in the United States became one of amelioration of social ills, instead of the institution of a police state, was to a great degree the result of the spread of the social gospel.

Reform efforts in the United States had been connected to waves of Protestant revival since colonial days. However, the earlier reform efforts focused on the individual's personal relationship to God. Even abolitionism merely expanded the older concept into a national relationship to God. The contribution of social gospel to reform was essentially a change in focus from relationships to God to relationships among people. Popular works like *Progress and Poverty,* (1879) and *If Christ Came to Chicago* (1893) called attention to the impossibility of the poor changing the economic circumstances that so inequitably distributed the wealth of the nation. The lengthy depression of the 1890s made urgent the need for prosperous Americans to accept the role of their brothers' keepers.

The middle-class reform movement launched a three-pronged attack on the problems of the day, starting at the grass-roots level. Decentralized, though often affiliated, groups in localities across the country grappled with political and social ills. The discovery that the problems were more complex than any private organization of well-meaning citizens could address prompted the first demands that government become part of the solution. As adequate resolution of each issue required greater degrees of coordination and power, the reformers turned from the city to the state and then to the federal government.

The earliest reforms were part of the campaign by political reformers known as mugwumps against local political corruption. In cities across America, political machines had learned to win and keep offices in municipal government by extending economic aid to the city's poor. At a time before acceptance of a governmental role in provision of social services, the act of helping a widow find rent money or getting an orphan a job, even when done on a random and sporadic basis, won the good will of most of the electorate. That such good deeds were meagerly awarded and that the machine politicians used political office to enrich themselves mattered little to people who knew there was no other source of assistance. However, to the privileged sectors of society, the atrocious condition of city streets and utilities and the inequitable system of property taxation found in most cities nullified any good the machines did. Most mugwump reformers in the period between the end of Reconstruction and the depression of the 1890s believed that political machines could be broken only if "unqualified" people were denied the franchise. Imposing literacy and lengthy residency requirements, the mugwump and, later, Progressive reformers of both the North and South continued well into the twentieth century the process of politically marginalizing poor native whites, immigrants, and blacks.

Important Progressive political reforms carried on the process of marginalization. Wherever the reformers took control, they altered the basis of city government from representation by ward or borough to city-wide election, effectively raising the cost of winning by distribution of assistance, while removing office holders from direct accountability to impoverished voters. Many analysts now believe that the American apathy surrounding local elections emerged during the waning years of the nineteenth century as reforms rendered large sectors of society impotent to gain effective representation.

Of course, not all the reforms enacted by the Progressives, or even the mugwumps, were detrimental to democracy. Many reforms were directed at improving democratic practices. The institution of the secret ballot and the banning of campaigning from the polling place are but two of the reform efforts begun under mugwump auspices and continued by Progressives in an effort to end retribution by employers and politicians against voters. The campaign for the direct election of senators, rather than their appointment by state legislatures, ultimately successful with the ratification of the Seventeenth Amendment, is an excellent example of Progressive hopes that better popular representation would decrease corruption at the state and national levels. Many states and localities, especially in the West, added initiative and referendum for legislation and recall of public officials to the tools of representative democracy.

Of all the Progressive political reforms, the one that has had the greatest impact on the ordinary citizen to this day was public ownership of public services. Private providers ran often dangerous public transportation at prices well in excess of value received. Others held city refuse collection contracts and dumped the refuse in the alleys and vacant lots of tenement districts. Whatever the service—transportation, sanitation, street maintenance, water and sewerage, gas and electricity—taxpayers came to associate private contracts with haphazard service, high prices, and political corruption. In exasperation, voters cast their fears about socialism aside in order to put public services directly under public control. Since then, municipal waste collection, city-owned utilities, and city and county road maintenance departments have been the norm throughout the United States. Building on the successful results of their foray into public ownership, the Progressives also pressed for public ownership of amenities such as parks, concert halls, libraries, and, in the South for the first time, grammar schools.

Despite the flurry of political reforms at the local and state levels, poverty and social unrest continued unabated. While this may not seem surprising from our present point of view, many reformers initially had sincerely believed that social ills would be remedied simply through efficient and honest government. Now politically ready for government intervention in social matters, Progressives sought the underlying causes of the rebellious discontent so obvious in the Haymarket affair and Homestead Strike. From the mid-1880s on, much of the investigation took place in the neighborhoods of the poor, often directed by the men and, especially, women of the settlement house movement.

Settlement houses developed first in England; they were started in the United States in the mid-1880s. The most famous, Hull House in Chicago, exemplified many of the characteristics of the Progressive era. It was founded by young women of the upper-middle class who found an answer for a meaningful use of their education in the social gospel's directive to reach out to the less fortunate. Both young men and women boarded within Hull House's walls, in many ways acting as emissaries of the American middle class in the often alien realm of the working class. Settlement house residents not only offered educational programs to their neighbors designed to introduce middle-class habits and rudimentary civics lessons but also kept painstaking records of the living and working conditions of the poor.

The records accumulated by the settlement houses provided ammunition in the battle for social legislation. Adding to the written record visual evidence made possible for the first time by flash photography, Progressive social workers showed how the poor lived in filthy, stifling quarters. The disease-ridden tenements presented to local reformers and municipal governments an immediately remediable situation. With a reputation as a breeding ground for epidemics, the slums provoked a concerned response from even the most self-concerned individuals. City planning commissions developed housing standards requiring at least minimal levels of light and fresh air and sanitary access to water supplies. Campaigns involving entire communities set out to remove filth and manure from the streets while instilling pride in the populace.

Labor conditions proved more intractable than living conditions. Tradition insisted that the relationship between worker and employer was a private contract. Working families and labor unions were as adamant about maintaining that relationship as the employers themselves. While legislators were inclined to support the concept of contract where it concerned adult men, they were more open to regulation of the working conditions of women and children. At the state level, paternalistic legislators passed restrictions on the labor of women and children. Yet such laws were regularly declared unconstitutional until 1908, when the U.S. Supreme Court finally upheld Oregon's cap on women's work hours.

The federal government first entered the arena of regulation of businesses as an extension of its role in interstate commerce. Responding to farmers' complaints about rebates to big businesses while small shippers' charges appeared to subsidize the discounts, Congress passed the Interstate Commerce Act in 1887. Expansion of the federal role in interstate commerce underlay subsequent federal Progressive reform of business practice, including areas of consumer protection. Thus, the Sherman and Clayton Acts forbade certain kinds of business combinations because they were in restraint of trade, while the Meat Inspection Act and Pure Food and Drug Act, both passed in 1906, regulated the quality of goods that passed across state borders.

Sometimes the motivation for particular reforms may seem quaint to modern students. A good example of this is the background to the Sixteenth Amendment, which authorized an income tax. The politics of the nineteenth century had been concerned to a remarkable degree with one question: What was the proper level for the tariff? The tariff was the chief source of government income and an important means of protecting American industries from being undercut by foreign goods. Maintaining a high tariff kept the government solvent, benefited certain industries and farmers, and kept prices higher than many Americans could afford. Ratifying the income tax amendment in 1913 separated the issue of government funding from protectionism, allowing Congress to risk foreign competition without undermining the financial security of the national government.

At the national level, Progressive reform retained a mugwump character in that major reforms often focused on the character of the poor rather than the problems they faced. The simplest way to have the right kind of working class, many reformers thought, was to allow into the United States only the "right" kind of immigrants. In 1882 and again in 1902, Chinese immigration was forbidden outright, while efforts to restrict immigration from elsewhere were defeated only by the presidential vetoes of Taft and Wilson. In 1917, Congress finally had the votes to override Wilson's veto, marking the beginning of a new era of unrepentant xenophobia. Two years later, this time with Wilson's blessing, the constitutional amendment prohibiting the manufacture and sale of alcohol was ratified. Supporters, who tended to believe that alcohol, frequently manufactured by immigrant-run enterprises, was the root cause of poverty and crime, were wholly unprepared for the levels of lawlessness ushered in by Prohibition.

The amendment granting women the right to vote may have drawn as much from growing nativism, or opposition to immigrants, as it did from the arguments of feminists. After over fifty years of agitation for female suffrage, women's efforts on behalf of Progressive reform had clearly demonstrated both that women were capable of intelligent decision-making and that office-holders were unresponsive to the petitions of voteless segments of society. Sadly, the most persuasive argument to many was that it was unfair and unwholesome that women from nice native-born prosperous households could not vote while immigrant and African-American men could. The ratification in 1920 of the Nineteenth Amendment, which granted women the vote, thus stands as peculiar testimony to the convergence of reform and reaction.

Little was done in the way of national legislation to improve the circumstances of life for the poor, whose distress had prompted the initial call to reform. While Theodore Roosevelt may have begun using the presidency as an ostensibly neutral mediator in disputes between labor and capital, striking workers during and after World War I found that the federal government would be impartial only when convenient. Antitrust legislation, one of the main victories of the Progressives, soon was used more to impede the development of labor unions than to stop predatory business practices. Real reform for workers had to wait until the New Deal's response to the Great Depression in the 1930s.

African Americans benefited from the Progressive era more from the circumstantial prosperity of the two decades after 1897 than from any activity pursued by governments at any level. In fact, the 1896 *Plessy* v. *Ferguson* decision and the segregation of the federal workforce under Wilson reinforced black Americans' conviction that they were on their own in the fight for civil rights. Taking advantage of the relatively tolerant mood prevailing in the North, African-American leaders, with the financial and moral support of a few sympathetic whites, inaugurated the Niagara Movement (1905) for civil rights and integration; and, five years later, they launched the National Association for the Advancement of Colored People (NAACP). In this way, perhaps the most important reform in the twentieth century—federally protected extension of civil rights—was planted fifty years before bearing fruit in the 1960s.

The Progressive era also inadvertently spawned another movement that came to fruition in mid-century. The 1890 census had dramatically pointed out that there were territorial limits even in America by demonstrating the closing of the frontier. Aware as a nation for the first time that nature's bounty was not bottomless, Progressive reformers, especially under Theodore Roosevelt, worked to apply theories of scientific management to the conservation of remaining public lands. Woodrow Wilson's administration expanded the concept of conservation to recreational resources when it established the National Park Service in 1916. After the end of the Progressive era, concern over pollution in the cities and maintenance of public lands fell dormant until the population and technological pressures of the 1950s transformed the latent Progressive conservationism into modern environmentalism.

If progressivism degenerated into a confused morass of half-starts and nativism at the federal level, the grass-roots origins of the movement remained alive. Local women's clubs continued to fight for sanitation and education. State-appointed factory inspectors relentlessly gathered statistics on child labor and hazardous working conditions. African Americans painstakingly brought suit in court for equal access to the resources of American society. Individual chapters of wilderness clubs readily heard and supported the new professional ecologists. The Progressive era ended with World War I, but reform efforts continued. The experiments in governmental activism left a legacy of official willingness to regulate social interactions.

Self-confident, educated, financially independent, and spiritually driven, the Progressives breached the traditional wall between the public and private sectors. Though unable to take full advantage themselves of the new responsiveness of government, the young middle-class adults of turn-of-the-century America opened a path that later generations were to pave.

SELECTED BIBLIOGRAPHY

Boyer, Paul. *Urban Masses and Moral Order in America, 1820–1920.* Cambridge: Cambridge University Press, 1978. Chronicles attempt to instill traditional, rural moral values into the people of the new urban centers.

Bryan, Mary Lynn McCree, and Allen F. Davis, eds. *One Hundred Years at Hull House.* Bloomington: Indiana University Press, 1990. Essays celebrating the centennial of the first and most noteworthy settlement house.

Buenker, John D. *Urban Liberalism and Progressive Reform.* New York: Scribner & Sons, 1973. Study of the contribution of urban Democrats to Progressive reform through cooperation with other groups interested in reform.

Cooper, John M., Jr. *The Warrior and the Priest.* Cambridge, MA: Harvard University Press, 1983. A very readable dual biography of Theodore Roosevelt and Woodrow Wilson.

Crunden, Robert. *Ministers of Reform: The Progressives' Achievement in American Civilization, 1889–1920.* New York: Basic Books, 1982. An analysis of twenty Progressive era figures demonstrating the cultural side of the movement.

Frankel, Noralee, and Nancy S. Dye, eds. *Gender, Class, Race, and Reform in the Progressive Era.* Lexington: University of Kentucky Press, 1991. Collection of essays dealing with women in the Progressive era.

Ginger, Ray. *Altgeld's America: The Lincoln Ideal Versus Changing Realities.* New York: Funk & Wagnalls, 1958. Study of Chicago's liberal reformers in the 1890s, centered around Illinois governor John Peter Altgeld.

Goodwyn, Lawrence. *The Populist Moment: A Short History of the Agrarian Revolt in America.* New York: Oxford University Press, 1978. History of the farmer-based movement that lent much to progressivism.

Gould, Lewis L., ed. *The Progressive Era.* Syracuse, NY: Syracuse University Press, 1974. A variety of essays analyzing the Progressive era from different perspectives.

Harbaugh, William H. *The Life and Times of Theodore Roosevelt.* New York: Collier, 1961. Balanced biography of the president most closely associated with progressivism.

Hareven, Tamara K., and Randolph Langenbach. *Amoskeag: Life and Work in an American Factory-City.* New York: Pantheon Books, 1978. A case study of management and labor in what was the world's largest textile factory.

Hofstadter, Richard. *The Age of Reform: From Bryan to F.D.R.* New York: Vintage Books, 1955. Classic analysis of American politics in the early twentieth century.

Kolko, Gabriel. *The Triumph of Conservatism: A Reinterpretation of American History, 1900–1915.* New York: Free Press, 1963. Argues that the Progressive era reforms were really just what conservative forces wanted.

Lamoreaux, Naomi R. *The Great Merger Movement in American Business, 1895–1904.* Cambridge: Cambridge University Press, 1985. A statistical analysis of the business combination movement at the turn of the century and its impact on antitrust activity.

Link, William A. *The Paradox of Southern Progressivism, 1880–1930.* Chapel Hill: University of North Carolina Press, 1992. Argues that Southern Progressives had only limited success because they tried to impose reform through coercion and control.

McCormick, Richard L. *From Realignment to Reform: Political Change in New York State, 1893–1910.* Ithaca, NY: Cornell University Press, 1979. Study of the impact of progressivism on an important northeastern state.

———. *The Party Period and Public Policy: American Politics from the Age of Jackson to the Progressive Era.* New York: Oxford University Press, 1986. A study of the changes brought by Progressive politics on U.S. political parties.

McGerr, Michael E. *The Decline of Popular Politics: The American North, 1865–1928.* New York: Oxford University Press, 1986. Argues that the partisan politics of the Gilded Age was replaced by the politics of personality, despite Progressives' efforts to create an educated, issue-oriented electorate.

Meltzer, Milton. *Bread and Roses: The Struggle of American Labor, 1865–1915.* New York: Alfred A. Knopf, 1967. Survey of the development of organized labor.

Painter, Nell Irvin. *Standing at Armageddon: The United States, 1877–1919.* New York: W.W. Norton, 1987. Survey text from a working-class point of view, with emphasis on political and labor history.

Riis, Jacob A. *How the Other Half Lives: Studies among the Tenements of New York.* New York: Dover, 1971. Originally published in 1890, this was a pioneer photographic exposé of immigrant poverty in New York City.

Weinstein, James. *The Corporate Ideal in the Liberal State, 1900–1918.* Boston: Beacon Press, 1968. Radical interpretation asserting that progressivism developed under the banner of corporate capitalism and its financial institutions.

This photograph conveys a sense of the filth and destruction that were the hallmarks of trench warfare on the Western front during World War I. (Photographic Archives, University of Louisville, Jon Kegelman Collection)

2

World War I, 1914–1918

INTRODUCTION

When World War I broke out in Europe in early August 1914, President Woodrow Wilson asked the American people to be neutral in thought as well as in deed. While the vast majority of Americans had absolutely no interest in joining in the conflict—indeed, most thought Europe was decadent and corrupt—many of them, including the Wilson administration, were pro-British in sentiment. This was not surprising in view of the fact that many Americans traced their roots back to England, Scotland, or Wales. Moreover, the United States and Great Britain shared a common language, were major commercial partners, and had enjoyed a diplomatic rapprochement since the turn of the century.

Although Wilson proclaimed U.S. neutrality, both sides in the war violated it with impunity. Great Britain used its control of the seas to prevent American goods from reaching German-controlled areas of the Continent; this was inconvenient but caused no loss of life. Germany, however, embarked on a campaign of submarine (or U-boat, for *Unterwasser-Boot*) warfare, declaring a war zone around the British isles and sinking ships that tried to sail through. The danger of the campaign was dramatized in May 1915 with the sinking of the luxury-liner *Lusitania* off the Irish coast, which incurred the loss of over 1,100 lives, including 128

Americans. Wilson strongly condemned the German action against a civilian ship; and Germany, not wanting the United States in the war,
promised that in the future, warnings would be given and passengers
and crew members would be provided for. Wilson presented Germany
with a virtual ultimatum in March 1916 after the sinking of the U.S.S.
Sussex; and, once again, the Berlin government backed down.

In January 1917, however, with the land war on the Western Front
stalemated and with resources running low, German leaders felt they
had to force the issue. They declared a policy of unrestricted submarine
warfare against Atlantic shipping, knowing that this would inevitably
draw the United States into the war. Their calculated risk was that such
a program would starve the British and French into submission in six
months, while it would take the United States at least nine months to
mobilize sufficiently to make a military difference in the war. By then,
it would be too late. If Americans needed to be coaxed further toward
entering the war, the Zimmermann Note did that. This diplomatic message from the German foreign ministry to Mexico, intercepted and publicized by the British, promised the Mexicans that if they joined Germany
in war against the United States, they would be given back the territory
annexed by the United States following the war with Mexico in 1846–
1848.

By early April 1917, Wilson's hand was forced. The president, who
had made several earlier attempts to end the conflict through diplomacy,
concluded that the submarine war, the security threat suggested by the
Zimmermann Note, and his personal interest in participating in the postwar peace conference made American entry into the war necessary. On
April 2, 1917, at Wilson's request, Congress declared war on Germany
to "make the world safe for democracy."

Although Wilson's successful reelection campaign of 1916 had been
based in part on the slogan "He kept us out of war," the president had
taken measures to prepare the country for possible future involvement.
Part of the rationale for this was political: the ever-popular Theodore
Roosevelt had emerged as the leader of a campaign urging national pre-
paredness; and Wilson, a bitter political rival, could not permit Roosevelt
to capitalize on this issue in an election year.

Congress granted Wilson extraordinary powers to mobilize the country for a possible war, and the president wasted little time in carrying
out measures that effectively concentrated authority in the executive
branch through the creation of several important agencies. In August
1916, Wilson established the Council for National Defense, a civilian

board responsible for overseeing the entire war-preparedness effort. Other agencies were more specific. The U.S. Shipping Board mobilized shipyards in an intensive shipbuilding program that soon was providing twice the number of ships sunk by the Germans. The Food Administration, headed by future president Herbert Hoover, worked on ways to increase the amount of food available for soldiers and civilians in Europe. The Fuel Administration was primarily concerned with conserving coal so that it would be available to fuel naval vessels; one of its measures was the introduction of Daylight Savings Time. The Railroad Administration took over operation of the nation's rail system to facilitate the rapid movement of military personnel and equipment.

Of particular importance were the War Industries Board and the Committee on Public Information. The War Industries Board, created after the declaration of war and chaired by Bernard Baruch, a prominent financier, was given extensive powers over American industry to maximize production for war needs. Among other powers, the board could fix prices and schedule industrial priorities. As the government wanted to make certain needed supplies were available, prices were set at levels calculated to guarantee high profits; the aptly named Savage Arms Corporation reported profits of 60 percent in 1917, and the Bethlehem Shipbuilding Company saw its annual profit rise from $6 million to $49 million once the war got underway.

The Committee on Public Information served as a propaganda agency to maintain unified public support for the war effort. Under the leadership of journalist George Creel, the committee, helped by many local patriotic organizations, inspired a highly emotional campaign designed to persuade all Americans to hate the enemy. The brunt of this effort fell on the German-American community, the largest and best-organized foreign-language group in the country. Prior to the war, German Americans were generally thought of as hard-working, law-abiding people whose racial stock was only one small step removed from the superior Anglo-Saxon race.

But when, in the early months of the war in Europe, German Americans argued for a strict adherence to the policy of neutrality, they were branded as suspicious and disloyal; and the hostility against them gradually increased as German submarines sank American ships or an alleged act of German sabotage was reported. By April 1917, German Americans were scorned throughout the nation, and some were the victims of violent acts against their persons or property. The Wilson administration dusted off old acts or induced Congress to pass new ones that led to the arrest (and, in some cases, the deportation) of several thousand German Americans or their sympathizers on the grounds of disloyalty, espionage, or sedition.

Fighting World War I cost the United States $33.5 billion, including some $7 billion loaned to American allies and spent in this country. The sale of war bonds through five public campaigns, using high-pressure sales techniques based on appeals to patriotism, raised about two-thirds of the war's cost, while increased taxes accounted for the balance. Personal income taxes rose to a maximum of 75 percent on the wealthiest Americans, and a 65-percent excess profits tax and a 25-percent federal inheritance tax were both instituted. A federal excise tax was imposed on other items.

From a military standpoint, the United States was unprepared for war in 1914, when it began in Europe, and not much better prepared when Congress declared war in the spring of 1917. After a long public debate, a Selective Service Act was passed in 1917, providing for a draft. Through this means and through volunteer enlistments, the United States raised an army of over four million, of whom about half were eventually sent to France. An enlarged navy undertook important blockading, convoying, and antisubmarine warfare tasks.

The American Expeditionary Force, or AEF, was headed by General John J. Pershing. After some inter-allied conflict about the command structure, a good working relationship was established, and the AEF generally took responsibility for the southern sector of the western front. At the time American forces began to arrive in significant numbers, the Allied effort was weakening; and most historians believe that the contribution of the AEF was essential in bringing about an armistice on Allied terms, even if that contribution lasted less than a year. The AEF was instrumental in helping repel a series of German offensives in the spring and summer of 1918 and then pushing through the front lines in the early fall of 1918 as the German effort collapsed both at the front and within Germany itself. The armistice of November 11, 1918, found the Allies in a highly advantageous military position from which they were able to dictate the terms of peace.

One of Wilson's principal motives for entering the war was his desire to play a major role at the peace conference, steering it toward his preconceived notions of what would make a lasting and fair peace. These notions, spelled out in a January 1918 speech, came to be known as his "Fourteen Points." Of these, five were general principles of diplomacy, including disarmament, which the president felt would avert future wars

if implemented. Eight of the points dealt with specific European territorial settlements, based on the principle of national self-determination,
whereby people could decide, by means of a special election called a
plebiscite, under what government they wished to live. The fourteenth
point, most important to Wilson, was the creation of a League of Nations,
an international organization based on the concept of collective security,
in which the organization's members would work together to maintain
a peaceful world.

By the time of the armistice, the peace conference, to be held in Paris
beginning in December, and the League of Nations had become so important to Wilson that he determined to lead the American delegation
himself, even though this meant that he would be out of the United
States for an extended period of time. Although there was general public
approval of Wilson's personal participation, the president, in his growing
obsession with the peace process, failed to take into account the political
necessities connected with ratifying the eventual treaty. The Senate was
nearly equally divided between Democrats and Republicans, and, with
a two-thirds vote needed for ratification, Wilson needed Republican support. But he complicated matters for himself by making peace a partisan
issue in the November 1918 midterm elections and then worsened his
political prospects by failing to include any important Republicans
among the top echelon of the delegation that accompanied him to Paris.

Wilson spent all but six weeks of the period between December 1918
and June 1919 in Paris, working out the details of the enormously complex Treaty of Versailles. It was exhausting work, but, in the end, the
president brought home a treaty that included his coveted League of
Nations. Initial American reaction to the treaty was quite favorable, but
as the summer of 1919 wore on, opposition began to mount. Part of it
came from returning troops, who told stories about the immoral and
ungrateful Europeans whom they had tried to help; part came from journalists and others who revealed tales of the vengeful-minded diplomats
fighting for nationalistic gain throughout the peacemaking process. Most
of the opposition, however, developed among various factions of senators, who, as they studied the treaty, saw many aspects they considered
unsatisfactory.

By late summer, the Senate appeared to coalesce into three groups
with widely differing attitudes toward the treaty. First, there were the
so-called irreconcilables, about sixteen senators, mostly Republican, who,
for one reason or another, were unalterably opposed to ratification. A
larger group of perhaps forty had reservations about certain parts of the

covenant of the League of Nations, included within the treaty, and would not vote for ratification until Wilson satisfied their concerns by agreeing to modifications in the document. A final group of senators, some forty Democrats, were internationalist-minded followers of the president, who would do his bidding on the Senate floor.

As Wilson saw opposition rising to ratification of the treaty, he decided to take his case directly to the people by means of a national speaking tour. This was a physically demanding effort, and the president, already weakened by his work in Paris, collapsed four weeks into the tour and had to be taken back to Washington. Shortly after his return to the White House, he suffered a crippling stroke that totally incapacitated him for several weeks. After Wilson's recovery to a point where he could participate in the treaty debate again, he seemed to be much more inflexible in his demand that no changes be made to the treaty. Consequently, when the reservationists introduced their modifications on the floor of the Senate, the internationalists were instructed to vote against them; and when the internationalists called for a vote on the unsullied treaty, enough of the reservationists voted against it to block its ratification. In two key votes on the treaty, one in November 1919 and the other in March 1920, the supporters failed to attain the two-thirds majority they needed, and the treaty went unratified.

The election of 1920, a massive Republican victory, was seen as a repudiation of Wilsonian internationalism and ushered in a period of political isolationism characterized by a refusal to have anything to do with the League of Nations or its auxiliary bodies, such as the World Court. Although the United States remained an active player in global economic matters, even helping to bring a semblance of economic stability to Germany in the 1920s, the political events that gathered momentum in the 1930s and set the stage for World War II took place in the absence of American involvement.

INTERPRETIVE ESSAY
Jacob Vander Meulen

History students interested in American battlefield action or in America's relations with other nations naturally give special attention to major wars like World War I. But so too do students interested in the nation's history at home because major wars mean just as many challenges for those who do not fight as they do for soldiers and diplomats.

Times of major war pose unusually heavy demands and strains on a nation. How a nation handles such emergency challenges reveals much about its social, cultural, and political patterns over longer periods of time. The twenty-month period from April 1917 to November 1918, when the United States was officially involved in World War I, offers a kind of laboratory for students interested in how America works at home and for the broader patterns of American life during the early twentieth century.

For a nation fighting a major war, success, or even just survival, requires a strong economy. That means steady supplies of farm products and raw materials, the best factory, energy, and transportation systems, and the latest technology. The United States was well-positioned here. It had these ingredients in abundance and boasted the world's strongest economy during World War I. Also essential are plenty of skilled and hard-working men and women to bring these requirements together and turn out the supplies and weapons needed by the soldiers in the field and the sailors at sea.

People are the key ingredient in a war economy, and here again the United States was very strong. At the time of the war, the U.S. population was about 102 million. Among the principal countries at war, only Russia had more people. But large numbers of people are just part of the story. Equally important are people's attitudes. A strong war economy and national success in war depend on a people's sense of unity and commitment to national goals. People must be willing to sacrifice personal interests and goals that they might pursue under normal peacetime conditions. And they must be willing to yield to the kind of new political power and authority over their day-to-day lives that a national government usually needs to assert during a war emergency.

Building unity, national commitment, and a strong wartime federal government in Washington, D.C., proved to be the biggest challenges for Americans during World War I. Most Americans supported the war effort against Germany, but at different levels of commitment. Many other Americans opposed the war, while still others didn't care one way or another.

When the war started for Americans in 1917, a large army and navy had to be built up, equipped with the best weapons and supplies, and sent to the battlefields across the Atlantic—all in time for the United States to have an impact on the war before its enemies won it. However, the government in Washington was in no position to take on the powerful central political role that the war economy required if it were to be managed and organized in a logical way.

In 1917, Woodrow Wilson, a Democrat, was president of the United States. As commander-in-chief of the Army and Navy, he set the nation's basic military strategy. He was also responsible for making sure the war economy worked effectively. Here, the president was assisted and supported by his cabinet, made up of top officials of the various departments of the federal government's executive branch. But, as Wilson and his cabinet tried to organize the country for war, they came up against four main obstacles to strong national government in the United States.

The first two of these were obstacles that American presidents had always faced and always would face—the fact that America was a democracy and the fact that the government's authority was divided between the president and Congress as required by the Constitution. Thus, President Wilson's policies, even with a war on, had political limits; his policies and programs had to meet the concerns of representatives and senators who were elected by the people. Many of these individuals opposed the war on principle or opposed aspects of the president's management of the war. Many were Republicans who opposed the president for simple partisan reasons. They wanted the Democratic president to falter so that people would vote Republican in the next election.

The other two obstacles to the president's policies were not built-in, constant factors limiting the government's power; rather, these limits were unique to the times and experiences of Americans in the early twentieth century. In the first place, the government was very weak in a bureaucratic, administrative sense, only a fraction of its size today. Experienced government officials and agencies were scarce, and the Wilson administration had to start from scratch as it organized itself to deal with the war economy's many complicated problems.

The fact that Americans had deeply mixed feelings about how powerful the federal government ought to be posed the fourth obstacle. It also helps explain why the federal government was so small. In American politics, there always had been strong opposition and resistance to powerful government in Washington. Most Americans believed in weak government, fearing that a strong federal government would threaten individual liberties, free enterprise, and the powers of the states.

In terms of its impact on their day-to-day lives, most Americans now would barely recognize the government in Washington during the first decades of the twentieth century. Indeed, most Americans today would find it hard to understand how Americans of that period thought of themselves as national citizens. Partly because the federal government's reach into their lives was so limited, most Americans then had a much weaker sense of national identity, or nationalism, than they have today. The United States is a large country made up of many different regions. Then, the overall sense of Americans as parts of a single national entity was not nearly as strong as it is today. People often thought of themselves as Texans, Californians, New Yorkers, Georgians, or Kansans before they thought of themselves as U.S. citizens.

The experience of World War I brought Americans a long way toward building a stronger sense of nationalism and national purpose, especially among those young men who were gathered up from across the land, trained as soldiers, and sent abroad to fight for their country. Still, deeply held old values and principles, along with the built-in weaknesses of the government, meant that the Wilson administration had to rely mainly on the willingness of workers, farmers, businessmen, politicians, and other Americans to cooperate voluntarily with its war policies. There were important exceptions to this rule, especially when Congress approved conscription, or the draft, of young men into the military. But, for the most part, the Wilson administration had to be careful not to violate popular attitudes toward the proper role of government, which most Americans thought should be as minimal as possible.

The political problems faced by the government became clear even before the United States formally entered the war in April 1917. President Wilson barely won the election of November 1916. He would have lost if just 4,000 people in California had voted instead for his Republican opponent, Charles Evans Hughes. The voters also sent many Republicans to Capitol Hill, giving the Democrats an uncomfortably small majority in Congress.

That closely fought election reflected deep divisions among Americans despite the fact that most of them were prospering, thanks to the economic stimulus of so many orders from the British and French for war supplies and food. Americans disagreed sharply about what position the United States ought to take toward the war in Europe, which had been raging for more than two years.

The election also reflected the concerns, confusions, and frustrations Americans felt about the many ways their country had changed since the end of the nineteenth century. There was concern about the new influence of big business corporations and about how the government ought to control that power. There had been many major strikes by workers against their employers. There were loud campaigns to amend the Constitution so that women could vote and to prohibit the sale of alcoholic beverages in the United States. Also unsettling were the various problems of America's big cities, especially the very rapid growth in the numbers of people who had emigrated from countries and cultures that were unfamiliar and confusing to many Americans.

President Wilson had to view the results of the 1916 election as a voters' backlash against the turbulence of recent political life and as a warning of the sorts of limits there would be on his foreign policy and on his management of the war economy should the United States join the fighting. These limits help explain why he continued to stall into April 1917 his request that Congress declare war on the Germans even though they had sharply increased their U-boat attacks on technically neutral American ships delivering supplies to the Allies.

After America's declaration of war, Wilson announced that "politics is adjourned" for the war's duration. It seemed essential that Americans and their representatives forget old controversies and political differences and pull together in the national emergency. As matters turned out, however, politics were not adjourned and the way Americans went about organizing themselves for the war actually reproduced their old political differences.

For example, many Americans agreed that a new government agency with broad powers to oversee the war economy was needed. It seemed that America's unregulated, free-enterprise economy would never be able quickly to turn out everything that millions of soldiers required. Farmers would have to produce much more. Privately owned factories would have to be converted to military production. The flow of raw materials into the factories and the many new military construction projects had to be steady and reliable. The nation's transportation systems would have to be able to carry the heavy extra loads and get material where it was needed when it was needed. And finished products would have to find their destinations on time.

The economy would be stretched to the maximum because of so many new military orders adding to the usual demands on the economy from people in civilian life. Efforts to control price inflation would be needed. Decisions would have to be made on which industries and products were essential to the war effort and which should get priority claims on raw material supplies. Overall, the job seemed immense and very complicated. Careful planning and a powerful government agency seemed unavoidable.

President Wilson recognized this as early as the summer of 1916 when he appointed the Council of National Defense (CND) to oversee the buildup of the nation's peacetime armed forces. The CND was the first of a stream of new federal agencies created to cope with the war's economic and social problems. These agencies amounted to a very large extension in the role of government in the day-to-day lives of Americans. But the amount of actual power they had also reflected the deep suspicion Americans had about strong government.

The CND, for example, had no formal or legal power, even after the nation formally entered the war. It comprised President Wilson's cabinet members and representatives of the economy's main economic functions, such as banking, industry, mining, labor, transportation, and health care. But all the CND could do in terms of overseeing the war economy was to give advice and encouragement to private businessmen and operators. The CND could point out problems, suggest solutions, and make appeals for everyone to work together, but it could not give orders.

Congress would not give the CND any real authority. Representatives and senators worried about how new executive war agencies might disrupt the traditional "checks and balances" of the federal government. Most importantly, Congress insisted that the army and navy keep full control over how military contracts were given out to businesses. This was the government's principal lever in the private economy, and Congress wanted this power to stay where it always had been, in the military services where the people's representatives could easily keep their eyes on things.

The CND was replaced by the War Industries Board in July 1917, but this new agency was not much more effective. The lack of a central coordinating mechanism over America's war economy led to many difficulties, delays, shortages, and "bottlenecks" as businessmen and industries competed with one another for the supplies and materials they needed to do their jobs.

To deal with specific problems, other federal agencies were created, such as the Food Administration, the Fuel Administration, the Railroad Administration, and the Shipping Board. Each had roles of different degrees of importance and different levels of authority, but only rarely did they go much beyond encouraging voluntary cooperation. Legal regulations were avoided as much as possible. The fact that some five thousand new federal agencies were instituted during the war suggests the haphazard and often chaotic way Americans dealt with mobilization on the home front. The pattern continued even after loud complaints about "bottlenecks," waste, and mismanagement during the winter of 1917–1918 when American troops in Europe were using British and French equipment because suppliers at home had still not come through almost a year after the United States entered the war.

The Germans almost made the right bet. In early 1917, they knew that their U-boat attacks on American ships supplying the British and French would probably lead to a U.S. declaration of war against them. They gambled on crushing the Allied armies in Europe, blockading Great Britain, and winning the war before the Americans could get organized and become an actual military threat. But by the summer of 1918 the Germans had not won the war and the Americans were becoming much more powerful.

Despite the long delays and the confusions in the management and planning of their war economy, Americans did turn out a steady stream of war supplies, weapons, and ships. And the army and National Guard grew from only 380,000 men in early 1917 to about 3.7 million by the end of the war. About two million well-armed and well-trained U.S. soldiers gradually found their way onto the battlefields of western Europe. A total of 50,585 U.S. servicemen died for their country in combat; some 60,000 others died from war-related disease.

Americans eventually succeeded in mobilizing themselves for World War I without basic changes to their open and democratic system of government or to their national political values. Their successes point to the overall vitality of the national economy, which grew stronger day by day because of the war's stimulus. For example, the output of the nation's factories grew by a very large margin, about 33 percent, from 1914 to 1918.

The huge American economy easily absorbed the costs of poor planning and coordination. America's success also points to the fact that the United States was far removed from the actual fighting. For most Europeans the threat was much more immediate. The war devastated their homelands, and their resources were much more limited. European governments had little choice but to impose the kinds of controls and authoritarianism that Americans had the luxury of avoiding thanks to their country's size, resources, and geographical protection.

In areas of life apart from the war economy, however, Americans seemed much more tolerant of infringements on personal freedoms, individual expression, and radical ideas. The Wilson administration encouraged and led a national effort to foster patriotism, build popular support for the war, and stamp out opposition to it. In a sense, this campaign, with its many features of repressive intolerance, contradicted the government's effort to mobilize the war economy by relying on voluntarism and cooperation. To get people to cooperate, the Wilson administration tried to make noncooperation socially unacceptable and offensive for Americans.

The government heavily promoted the war effort and used aggressive advertisements to sell the nation's war aims. Agencies like the Food Administration campaigned to get Americans to eat less of certain kinds of foods so that shortages might be avoided. The Treasury Department persuaded many Americans to help finance the war by buying Liberty Bonds. And the government launched a national publicity, or propaganda, campaign to shape public opinion and to discredit war opponents. Americans proved broadly responsive to and supportive of this campaign, which seems something of a paradox, given their values of individual freedom in economic matters.

Support for this conformity campaign stemmed in part from anxieties among Americans about the way their society had changed in the years prior to the war, especially in its ethnic and cultural makeup. Americans who had been born in the United States and whose family roots went back several generations, were disturbed by the large numbers of people who had recently come to America and had built up a significant presence, especially in the large cities.

These immigrants seemed threatening because they came from countries and cultures with which Americans had little experience. Many came from Italy, Greece, and central and eastern Europe and practiced the Catholic and Jewish religious faiths, which some Americans considered inferior, even dangerous, to mainstream U.S. culture and values. The effort to build conformity of opinion during the war drew much energy from pre-war prejudices toward new Americans and from deep anxieties and confusions about what it now meant to be an American in a rapidly changing world.

The government's wartime campaign of intolerance also had roots in President Wilson's efforts to win the election of 1916 by countering criticisms of his pro-Britain and pro-France policies. The president played on the prejudices and anxieties of Americans and worked to foster divisiveness by calling for "100 percent Americanism" and dismissing his critics as "disloyal" Americans. He also spoke darkly about "hyphenated" Americans, referring to the hyphen in such expressions as German-American or Irish-American.

Only eight days after America's declaration of war in April 1917,

President Wilson created the Committee on Public Information, which became the government's main agency for propaganda and opinion-molding. George Creel, a well-known journalist, oversaw the committee's work, which included the production and distribution of anti-German movies with titles like *The Kaiser, Beast of Berlin,* and *The Prussian Cur.* The committee printed and distributed millions of pro-war brochures and pamphlets.

One of its major efforts involved an army of 75,000 volunteer speakers who roamed the nation appearing in any public forum they could find—churches, town squares, schools—to give spirited speeches intended to whip up support for the war. Audiences were encouraged to hate Germans and "slackers"—those who avoided what everyone assumed was their duty. Ethnic Americans were pressured to give up their old-country practices and to act like "100 percent Americans." These volunteers were known as the "four-minute men" because their speeches were always about the same length, carefully timed to raise the feelings of their audiences at just the right pace. The "four-minute men" often exaggerated, and even fabricated, stories of German atrocities and war crimes and enemy spies and saboteurs in the United States.

The propaganda campaign went well beyond the efforts of federal government officials, extending to state and local officials and other Americans all across the country. The campaign soon took on aspects of a nationalist frenzy and snowballed into a witch-hunt. Many states and local authorities, for example, passed laws banning the German language, German music by composers such as Beethoven, Bach, and Mozart, and German words like "pretzels," and "hamburger" (which became "Liberty sandwich"), or "sauerkraut" (which became "Liberty cabbage"). In New Orleans, Berlin Street became General Pershing Street.

Far more disturbing were the creation of citizen thought-control and vigilante groups with names like the American Protective League, Sedition Slammers, and Boy Spies of America. These oversaw local "agents" who watched friends and neighbors, opening their mail and tapping their phone lines, trying to detect any sign of "disloyalty"—a term that could mean anything. All too frequently, these efforts evolved into mob violence and attacks on innocent or harmless people. Americans of German descent were especially victimized by the witch-hunts.

Congress encouraged such intolerance by passing the Espionage Act in June 1917. It gave the government new powers to fight spies and sabotage, which would seem to be reasonable in time of war. But it also provided new powers to curb dissent and opposition to the war. The

Post Office, for example, was authorized to deny mail privileges to writers, magazines, and journals that it deemed responsible for "traitorous" writings. The Post Office's guidelines on what was "traitorous" were vague, and disloyalty could mean just about anything, including honest debate.

As the war went on, the Espionage Act was strengthened, most notably by the Sedition Act of May 1918, which made the expression of opposition to the war a federal crime. These acts, combined with new restrictive immigration laws, were energetically enforced by federal officials. The overall effects were the quashing of free speech and civil liberties even though America's stated aim in the war was to make the world "safe for democracy." In one case, a film director was given a ten-year jail sentence because he produced a movie about the American Revolution that a judge thought was too critical of America's ally, Great Britain.

These laws wrecked left-wing social and political movements in the United States, which voiced the opinions of Americans who thought their government and society were unfair to poor and working people. These radicals saw the war as the result of businessmen's efforts to increase their markets and profits—even if that meant the loss of many soldiers' lives. That was the position of the Socialist party, and its leader, Eugene V. Debs, was sentenced to ten years in prison when he gave an antiwar speech in Cleveland.

Also heavily suppressed were radical labor unions, like the Industrial Workers of the World (IWW), which sponsored strikes in western lumber camps and mines, trying to win better pay and conditions for workers. Thousands of IWW members were jailed. And many newcomers to America were jailed or deported without trial when the government deemed them threats to the war effort and to pro-war popular attitudes. The power, or perhaps the unnecessary excesses, of the government's pro-war and patriotic propaganda and its campaign to suppress dissenters is suggested by the fact that, of 3 million men drafted during the war, only about 170,000 tried to evade the draft.

Another important aspect of wartime control over social behavior and of the effort to build a stronger sense of nationalism and patriotism was the success of the Prohibition campaign. For years, reformers had tried to eliminate alcoholic beverages in the United States. They acted on genuine concerns about the serious social problems and health risks connected with heavy drinking. But they were often also motivated by dark antiforeigner feelings which the war intensified. Drinking was an important part of the social and religious practices of recent immigrant groups, and Prohibition was often aimed at suppressing differences and making immigrants more like mainstream Americans. The campaign was helped by the sense of wartime urgency. Beer and liquor used up scarce grains like barley, hops, and corn. Further, the major breweries had been established by German Americans like Pabst, Schlitz, and Anheuser-Busch; and putting them out of business seemed like another good way to strike out at "disloyal" Americans. In late 1917, Congress passed Prohibition legislation, outlawing the sale of alcoholic beverages in America, and in 1919, Americans ratified the Eighteenth Amendment to the Constitution to reflect the new policy.

In other areas of American life, World War I led to some very important steps toward greater tolerance, democracy, and opportunity. Wartime conditions helped push toward success the campaign for women's right to vote and also created new opportunities for black people.

Women's groups had struggled for decades for this basic right, but their efforts to change the law suffered a major defeat in the senate as late as October 1918. The contribution of women in America's defense factories, on the farm, and in various support roles in the military, however, were changing old-fashioned perceptions on the proper place for women in society. To many, it now appeared two-faced for Americans to be fighting for democracy in Europe while denying it to women who made up half the population. Further, it seemed that a world at war could use the caring, nurturing skills in which women were thought to be superior to men, a loving sense of mercy that could help avoid future wars if women were empowered. Thus in June 1919, Congress approved the vote for women, and a year later, Americans added the Nineteenth Amendment to the Constitution.

Like women, African Americans also suffered from having few political rights before the war. They also had few social and economic rights, as these were denied them by the states of the American South where the great majority of black Americans lived. Since the 1890s, southern states had enforced white supremacist laws, called "Jim Crow" laws, that segregated people by race and excluded blacks from voting and from all but the lowest educational and job opportunities. The war, however, produced new opportunities for blacks outside the South, and hundreds of thousands moved to big northern industrial cities like New York, Chicago, Detroit, Cleveland, and Pittsburgh to take up wartime jobs. By 1920, some 1.5 million southern blacks had moved north in the "Great Migration," taking on factory jobs or other city-based work. They also built strong urban neighborhoods, like Harlem in New York, which soon generated new political strength for black Americans.

For American blacks and women, the struggle for real equality and justice was far from over and would require steady efforts through the years and decades ahead. Still, World War I created new opportunities and an atmosphere inspiring progress. The possibilities for blacks and women presented by the war, but also the old, ongoing limits and obstacles against them, are symbolic of the war's overall effect on American life, especially on government and the sense of nationalism among Americans. The war forced major steps toward a modern federal government that could better deal with the kinds of complicated national problems that would develop in the decades ahead. And Americans more and more came to see themselves as members of a national community, with a more focused sense of their relation to the national government. Still, Americans took these steps forward without giving up their basic political values. And they came to view their future in terms of how they understood the past but with a new sense of anxiety and uncertainty.

SELECTED BIBLIOGRAPHY

Ambrosius, Lloyd E. *Wilsonian Statecraft: Theory and Practice of Liberal Internationalism during World War I.* Wilmington, DE: Scholarly Resources, 1991. A detailed analysis of the intellectual background of Wilson's diplomacy.

Arnet, Alex Mathews. *Claude Kitchin and the Wilson War Policies.* Boston: Little, Brown, 1937. An old, but still very useful, study of national politics during the war.

Beaver, Daniel R. *Newton D. Baker and the American War Effort, 1917–1919.* Lincoln: University of Nebraska Press, 1966. A history of efforts to mobilize the nation for war and of the role in these efforts played by the secretary of war.

Blum, John Morton. *Woodrow Wilson and the Politics of Morality.* Boston: Little, Brown, 1956. President Wilson and his view of the world are the topics of this study, written by a distinguished American historian.

Coben, Stanley. *A. Mitchell Palmer: Politician.* New York: Columbia University Press, 1963. Palmer became President Wilson's attorney general, the nation's top law enforcement official.

Coffman, Edward M. *The War to End All Wars: The American Military Experience in World War I.* New York: Oxford University Press, 1968. A vivid account of the war as experienced by American servicemen and women.

Cornebise, Alfred E. *War as Advertised: The Four Minute Men and America's Crusade, 1917–1918.* Philadelphia: American Philosophical Society, 1984. An account of the public speakers who tried to persuade Americans to work harder and support the war effort and the government's goals.

Cuff, Robert D. *The War Industries Board: Business-Government Relations during World War I*. Baltimore: Johns Hopkins University Press, 1973. This book carefully traces the policies and politics of one of the leading civilian government agencies for managing America's wartime economy.

Freidel, Frank. *Over There*. New York: McGraw-Hill, 1990. An illustrated survey of America's role in World War I.

Fussell, Paul. *The Great War and Modern Memory*. New York: Oxford University Press, 1975. One of the best readers available for students of the war.

Gilbert, Charles. *American Financing of World War I*. Westport, CT: Greenwood Press, 1970. An important study of economic relations among the Allies and of wartime taxes and revenues in the United States.

Granatstein, J.L., and R.D. Cuff, eds. *War and Society in North America*. Toronto: Thomas Nelson, 1971. A series of essays that compare the different approaches taken toward managing the war effort at home in the United States and in Canada.

Greenwald, Maurine W. *Women, War and Work*. New York: New York University Press, 1980. A fine account of the war as experienced by American women.

Grubbs, Frank L. *The Struggle for Labor Loyalty: Gompers, the American Federation of Labor, and the Pacifists, 1917–1920*. Durham, NC: Duke University Press, 1968. This book traces the policies and political struggles of organized labor's main voice during the war.

Hartmann, Edward George. *The Movement to Americanize the Immigrant*. New York: AMS Press, 1967. A study of the American response to the "new immigration" of the late nineteenth and early twentieth centuries.

Hawley, Ellis. *The Great War and the Search for a Modern Order: A History of the American People and Their Institutions, 1917–1933*. New York: St. Martin's Press, 1979. One of the most important interpretations of the war's consequences for institutional life in America.

Johnson, Donald. *The Challenge to American Freedoms: World War I and the Rise of the American Civil Liberties Union*. Lexington: University of Kentucky Press, 1963. A very useful study of the challenges to basic individual freedoms during the hysteria of World War I and the efforts of some Americans to defend them.

Kennedy, David M. *Over Here: The First World War and American Society*. New York: Oxford University Press, 1980. The author provides a broad overview of the results of the war for American society, economy, and culture.

Kerr, K. Austin. *American Railroad Politics, 1914–1920*. Pittsburgh: University of Pittsburgh Press, 1968. This book focuses on the relations between the federal government and the railroad industry during the war, which posed some of the biggest problems for the government and the war economy.

Lasswell, Harold D. *Propaganda Technique in the World War*. New York: Peter Smith, 1938. A study of the government's efforts to shape and control public opinion by a famous American political scientist.

Leuchtenberg, William E. *The Perils of Prosperity, 1914–32*. Chicago: University of Chicago Press, 1958. An important overview of American history from the Wilson years through Herbert Hoover's presidency.

Link, Arthur S. *Wilson: Campaigns for Progressivism and Peace. 1916–1917.* Princeton, NJ: Princeton University Press, 1965. This is just one title among Professor Link's many important studies of Woodrow Wilson and his policies.

Livermore, Seward. *Politics is Adjourned: Woodrow Wilson and the War Congress, 1916–1918.* Middleton, CT: Wesleyan University Press, 1966. Essential reading on wartime national politics.

Luebke, Frederick C. *Bonds of Loyalty: German-Americans and World War I.* De Kalb: Northern Illinois University Press, 1974. This study traces the experiences and outlook of Americans who immigrated from Germany or were of German ethnic descent.

Mock, James R., and Cedric Larson. *Words That Won the War: The Story of the Committee on Public Information, 1917–1919.* Princeton, NJ: Princeton University Press, 1939. A history of the main government agency for information on the war and for shaping public opinion.

Paxson, Fredrick L. *American Democracy and the World War.* 3 vols. Boston: Houghton Mifflin, 1936–1948. A major study of the war's impact on American life.

Rudwick, Elliot M. *Race Riot at East St. Louis, July 2, 1917.* Carbondale: Southern Illinois University Press, 1964. This book focuses on one of the most violent domestic events of the war years and relates it to larger developments in race relations.

Stooksbury, James L. *A Short History of World War I.* New York: William Morrow, 1981. A good, comprehensive survey of the war, with emphasis on its military history.

Walworth, Arthur. *Wilson and His Peacemakers: American Diplomacy at the Paris Peace Conference, 1919.* New York: W.W. Norton, 1986. An excellent comprehensive treatment of the American diplomatic role during the long Paris Peace Conference.

As this photograph of a small Mississippi town in 1936 suggests, unemployment was a major social and economic problem during the Great Depression. (Photographic Archives, University of Louisville, Roy Stryker Collection)

3

The Great Depression, 1929–c. 1939

INTRODUCTION

Although the stock market crash of October 1929 is usually cited as the end of the prosperous 1920s and the beginning of the Great Depression, it may better be seen as a symptom of several serious economic problems that developed in the American economy during the late 1920s. Among these was a large and uncontrolled speculative boom on Wall Street, with stock prices rising out of any reasonable relationship to the financial soundness of the corporations whose stock was being traded. No regulatory agency existed that could work to prevent excessive speculation and police other malpractices in the stock market.

Another significant problem was an agricultural depression that had begun shortly after World War I and lasted throughout the decade. From this depression came a decline in farm income, land values, and, ultimately, in the purchasing power of people living in rural areas. Many country banks failed during the 1920s, and despite the efforts of sympathetic congressmen, the federal government provided little relief. The plight of the farmers contributed to an unequal distribution of income across America in the 1920s, with high industrial profits and low taxes enabling the rich to get richer much faster than the poor got less poor. This meant that the economy was dependent on a small percentage of people for the investment necessary to maintain or expand industrial productivity; when these people were no longer investing, the economy was bound to suffer.

Finally, there was an international dimension to the growing economic problems of the late 1920s. The United States had emerged from the war with the strongest economy in the world, and most of Europe, because of the problems inherent in postwar reconstruction, was dependent on American loans and trade. Should the United States withdraw from involvement in the greater European economy, there would be dire consequences.

The October 1929 stock market crash was significant in the coming of the Depression because it struck at the fortunes of the wealthy and caused them to stop investing. The crash exploited the weakness of corporate structure in the United States, which also dampened investment. Perhaps most importantly, the crash had a major psychological impact, creating an attitude of hopelessness and the feeling that nothing could (and, some thought, should) be done.

President Herbert Hoover, a Republican of conservative economic beliefs, knew that the Depression, as it worsened in 1930 and 1931, was a serious economic crisis; but he felt strongly that it was a consequence of the economy's natural development and that the government had no role to play in bringing about recovery. He also felt that the mood of the country was important to recovery, and thus he spent a good deal of time trying to create a positive atmosphere through optimistic predictions and participating in upbeat activities, such as attending the 1931 World Series. Privately, he urged business leaders to be socially cooperative in maintaining employment at reasonable wages, while cutting other expenses in order to lower production costs.

But when in 1930 conditions worsened and public hostility began to focus on the president, the administration decided that the Depression was a result of foreign causes. To counter that, Hoover urged Congress to pass the Smoot-Hawley tariff bill, a measure designed to protect American commerce from foreign competition by raising customs duties to record high levels. Against the advice of most economists, the bill passed; it had a chilling effect on European economies, while doing little to help the economy in the United States.

Conditions in the United States worsened each year in the early 1930s. This was most clearly evident in the unemployment rate, which rose from 9 percent in 1930 to 16 percent in 1931 to 24 percent in 1932. Many other Americans were underemployed, working only a few hours per week, or had had their wages severely cut. By late 1931, there was real distress in some parts of the country. Hoover proposed the creation of the Reconstruction Finance Corporation (RFC), a government agency empowered to lend money to banks, railroads, and major industries as a way to hire back workers and stimulate the economy. But the RFC, run by conservative bankers, dispersed only a fraction of the money it was authorized to lend, and the suffering continued. In 1932, much against his personal beliefs, Hoover allowed the RFC to lend money to states for relief purposes. Again, the agency was frugal with its money, and little relief was provided. The seriousness of the crisis was etched most sharply by the plight of the "bonus army," a motley band of 22,000 unemployed World War I veterans who came to Washington in the summer of 1932 to demand immediate payment of a bonus for their military service that had been promised for 1945. Congress voted down a bill to that effect, and the unsympathetic administration used currently enlisted troops, led by General Douglas MacArthur, to drive the veterans out of the capital.

In the presidential election of 1932, the Republican incumbent, Hoover, was matched against the Democratic governor of New York, Franklin D. Roosevelt. Unable to run on his record, Hoover could only try to persuade voters that the country would be doomed if the Democrats won. Although crippled by polio and unable to walk unaided, Roosevelt ran a vigorous campaign, based on a program called a "New Deal for Americans," of capitalism modified by economic planning that would prevent the booms and panics of earlier times and create a more even distribution of national wealth. The real issue was the Depression and the hardships it had brought on, and voters, frustrated by Hoover's inability to ease the problem, elected Roosevelt by a wide margin.

The transition period between Roosevelt's election in November 1932 and his inauguration in March 1933 saw conditions worsen still more. By inauguration day, the nation's banking system was in danger of imminent collapse, and Roosevelt's first action as president was to declare a "bank holiday," closing all the banks for five days while teams of inspectors checked the books. Most banks were allowed to reopen, and the crisis passed. Later, the Twentieth Amendment to the Constitution was adopted, shortening the "Lame Duck" transition period by moving inauguration day back from March 4 to January 20.

In practice, the New Deal was an avalanche of legislation, much of it passed during the first hundred days of Roosevelt's presidency. Although historians have discussed the New Deal in a variety of ways, it

may be noted that nearly all the legislation was related to the three principal objectives of the program: (1) a pressing need to provide *relief* for
the many thousands of Americans in genuine distress because they were
out of work and out of savings; (2) a need to bring about *recovery* from
the economic paralysis gripping the nation; and (3) a need to enact *reform*
measures to prevent it all from happening again. Although many of the
New Deal acts were hastily formulated and ineffective, and others were
found to be unconstitutional, the very fact that Roosevelt and the Congress were doing something provided a real psychological boost.

In May 1933, Congress created the Federal Emergency Relief Administration (FERA), which made money grants to states for welfare payments and supervised federal relief programs. One of the most popular
of these programs was the Civilian Conservation Corps (CCC), which
employed 2.75 million young men between 1933 and 1942. In the CCC,
men between the ages of 18 and 25 were taken from the cities and put
to work on reforestation, irrigation, and other conservation projects in
national parks, forest reserves, and other federally owned land. Workers
were given room and board in army-like encampments and were paid
$30 per month, of which $25 was sent back to their families. They generally thrived on the outdoor work, and, in most places, a strong sense
of camaraderie developed. Special CCC programs for Native Americans
and Eskimos allowed them to work on useful projects in their own reservations or villages.

By far the most important relief program was the Works Progress Administration (WPA), which gave work to more than eight million Americans between 1935 and 1941. For the most part, WPA workers built or
repaired public buildings, roads, and bridges. There were also special
WPA programs for different professions: for example, artists painted mu-
rals in post offices; historians wrote state and city guide books; and play-
wrights produced dramas for civic entertainment. Because of its large
bureaucracy, the WPA became one of the most politicized of the New
Deal agencies. Republicans accused Democrats of appointing state and
local administrators on the basis of their politics; and while Democrats
refuted the allegations, the issue was a factor in the midterm election of
1938, in which the Democrats suffered significant losses, and in the passage of the Hatch Act in 1939, which forbade political activity by federal
employees.

The National Recovery Administration (NRA), created in June 1933,
was the New Deal's principal effort to bring about economic recovery.
Under the NRA, business, labor, and government representatives were

to cooperate in drafting "codes of competition," which utilized planning to divide up markets and in other ways reduce open competition in a particular industry. Each code also included protection for labor in the form of collective bargaining rights, a shorter work week, and a minimum wage of forty cents per hour. Problems arose, however, as the codes were developed. In many sectors, large industries or businesses dominated and wrote the codes to their advantage. Labor and consumers had no voice in the code authorities, which administered the program. And everyone had trouble with General Hugh S. Johnson, the unstable and authoritarian head of the NRA.

In 1935, the Supreme Court, in the case of *Schechter* v. *U.S.*, found the NRA to be unconstitutional. The court ruled that Congress had improperly delegated to a voluntary association that was a part of the executive branch of the government powers that the constitution reserved for Congress itself. Later, in 1935, Congress passed the National Labor Relations (or Wagner) Act, which resurrected the beneficial provisions for labor that had been part of the NRA.

The administration attempted to bring about economic recovery for agriculture in the Agricultural Adjustment Act (AAA), passed in May 1933. This act authorized payments to farmers who took acreage out of production or killed off livestock. In either case, the purpose was to reduce the supply and thus increase prices to a point where they were in better balance with industrial prices. It worked; by 1935, prices for major grains had doubled and total farm income was up 54 percent. But in 1936, the Supreme Court, in *U.S.* v. *Butler,* declared the AAA unconstitutional on the grounds that the federal government was delegating powers reserved to the states. A second AAA, passed in 1938, resumed aid to farmers by providing cash subsidies to them when commodity prices dropped below a certain level.

A number of congressional acts contributed to the reform aspect of the New Deal. The Securities Exchange Commission (SEC) was created to regulate the operations of the stock market and end the abuses that had contributed to the 1929 crash. The Federal Deposit Insurance Corporation (FDIC), a part of the Glass-Steagall Banking Act of 1933, provided federally funded insurance for bank accounts up to $2,500. The Social Security Act, passed in 1935, coordinated state and federal old-age pensions and unemployment compensation, which varied widely among the states.

Even though Roosevelt had campaigned in 1932 on the importance of a balanced federal budget, it was clear by 1935 that deficit spending (then called "pump-priming") had been an important factor in stimulating the recovery. But the deficits, which ranged from $2.6 billion to $4.4 billion between 1933 and 1936, were unprecedented in peacetime and brought on some political opposition. After his reelection in 1936, the president declared that the Depression was over and cut spending sharply in order to bring the budget back into balance. The result was a sharp recession, beginning in the summer of 1937, and a renewed spurt of deficit spending in 1938. The federal budget deficits between 1929 and 1939 totaled some $40.4 billion and more than doubled the national debt.

Although Roosevelt was reelected in a landslide in 1936, there was opposition to the New Deal. Conservative Republicans decried the growth of the federal government and the annual deficit. On the left, Socialists and Communists argued for a more radical restructuring of the capitalist system. And Roosevelt himself created a good deal of opposition in 1937 with his "court-packing" plan. Upset with Supreme Court decisions invalidating various New Deal measures, the president urged Congress to approve legislation that would allow him to appoint one new justice to the court for each sitting justice over seventy years of age. By expanding the size of the court with his own appointees, Roosevelt hoped to win more favorable decisions. But Congress defeated the proposal, and the American public reacted with hostility to the president's attempt to tamper with such a revered institution.

The most vocal opponents of the New Deal were demagogues—charismatic politicians who were driven by a zeal for personal power and influence and whose messages were crafted to appeal to the desperate. Huey Long, a Louisiana politician, attracted many people with his "Share-the-Wealth" program before his assassination in 1935. Father Charles E. Coughlin, the "Radio Priest," spoke to large audiences over the radio, increasingly blaming America's problems on an international Jewish conspiracy. And Dr. Francis E. Townsend claimed ten million supporters of his Revolving Old Age Pension Plan, in which each American over the age of sixty would receive $200 per month, with the condition that the money be spent within thirty days.

By 1938, the country was hearing more and more about the war clouds gathering in Europe, and a national debate between isolationists and internationalists was taking shape. The New Deal was now rather old, and the administration, damaged by political problems with the WPA, the reaction to the court-packing plan, and the recession of 1937, found its majorities in Congress sharply reduced in the midterm election of 1938. Now an informal coalition of Republicans and conservative Democrats could block passage of any significant social welfare legislation. Clearly, the years 1939 and 1940 were a time of transition for the United States. The New Deal was over and the country was gearing up for World War II.

INTERPRETIVE ESSAY
Anders Greenspan

Herbert Hoover assumed the reins of government in March 1929 confident of a successful presidency, but a weakening economy and unchecked speculation in the stock market prevented this from happening. In addition, the government remained contracted as spending was held down, and the gold standard prohibited the expansion of the currency. An unequal distribution of income gave the wealthiest five percent of the population 26 percent of the nation's income. This concentration of wealth in the hands of so few lessened the spending power of the general population, which limited the amount of products that could be purchased. Black Thursday, October 24, 1929, was a harbinger of impending disaster. Nearly thirteen million shares of stock changed hands on the New York Stock Exchange that day, and prices dropped sharply, causing great alarm in the financial community. J.P. Morgan & Co. and other large banking interests did what they could to stem the day's losses, which threatened their financial futures. The next day, Hoover reassured a troubled country that the economy was on sound footing and that there was no need for alarm. Yet the crash, which occurred on October 29, was only a weekend away.

The loss of $40 billion as a result of the stock market crash in the last third of 1929 was horrendously damaging to the American economy. The dependence on business confidence was important, but that was now lost due to the economic tragedy that befell the nation. The stock market entered into every aspect of Americans' lives, and its collapse dealt a disastrous blow. By the end of 1930, industrial production was 26 percent below production in 1929. By the summer of 1932, the loss was approximately 50 percent below the 1929 figure. Construction and automobile production declined sharply. This was bad news, as both were prime economic indicators and major areas of growth prior to the crash. Due to this massive drop in production, unemployment skyrocketed. Wages and incomes were down all across the board, with industrial wages declining precipitously from $53 billion in 1929 to $31.5 billion in 1933. In addition, the group hurt worst, the farmers, lost more than half of their income, from $11.9 billion in 1929 to $5.3 billion in 1932. The economic collapse, coming after so much optimism and dreams of wealth in the post-World War I era, was psychologically crushing for many Americans. Many families were forced to double up as people lost their homes and families had to move in together. Many of the young people who were out of work married later and therefore had fewer children.

A disaster of this magnitude demonstrated that private relief agencies were not going to be able to handle the great suffering. Traditionally, Americans had relied on private agencies to help the poor, but as time went on and the Depression worsened, it became evident that they were not going to be able to shoulder the burden all by themselves. As private charity was unable adequately to help those in need, the poor congregated in "Hoovervilles," cardboard shanty towns across the country. Others traveled the country's rails, sleeping in box cars, searching for work or trying to escape their troubles. Existence was difficult, and more and more Americans began to blame their troubles on President Hoover's administration.

For many Americans, the reality of a country of such great abundance caught in a depression was difficult to comprehend. This was a country that had been able to feed and clothe its people with ease; yet clothing factories shut down and farmers had such great surpluses that they poured milk out in the streets in order to lower supplies, and raise its price. Meanwhile, some urban children were going without milk. Although many Americans felt Hoover did an inadequate job of handling the Depression, the reality is that he did do far more than the many presidents who had preceded him had done in similar situations. Many former presidents had faced economic collapses but had done virtually nothing to alter or correct their path. So when the Depression started, it did not seem logical that the government should step in quickly to fix the problems that, in the past, had been fixed by the business cycle. Many argued that any such governmental move would weaken the moral fiber of Americans and be detrimental to the country at large.

With the 1932 election looming, Hoover realized he needed to do something to strengthen the nation's gloomy economic outlook. The result was the Reconstruction Finance Corporation (RFC), the boldest antidepression measure ever taken by the federal government. RFC payments tended to go to many of the country's largest banks, insurance companies, and railroads, creating problems for many of their smaller competitors who could easily be forced out of business. As the suffering of American families grew worse, Hoover was hard–pressed to explain why the federal government was able to help many large corporations, but not smaller ones, or families and individuals. The purpose of the RFC was not to give massive federal aid, but, rather, to help people through firming up employment opportunities in the private sector. This, to Hoover's mind, would be enough of a stimulus to ease these businesses out of their temporary problems without huge amounts of government spending. In addition, the Emergency Relief and Construction Act of 1932 was meant to avoid the specter of federal relief, yet help states provide some type of employment for those who were desperately in need of work. These measures were weak, but the Congress, as a whole, was not pushing for welfare relief.

The two actions that sealed Hoover's fate, however, were the breaking up of the Bonus Army's march on Washington and the raising of federal income taxes during a depression. Due to larger federal outlays through these loans programs and declining tax receipts, the federal deficit rose to more than $2 billion. With strong sentiment that the federal government should not run at a deficit, the obvious answer seemed to be an increase in income tax rates. On June 6, 1932, Hoover signed into law the Revenue Act of 1932. This proved to be a totally counterproductive bill, as it took money out of people's hands and strengthened opposition to a president who was seen as being insensitive to the public's concerns. A similar problem occurred with the Bonus Army. The Senate's rejection of the demand of World War I veterans to advance by several years the payment of promised bonuses was based on the argument of fiscal responsibility. The veterans argued, however, that disbursement of the bonus money would have increased consumer spending and, therefore, would have boosted the economy. So entrenched was the philosophy against deficit spending that even this relatively modest attempt to placate the country's veterans was turned down.

To add insult to injury, Hoover refused to meet with the veterans or their representatives, a clear rebuff and an indication that Hoover did not take the Bonus Army seriously. Although the House supported the veterans, the Senate refused to do so, and Secretary of War Patrick Hurley and Secretary of Treasury Ogden Mills moved to tear down the veterans' encampment in the Anacostia flats. Although the superintendent of the District of Columbia police was opposed to a confrontation, Hurley obviously wished to provoke one with the Bonus marchers. As the veterans refused to leave, a struggle broke out, and Hoover ordered federal troops under Douglas MacArthur to settle the streets. Heavily armed, MacArthur and his men attacked the camp in Anacostia, and the veterans fled into the countryside. This inept handling of a volatile situation, combined with the imposition of higher taxes, drove voters away from the Republicans in the election of 1932.

Franklin Delano Roosevelt's victory in the fall of 1932 signaled a turning point in American politics. For although FDR was basically a fiscal conservative, his administration altered the relationship of the people to the government. The depth and suffering of the Depression gave Roosevelt immense presidential powers. Congress was anxious for any plan or program to help soften the blow of the Depression, and Franklin Roosevelt was ready—along with his advisers, known as the "Brain Trust." As president, FDR had to work to create a cohesive coalition to promote his platform. The Democrats were a diverse group ranging from northern union members to old-line southerners. Through wise moves and political craftsmanship, FDR was able to create a cohesive Democratic party that would control the presidency for two full decades.

When Roosevelt took office on March 4, 1933, he had unprecedented power for a president in peacetime. On March 6, the president announced a five-day bank holiday and forbade gold payments and exports of the precious metal. On March 9, Congress quickly enacted the Emergency Banking Act. Roosevelt pushed for the maintenance of private control of the banking and finance sectors of the economy, seeking to preserve the market system with an eye toward government regulation rather than control.

FDR informed the nation of his plans to improve the economy in his first "fireside chat" on March 12, 1933. These radio broadcasts became an integral part of the New Deal, as FDR used them to keep in close communication with the American people and inform them of the changes being made in Washington. Never before had Americans felt so close to their government. Indeed, FDR's greatest talent was his ability to communicate with Americans through the media: radio and newsreels. He was able to convey ideas in simple language and with a voice and style appealing to his vast audiences. As is often required of a successful politician in a democracy, he knew what Americans wanted and sought to give it to them. FDR also believed in the old Progressive notion that government has a positive role to play and that it can do much to better people's lives and promote the growth of the country.

The first policies of the New Deal relied heavily on cooperation among those who were the major partners in the country's economy. Roosevelt took the country off the gold standard and initiated a policy of controlled inflation, which raised prices and increased incomes for business. This led to increased wages and the possibilities of employment. The most important of these cooperative programs were the National Recovery Administration (NRA) and the Agricultural Adjustment Administration (AAA), which changed the relationship between the government and the business community. Although both programs would eventually be declared unconstitutional, these acts demonstrated Roosevelt's power and the innovations of the New Deal.

The two programs expressed the philosophy of the first part of the New Deal. The idea behind them was to end the deflationary spiral that had brought farm prices and industrial wages down. They were aimed at getting the economy rolling again through emphasis on the private sector. Hard economic times had combined with the severe drought and "dustbowl" conditions of the plains states to create a great danger of foreclosure, as prices for farm products remained low and many farmers had trouble paying off their debts. Many states moved to halt the rush, passing legislation that placed a moratorium on farm foreclosures or forbade the forced sale of a bankrupt farmer's land and equipment. When forced sales, usually auctions, were held, friends and neighbors intimidated outside buyers and purchased the foreclosed farmer's property for pennies an acre. Then they returned the property to the original owner. This was a demonstration of local community action to prevent the loss of farms and people's livelihoods.

The AAA was a new approach to problems that had plagued farmers for half a century. The crux of the plan was to stabilize the production and the consumption of foodstuffs in order to preserve the nation's farmers from bankruptcy. As many farmers were deeply in debt, there had to be enough of a profit to repay debts as well as allow for the sustenance of the family to keep them from going under. This would be achieved by placing production limits on major commodities to prevent flooding of the market, which would drive prices down.

The NRA sought to handle and improve the lives of those who labored in the industrial sector of the economy by controlling cutthroat competition, raising prices, and providing decent working conditions. The basic structure of the NRA called for an intricate set of codes that would establish guidelines to ensure the above practices. Here was direct evidence of government closely regulating labor and businesses to help improve the economy and people's lives. Perhaps the most important element of

NRA was Section 7a, which affirmed the right of labor to organize and bargain collectively. This aspect of the legislation was seized upon by labor leaders to help foster membership and promote the power of the unions. Symbolized by the blue eagle, the NRA set quickly to work signing up employers who would agree to abide by a general set of codes until more specific ones could be drawn up for the multitude of businesses involved in the plan. The NRA's motto, "We do our part," emphasized that everyone needed to chip in to make the system work.

By 1935, the policies of the early New Deal appeared to be weakening. Businesses resented the increasing power of the federal government, and other critics argued that the New Deal was not doing enough to help those who were really hurting. The economy was simply not growing at a pace quick enough to promote long-term recovery. The role of the politician is to be reelected, and for Roosevelt to do so he had to ensure that his policies were effective enough to capture the interest of large numbers of Americans. He had promised Americans a New Deal and needed to make good on his commitment. FDR engineered a shift to the left to bring about greater governmental responsibility to ensure a happier public. While the early New Deal had depended to a large extent on old-style Hooverian voluntary cooperation, the later New Deal placed more authority in the hands of government. The government now became more directly responsible for the welfare of its citizens and acted as an arbiter of conflict.

Roosevelt faced his greatest opposition from Huey Long, a Louisiana senator, who reached national prominence in 1934 with his "share the wealth" plan. Long's critics pointed to several deficiencies in his program, but Long was clearly more interested in playing to the crowd for popular support than he was in making all of the numbers match. The "Kingfish," as he was popularly known, was accused of promoting a Communist or Socialist plan, and was attacked as being inherently un-American. Roosevelt saw Long as a harbinger of American fascism, as the Kingfish seemed to want absolute political power. Long, however, ceased to be a threat when he was assassinated on September 8, 1935, as he strolled through the halls of the Louisiana capitol building. How great a threat Long would have been in 1936 is uncertain. He had substantial grassroots support, but that would not necessarily have translated into votes on election day.

Long's plans were also muted by important changes that Roosevelt made in the New Deal as it swung to the left in 1935. The Congress supported Roosevelt's move for greater reform and greater governmental action to soften the blow of the Depression. The Works Progress Administration (WPA), started in May 1935 under the direction of Harry Hopkins, employed approximately eight million Americans over a six-year period in a variety of jobs all across the country. Approximately 78 percent of WPA funds were allocated to construction projects, with the remainder going to employ artists, writers, photographers, and actors, who expanded the horizons of millions of Americans with their paintings, plays, and books. Of particular interest are the oral recollections of former slaves recorded by WPA researchers, which form an enduring resource for our understanding of slavery.

The massive WPA expenditures were paid for through the application of Keynesian economics. Promoted by the British economist John Maynard Keynes, this policy was based on the government spending large sums of borrowed money to prime the pump of the economy and bring about recovery during hard economic times. It meant that the government engaged in deficit spending, which was politically unpopular, but the administration felt that the economic crisis necessitated this measure. It was hardly revolutionary; there was no real attempt to redistribute wealth, as Long was urging, although the wealthy were obliged to pay higher taxes.

Another major new initiative, the Social Security Act, became law in August 1935. The Social Security Act provided old-age insurance, which was compulsory for all but a small percentage of American workers. The government would share equally with states the cost of helping to care for people over the age of 65 who could not care for themselves. The act also offered care on a matching basis for the infirm. The most long-lasting New Deal program, Social Security has become a major cornerstone of the modern welfare state.

Roosevelt's strong victory in the 1936 election against Alf Landon, the governor of Kansas, gave him the sense that all he needed to do to promote the full power of the New Deal was to get the Supreme Court in line. The resultant scheme to pack the Supreme Court in order to steer decisions his way was Roosevelt's most severe political blunder, as it undermined his credibility and reinforced claims that he sought absolute power. Roosevelt, however, saw the action as necessary for him to carry out his New Deal mandate to aid the people who had elected him. Four Supreme Court justices were the primary opponents of the Roosevelt administration and its attempt to expand the New Deal; three justices, Louis D. Brandeis, Benjamin Cardozo, and Harlan Stone, were generally tolerant of many of the New Deal plans, although Roosevelt did not get their support during the battle over the Schecter case through which the NRA had been declared unconstitutional.

After the court found both the NRA and the AAA unconstitutional, Roosevelt thought it important that he act. His plan would allow him to appoint a new federal judge when the incumbent failed to resign within six months of turning seventy years of age. Supposedly, this action was geared to clear the courts of a backlog of legislation, but it was obviously an attempt to get older, more conservative judges off the bench in favor of younger ones who Roosevelt felt would support his policies. Roosevelt assumed that he would be able to control the Democratic majorities in both houses and get the bill through Congress, but he faced strong opposition from both parties and the bill was defeated. Nevertheless, with the retirement of one of the more conservative justices, Roosevelt was able to appoint a new, liberal justice and create a New Deal majority that supported his decisions. He could therefore proceed virtually unhindered in his actions in the last phase of the New Deal.

Even though the New Deal had saved capitalism and kept Americans fairly well-satisfied, by the time of Roosevelt's second inauguration, in January 1937, one-third of the nation still remained "ill-housed, ill-clad, and ill-nourished." As FDR indicated in his inaugural address, "The test of our progress is not whether we add more to the abundance of those who have much; it is whether we provide enough for those who have too little." This notion was very much the point of Roosevelt's second term. Building on the framework that had already been established, Roosevelt wished to extend the chance of the American Dream to everybody—a dream that had been shattered by the harshness of the Depression.

Across the country, the economy began to pick up under the New Deal, albeit rather slowly. Production, employment, and manufacturing payrolls increased from the spring of 1933 through the spring of 1936. Disposable income levels for households rebounded to their 1929 level by 1937, and there was increased speculation in the stock market as well. There was a bit of a shock in the fall of 1937, however. Referred to as the Roosevelt Recession, this decline threatened to wipe out all the benefits of the second phase of the New Deal. Following a reduction in federal expenditures and increased credit restrictions, the economy went into a tailspin in September and October of 1937. Clearly the patient was not yet well enough to be taken off treatment, so the doctor had to step in again.

Roosevelt moved quickly to halt the decline that could send the country into a second depression. He recalled Congress, and, in an address to the nation, he moved to complete the New Deal by further promoting bills to end child labor, to establish minimum wages and maximum hours, and to attempt to root out monopolies, effectively including old Progressive ideas as part of the New Deal package. These measures did not halt the recession, however. Only with a further injection of federal borrowing, about $3 billion to expand the WPA, did income levels return to 1937 levels by the spring of 1939.

With the Depression in check in the United States, attention turned more to the international sphere and the dangers posed by the German response to the worldwide Depression: Adolf Hitler and fascism. Although the United States had failed to join the League of Nations, the country could not be completely isolated from events occurring around the globe. A major industrial power, and the creditor of the British and the French, the United States was inexorably forced into world affairs. In Europe, the Depression had severely aggravated the debt situation, so as to cause a major financial crisis in the early 1930s. Germany ceased its payments after the Lausanne Conference in 1932, and all American debtors, except Finland, defaulted on their payments to the United States by 1934.

When FDR assumed the presidency in 1933, he built upon a policy begun by Herbert Hoover to create greater rapport between the United States and its Latin American neighbors. The Good Neighbor policy, as it was known, sought to decrease U.S. control over the internal affairs of Latin American countries and to renounce intervention. In addition, a series of reciprocity treaties negotiated by U.S. Secretary of State Cordell Hull was designed to increase hemispheric trade. All in all, the Good Neighbor policy was not a complete success. Although trade did increase significantly with the reciprocity treaties, Latin Americans still remained wary of U.S. power and the possibility of intervention, especially in the Caribbean and Central America. The United States was less open about its influence in Latin American affairs, but its presence remained quite strong in many countries south of the border.

During the 1930s, the American public's sentiment toward events abroad was very much one of political isolationism, and this hampered Roosevelt's ability to alter events overseas. Many intellectuals argued that the United States could do the most good by staying out of Europe's troubles and strengthening democracy at home. The results of this fervent isolationism were quite serious, as the Germans and Japanese were able to make territorial gains with the secure knowledge that the United

States, the only country capable of stopping them, had buried its head in the sand.

German military capacity had been contained by the Treaty of Versailles ending World War I, but Adolf Hitler's rise to power in Germany brought renewed militarism. Hitler ended the state of disarmament; and, in a move to assert German power, he remilitarized the Rhineland, the border area between France and Germany, in March 1936. Reaching out for more territory in 1938 under a policy called the *Anschluss,* Hitler took control of Austria and occupied the German–speaking Sudetenland, which was part of Czechoslovakia. He brought these territories into his conception of a greater Germany, enlarged to provide more "living room" for the German people. In an attempt to prevent the outbreak of war in Europe, the British and French agreed to the cession of the Sudetenland to the Germans. In return, Hitler promised no more territorial demands, and the British prime minister, Neville Chamberlain, felt certain that he had secured "peace in our time."

With the realization of impending international problems, Roosevelt moved to bolster American military spending late in the decade. Billions of dollars were allocated for naval and air buildups during 1938 and 1939. Although there was significantly increased military production, this did not necessarily signal American participation in a foreign war. In Europe, Hitler and the Soviets signed the Nazi-Soviet Nonaggression Pact (1939), which protected Hitler's eastern flank and allowed him to invade areas to the west of the Soviet Union. On September 1, 1939, Hitler invaded Poland, easily defeating the outdated Polish military. By September 3, the great European powers were at war. The Roosevelt administration invoked the Neutrality Act, although the president wished to repeal the arms embargo feature of the act. In November, Congress passed a new neutrality act, allowing any nation to buy arms from the United States as long as it paid cash and carried the goods away in its own ships. In this way, the United States would not be drawn into the European war because of credit extended to belligerents or merchant ships sunk delivering supplies across the ocean.

In the end, of course, the United States could not avoid entering World War II. The greatest conflict the world has ever known had its roots in the Great Depression, as hard economic times prompted a shift to strong leaders—some of whom embraced territorial gain as part of their political strategy. In the end, it was those countries that retained their democratic structure in turbulent times that were forced to restore some semblance of order in the world. Franklin Roosevelt's presidency had strengthened Americans' faith in their government and their economic system. In this way the New Deal served a dual purpose: it improved the nation's domestic economy and enabled the country to maintain its tradition of democratic values and its commitment to individual freedom, allowing it to be a powerful foe of fascist aggression.

In conclusion, the Great Depression had an undeniably lasting effect on virtually all sectors of American society. Most notably, it changed the relationship of the individual to his or her government. Previously, the traditional belief in society dictated that the government bore little or no responsibility for the economic welfare of its inhabitants. Before the New Deal era, if people were starving or homeless, the responsibility for these individuals lay with private relief organizations and local charities. The massive suffering of the Depression, combined with a desire by the public for greater government assistance, propelled the New Deal into being. With it came the transition of the United States to a limited welfare state, one in which Americans could count on some degree of assistance in time of need.

The welfare state grew in the four decades following the New Deal. Under postwar Democratic and Republican administrations, Americans received greater assistance from federal agencies and programs. In this way, FDR's legacy surpassed his twelve years in office. The New Deal itself was in many ways a temporary measure, as programs such as the CCC, WPA, and NRA did not survive into the postdepression era. But others, such as Social Security, farm subsidies, and stock market regulation, still exist today. Greater federal funding for education and the arts grew out of the New Deal, as did the Great Society programs of Medicaid and Medicare, which provide medical assistance to the poor and elderly.

In recent years, many government-funded social programs have come under attack as being too costly and, in some cases, unnecessary. Mounting budget deficits in the 1980s forced the United States to borrow heavily, requiring a greater amount of revenue to be spent paying off those loans. Increased defense spending also contributed to a lack of funds available for federal social programs. In addition, many states found it harder to meet their social welfare demands, leading them to seek assistance from the federal government. These financial factors, and a growing conservative political mood, have caused many Americans to question the need for such a large government role in people's lives. Plans to have a balanced budget by the early twenty-first century would necessarily mean the cutting of significant amounts of funding from social welfare programs, changing once again the relationship of Americans and their government.

SELECTED BIBLIOGRAPHY

Barber, William J. *From New Era to New Deal: Herbert Hoover, The Economists, and American Economic Policy, 1921–1933.* Cambridge: Cambridge University Press, 1985. A sympathetic look at an often maligned president and his economic views.

Bennett, Edward Moore. *Franklin D. Roosevelt and the Search for Security: American-Soviet Relations, 1933–1939.* Wilmington, DE: Scholarly Resources, 1985. A useful study of how the United States drew closer to this future world power during the Roosevelt administration.

Blum, John Morton. *Roosevelt and Morgenthau.* Boston: Houghton Mifflin, 1970. A compelling account of the relationship between the president and his secretary of the treasury.

Brinkley, Alan. *Voices of Protest: Huey Long, Father Coughlin, and the Great Depression.* New York: Alfred A. Knopf, 1982. An examination of two of Roosevelt's most virulent opponents.

Brock, William R. *Welfare, Democracy and the New Deal.* Cambridge: Cambridge University Press, 1988. A critical look at FDR's welfare policies.

Cashman, Sean Dennis. *America in the Twenties and Thirties: The Olympian Age of Franklin Roosevelt.* New York: New York University Press, 1989. A well-written survey of two complex decades.

Cohen, Lizabeth. *Making a New Deal: Industrial Workers in Chicago, 1919–1939.* Cambridge: Cambridge University Press, 1990. An important discussion of industrial workers and the growth of unionization.

Conkin, Paul K. *The New Deal.* New York: Crowell, 1967. A critical look at the accomplishments of the "Roosevelt Revolution."

Dallek, Robert. *Franklin D. Roosevelt and American Foreign Policy, 1932–1945.* New York: Oxford University Press, 1979. A comprehensive examination of FDR's dealings overseas through the Depression and World War II.

Freidel, Frank. *Franklin D. Roosevelt: A Rendezvous with Destiny.* Boston: Little, Brown, 1990. A compelling one-volume biography by an eminent historian.

Hoff-Wilson, Joan. *Herbert Hoover, Forgotten Progressive.* Boston: Little, Brown, 1975. A sympathetic treatment of an often disparaged president.

Kurzman, Paul A. *Harry Hopkins and the New Deal.* Fair Lawn, NJ: R. E. Burdick, 1974. A short, readable biography of the WPA chief.

Lash, Joseph P. *Dealers and Dreamers: A New Look at the New Deal.* New York: Doubleday, 1988. A look back at the New Deal's accomplishments, focusing on two of Roosevelt's brain trusters.

Leuchtenberg, William E. *Franklin D. Roosevelt and the New Deal, 1932–1940.* New York: Harper & Row, 1963. A classic one-volume study of the New Deal, well written and easily understood.

———. *The Perils of Prosperity, 1914–1932.* Chicago: University of Chicago Press, 1958. An important study of the era preceding Roosevelt's presidency.

Olson, James Stuart. *Herbert Hoover and the Reconstruction Finance Corporation, 1931–1933.* Ames: Iowa State University Press, 1977. The early history of Hoover's main vehicle for economic assistance.

———. *Saving Capitalism: The Reconstruction Finance Corporation and the New Deal, 1933–1940.* Princeton, NJ: Princeton University Press, 1988. The corporation and its functions under the Roosevelt administration.

Parrish, Michael E. *Anxious Decades: America in Prosperity and Depression, 1920–1941.* New York: W. W. Norton, 1992. A clear and useful survey of events during these two "anxious decades."

Romasco, Albert U. *The Politics of Recovery: Roosevelt's New Deal.* New York: Oxford University Press, 1983. An accessible tribute to Roosevelt and the New Deal.

Rosen, Elliot A. *Hoover, Roosevelt and the Brains Trust: From Depression to New Deal.* New York: Columbia University Press, 1977. A study of the leading minds assembled to help solve the country's problems.

Schlesinger, Arthur M. *The Coming of the New Deal.* Boston: Houghton Mifflin, 1958. This eminent historian's middle book of the "Age of Roosevelt" series.

———. *The Crisis of the Old Order, 1919–1933.* Boston: Houghton Mifflin, 1957. The first book in the three-part "Age of Roosevelt" series examines the causes and effects of the Great Depression.

———. *The Politics of Upheaval.* Boston: Houghton Mifflin, 1960. The third part of the "Age of Roosevelt" series.

Terkel, Studs. *Hard Times: An Oral History of the Great Depression.* New York: Pantheon Books, 1970. A compilation of interviews with a wide variety of people who remember the Depression years.

Ware, Susan. *Beyond Suffrage: Women in the New Deal.* Cambridge, MA: Harvard University Press, 1981. An examination of the important roles women played during the Depression.

Watkins, T. H. *Righteous Pilgrim: The Life and Times of Harold L. Ickes, 1874–1952.* New York: Henry Holt, 1990. A lengthy biography of FDR's secretary of the interior.

Williams, T. Harry. *Huey Long.* New York: Alfred A. Knopf, 1969. An extensive biography of the flamboyant Louisiana politician.

The surrender of Japan marked the end of World War II and was a happy occasion for all Americans. (Photographic Archives, University of Louisville, Lin Caufield Collection)

4 ───────────────────────────────────────

World War II, 1939–1945

INTRODUCTION

As war clouds gathered in Europe in the late 1930s, most Americans felt confident that the disillusioning experience of World War I could be avoided this time. In 1934, Congress had investigated the causes for America's entry into World War I and had passed a series of Neutrality Acts in 1935, 1936, and 1937, designed specifically to avoid the problems that had led the nation into the earlier conflict. The State Department pursued an irresolute course during these years, with some officials urging the sponsorship of an international conference to settle Europe's problems and others preferring to maintain strict political isolationism.

President Franklin D. Roosevelt, who was internationalist-minded but forced by the economic crisis and public opinion to concentrate on domestic policy in his first term, suggested in a 1937 speech that the United States, along with other friendly nations, should somehow "quarantine" aggressor nations to block their ambitions. Although public reaction to the speech was generally favorable, the administration had no practical plan for doing what the president proposed.

Not until the outbreak of the European war in September 1939 did U.S. foreign policy begin to take official note. Late in 1939, Congress passed a revised Neutrality Act that favored Britain and France by allowing arms sales on a "cash-and-carry" basis; the British Navy's control of the sea ensured that the vast majority of sales would go to our two closest European friends.

Following the fall of France in the summer of 1940, the Roosevelt administration pursued a more open policy of aid to the British, the nation seen as the last bastion between Hitler and the United States. In September, Roosevelt and Prime Minister Winston Churchill of Britain concluded a deal by which the United States would acquire leases on eight British military bases in the Atlantic and Caribbean in return for fifty of the oldest destroyers in the U.S. Navy.

After his reelection in November 1940, Roosevelt was freer to aid the British. He solidified his relationship with Churchill and allowed U.S. naval vessels to participate in convoying merchant ships farther and farther across the Atlantic. By November 1941, U.S. ships were sailing all the way to Britain and were increasingly coming under German attack. Meanwhile, in March of that year, Congress passed Lend-Lease, a military aid bill that authorized the lending or leasing of military equipment to Britain with the understanding that it would be returned or paid for after the war. Roosevelt likened Lend-Lease to allowing one's neighbor to use one's garden hose if his house was on fire, and the measure was generally accepted by the public. Later, Lend-Lease was extended to the Soviet Union and other wartime allies.

In the Pacific, U.S. relations with Japan had been deteriorating almost since the beginning of the century when President Theodore Roosevelt had to settle racially-oriented disputes in California. War between China and Japan began in 1937 (and was the immediate cause of the quarantine speech), but the United States hardly took notice. By the summer of 1940, however, the Roosevelt administration began to focus on Japan's activities in the Far East. By this time, Japanese forces had occupied much of eastern China and were menacing French Indochina and other European colonies in the region; the United States responded by imposing limited economic sanctions on Tokyo. That fall, Japan signed the Tri-Partite Agreement with Germany and Italy, formally creating the Axis, as the alliance was popularly known in the United States.

When Japan moved troops into southern Indochina in July 1941, the Roosevelt administration cut off all trade with Japan and froze Japanese assets in the United States. Japan proposed a "summit" conference, an idea that Roosevelt personally liked, but regard for China, considered an American ally, forced him to abandon the idea unless Japan withdrew its troops from China. Japan was not at all willing to do that and, instead, continued planning a secret attack on the U.S. military installation at Pearl Harbor in Hawaii. When the Japanese carried out that attack on December 7, 1941, the United States was catapulted into a world war.

Prior to the war, military planners had concluded that the United States should fight a holding action in the Pacific while putting forth most of its effort to defeat Hitler in Europe, the more important theater. But early naval successes at the battles of Midway and the Coral Sea weakened Japanese forces sufficiently to allow for a two-ocean war to be fought simultaneously. While American naval and marine forces gradually pushed the Japanese back toward their home islands in a two-pronged, island-hopping campaign across the Pacific, American land forces fought in North Africa and Europe, beginning with the invasion of Algeria and Morocco in November 1942 and continuing with the Italian campaign in 1943 and the D-Day invasion into northern France in June 1944.

While the fighting was going on, Roosevelt, Churchill, and the Soviet premier, Joseph Stalin, engineered the geopolitics of the war through a series of conferences. Many such conferences were held, planning military strategy, organizing the United Nations, and anticipating the economic costs of postwar reconstruction. But the "Big Three," as Roosevelt, Churchill, and Stalin were popularly known, met together only twice: at Teheran (now Tehran), Iran, in November 1943, and at the Soviet Black Sea resort of Yalta, in February 1945.

The Teheran Conference marked a turning point in the war from military considerations to postwar political issues. At this conference, the final strategy to defeat Hitler was confirmed, but whenever political questions were raised, signs of discord appeared. As a consequence, these matters were postponed until the military situation was clearly under control.

The Yalta Conference, held just three months before the end of the war in Europe, was far more political in nature and far more controversial. By this time, it was clear that Allied victory was near, and each leader came to the conference with postwar objectives. For Roosevelt, now in visibly bad health, it was to smooth out plans for the United Nations. For Churchill, it was to do what was necessary to maintain British primacy in Europe. And for Stalin, it was to assure the Soviet Union of postwar control over the states of east-central Europe, which would serve as a buffer zone between the Soviet Union and the nations of western Europe.

In a rather narrow sense, both the United States and the Soviet Union won their objectives at Yalta, while Britain did not. The United States got its way on most of the sticky points regarding the charter of the United Nations, which, it felt, would ensure a peaceful postwar world. To the great dismay of many Americans, the Soviet Union managed to seize control of Poland, Czechoslovakia, Hungary, Romania, and Bulgaria by leaving troops in those countries and making vague promises about interim governments and democratic postwar elections. When, after the war, these formerly independent countries appeared to be no more than Soviet "satellites," many Americans felt that Yalta had been a diplomatic disaster of the first order.

In a secret agreement made at Yalta, Stalin agreed to bring the Soviet Union into the war against Japan within three months after the end of the war in Europe. That came in early May 1945, when Hitler committed suicide in a Berlin bunker and remaining German resistance collapsed. In the Pacific, American forces continued to push the Japanese back, but intelligence estimates in early 1945 held that final victory would not come until an invasion of the Japanese home islands had occurred. Soviet assistance would be helpful in speeding that process toward a successful end.

What was not known in early 1945 was that the atomic bomb, under development in the United States since 1940, would be ready for use by that summer. After a successful test of the bomb in July, Harry S Truman, who had become president following Roosevelt's death in April, decided to use the bomb to end the war. Atomic bombs were dropped on Hiroshima on August 6 and on Nagasaki on August 9, with devastating effect; and at the emperor's behest, the Japanese surrendered shortly thereafter. Ironically, the Soviets had formally entered the war on August 8.

In terms of manpower and cost, World War II was by far the largest conflict in U.S. history. Between December 1941 and August 1945, 14.9 million men and women served in the military, of whom about 292,000 were killed in combat. Another 115,000 died of other causes, and about 670,000 were wounded. Estimates of the cost of the war range upwards of $360 billion, nearly three times the cost of the Vietnam War and eight to ten times the cost of World War I.

On the home front, World War II brought about the same sort of augmentation of power in Washington as had World War I. Even before Pearl Harbor, preparations for eventual entry in the war were underway. In 1940, an Office of Production Management was created to speed up production of war-related materials, and Naval and Military Supply Acts provided for the enlargement of the military services. And Congress approved, for the first time ever, a peacetime draft. All of this activity took place against a backdrop of vocal criticism from an active isolationist group, America First, which opposed any kind of intervention in the global conflict.

By the time of Pearl Harbor, the level of war production was still inadequate. In December 1941, Congress replaced the Office of Production Management with the War Production Board, which centralized control even further, and then created the Office of War Mobilization (OWM) in May 1943. Under the direction of James F. Byrnes, a former congressman and Supreme Court justice, this agency achieved maximum efficiency in wartime production. The OWM had sweeping powers to dictate production levels, remove items from the consumer market, and control domestic transportation. The automobile industry, for example, was diverted entirely to the manufacture of military vehicles.

Other agencies, allied with the OWM, altered American society in highly visible ways. The Office of Price Administration (OPA) controlled prices and rents and, after 1942, supervised a national rationing system by which Americans were allowed to buy only limited amounts of important commodities, such as gasoline, tires, shoes, coffee, meat, sugar, and butter, with the remaining production going for military uses. The War Manpower Board froze people in their jobs unless they were needed for more important war work, and the War Labor Board handled labor-management disputes so that war production would not be slowed by strikes.

As with World War I, this war was paid for by a combination of taxes and bond sales. In 1942, Congress passed a Revenue Act, which increased both corporate and personal income taxes; rates rose to 94 percent for those in the highest income brackets, and many people with low incomes found themselves paying income taxes for the first time. One lasting feature of wartime taxation was the introduction of withholding taxes, wherein income taxes were taken out of each paycheck, enabling the government to get its money much sooner. In all, some 40 percent of the cost of the war was covered by taxes.

This was not nearly enough, of course, and the remainder of the money was raised through a series of eight bond drives. Many Americans paid for bonds through payroll deductions, while others were subjected to high-pressure sales campaigns, often exploiting the looks and talents of show business personalities.

In general, Americans at home fared substantially better than they had during the Depression. Although many goods were difficult or impossible to obtain, there was relatively little black-market activity. Unemployment fell from about 14 percent in 1940 to less than 2 percent in 1943; and, although prices rose about 30 percent during the war, the average worker's wages rose 70 percent, due, in many cases, to abundant overtime work. About 45 percent of the labor force was engaged in some kind of war-related work.

One group of people who did not fare so well in the war was the 110,000 Japanese Americans living on the West Coast. Given the long-standing racial prejudice of whites toward the Japanese Americans, it was not surprising that after Pearl Harbor every person of Japanese descent was seen as a potential saboteur or spy. Consequently, in February 1942, President Roosevelt issued Executive Order 9066, mandating that all persons of Japanese descent, including those who had obtained American citizenship, be detained in internment camps, which were set up at isolated and inhospitable locations in the interior of the country. Most had little choice but to abandon their homes and businesses, often at great financial sacrifice, and follow the government's orders. Postwar claims by the Japanese Americans for their lost property netted them only about ten cents on the dollar. In 1988, the federal government paid each of the 60,000 survivors $20,000 as a belated gesture of apology.

World War II brought unalterable changes to the world. With much of western Europe devastated by the conflict, the United States, which had escaped physical destruction, and the Soviet Union, which had recovered from much of the damage caused by the German invasion early in the war, stood alone as global superpowers. Despite the hopefulness raised by the new United Nations, it would not be long before the widely differing political and economic systems of those two nations laid the groundwork for a very different kind of war.

INTERPRETIVE ESSAY
Larry Thornton

World War II marked the emergence of the United States as the world's most powerful nation. Although the war touched dozens of countries around the world, only the United States emerged virtually unscathed and unarguably stronger. American contributions were vital to the war effort and placed the nation in a position to shape much of the postwar world. World War II also fostered significant domestic social and political changes. By all measures, World War II unleashed developments that affected the identity and activity of the United States for the second half of the twentieth century.

Rooted in its geography and its republican experiment, the sense of American distinctiveness has been an enduring American myth: the United States is a unique, separate place looking out to the world. For most of its first century, while wary of the European powers, Americans focused their attention and energies on continental development and expansion. Europe, while important, remained beyond the scope of vital American interests; Asia was of even less concern. As the twentieth century drew closer, however, American interests expanded beyond U.S. boundaries where they jostled with the other imperial powers.

When World War I erupted in 1914, most Americans believed they could avoid the maelstrom as Europe's ills were not their concern. But these hopes were illusory. In 1917, President Woodrow Wilson asserted that German submarine attacks presented a *casus belli*. The Americans played a brief, but decisive, role in World War I, breaking the stalemate on the western front which led to an Allied victory.

In the aftermath of the war, many Americans shared the widespread revulsion against its horrors and hoped that war would never again plague the world. During the late 1920s, many Americans came to believe that the United States had been manipulated into belligerency against the nation's better interests and judgment. The general consensus asserted that the true interests of the United States would be best served by a cautious and reserved foreign policy, which could keep Americans from further political involvement in the conflicts among the hopelessly corrupt European states.

As events in Asia and in Europe became more and more unsettled in the 1930s and war appeared imminent, Americans hoped once again to avoid it. To this end, the Congress enacted the Neutrality Acts to prevent entanglements similar to those believed to have drawn the country into World War I. For example, sales of American arms to belligerent states were restricted, American ships were not to carry goods to belligerent states, and the president could prohibit Americans from traveling on belligerent ships.

The wars that came to Asia in 1937 and to Europe in 1939, however, did not mirror the conflicts of 1914; and the United States became increasingly embroiled as more and more people concluded that the outcomes of the two separate but coterminous wars did matter to the interests of the United States. Japan had long been an economic rival in the Pacific, and unchecked success of Japanese forces promised the diminution or exclusion of American trade in Asia. American sentiment clearly backed Great Britain in the European war, especially after the 1940 German victory over France and air assault on British cities. However, public opinion polls in 1940 showed that only 20 percent of the respondents favored American military involvement; these were not yet America's wars.

President Franklin D. Roosevelt, who did not believe that the country could avoid the war, suggested that aggression was, in essence, an attack on the United States. At the same time, Roosevelt, campaigning for his third term, pledged that no Americans would be sent to war unless the United States was attacked. In 1940, the United States, which had maintained a peacetime army roughly equivalent in size to Sweden's army, began to rearm and to aid those nations fighting the aggressors. Modified neutrality legislation allowed belligerent states to purchase American arms on "cash-and-carry" terms.

In 1940–1941 the United States shifted from neutrality with a profitable war-related business to nonbelligerency, doing everything short of war to aid the states fighting Germany and Japan. The British, the Chinese, and, later, the Soviets received loans and supplies through programs like Lend-Lease. In August 1941, Prime Minister Winston Churchill of Great Britain and President Roosevelt signed the Atlantic Charter, which proclaimed Anglo-American war aims of freedom and justice. To help secure British convoys, the U.S. Navy increased its Atlantic patrols and reported German submarine positions to the British. In September 1941, an order to "shoot-on-sight" placed the navy in an undeclared war with German submarines. Even so, the United States technically remained a nonbelligerent.

On December 7, 1941, in one of the most impressive military feats of the war, the Japanese struck a humiliating blow to the American Pacific fleet stationed at Pearl Harbor in Hawaii, destroying or damaging 18 battleships and their auxiliaries, along with 349 aircraft, and inflicting more than 3,600 casualties while suffering only 55 casualties and losing just 29 airplanes. On the same day, Japanese forces also launched successful attacks against American forces in the Philippines and British forces in Hong Kong and Malaya. Assuming the inevitability of war with the United States, the Japanese decided to launch this war sooner rather than later. Some Japanese policymakers were convinced that the Americans lacked the heart to rebound from such a crippling blow. Instead, the Japanese attack aroused the fury of the American people, and residual elements of that fury remain to this day. Like a match that flares brilliantly when struck, the Japanese war effort quickly sputtered in the face of its enemy's might.

Germany declared war on the United States on December 11, 1941. The German hope that Japan could force Britain out of the war while German forces focused their energies on a final assault on the Soviet Union, all before the United States became a serious factor in the war, was an illusion. The Germans did not recognize that Axis war efforts were doomed because their invasion of the Soviet Union had failed to achieve a quick victory, their forces could not knock out Britain, and, now, the entry of the United States introduced a power that, alone, could contribute to every theater of the war. Both the Japanese and the Germans grossly underestimated the United States and overestimated their own abilities in the face of the coalition they had forced into existence.

World War II was total war, a modern industrial war. With its enormous industrial base, large population, and efficient mobilization, the United States epitomized total war effort. Prior to the twentieth century, wars were limited in scale, organization, and cost. During the 1790s, the French revolutionary government proclaimed its authority to conscript all citizens, their labor, and their property in the people's war against the kings of Europe. But preindustrial societies could only produce limited quantities of war supplies and spare so many people from food production without the risk of widespread starvation and social collapse. The French proclamation of total war represented a dramatic expansion of the authority claimed by governments, a claim that increasingly would be utilized in the industrial age. With industrial production and expanded food cultivation, the inherent limits on the scale of war were set loose: increasingly, more soldiers and more weapons became available. The American Civil War previewed industrial war with its larger armies, unprecedented quantities of factory-produced supplies, and railroads delivering soldiers and supplies right to the front lines. By World War I, the expanded scale of war strained the strongest states and overwhelmed those states with weak industrial bases, Russia being the most obvious example.

World War II was a war between enormous industrial establishments, and the side better able to organize its economy effectively and disrupt its opponents' had a decided advantage. As the United States developed its wartime economy, the drive for efficiency or rationalization of production required a powerful authority to coordinate the efforts of so many different branches of society. The federal government assumed this role. One measure of its expanding authority was the enormous increase in federal spending. Annual finance acts raised income tax rates and increased the numbers of Americans required to pay income taxes, raised the corporate tax rates, and introduced various other taxes in an effort to keep pace with the rapidly expanding budget. Nevertheless, taxes could not keep up with spending, accounting for about 40 percent of expenditures during the war.

In the name of efficiency, the federal government claimed more and more prerogatives that had been the province of the individual states or outside the purview of government altogether. War needs brushed aside traditional American suspicion of big government. For example, faced with an impending miners' strike, the federal government nationalized the coal mines rather than allow a strike to disrupt essential war production.

The government exerted unprecedented supervision over the economy. Initial planning efforts, based largely on cooperation, lacked sufficient enforcement capability, which rendered them ineffective; but, by 1943, new agencies successfully extended federal authority throughout the economy. In January 1942, President Roosevelt announced tank, aircraft, and merchant shipping tonnage production targets for 1942 and 1943, part of the Victory Program. A plethora of new agencies, like the Office of Economic Stabilization and the Office of Price Administration, fixed priorities, allocated orders, and controlled inflation through price, wage, and rent controls. The Americans and the British also formed joint allocation boards to coordinate their two economies for greater efficiency.

The results were staggering. The United States built a military juggernaut second to none. More than 15 million men and women were mobilized for one or another of the services. These citizens in uniform were outfitted and armed. Over two million workers produced more than 275,000 airplanes for the war effort. Other workers built ships, tanks, landing craft, jeeps, and other items of war. American food, vehicles, medicine, clothing, and other aid to the Soviet Union exceeded $11 billion, and additional billions in aid went to China, Great Britain, and other nations.

World War II stimulated unprecedented growth in the American economy. The Gross National Product (GNP) nearly doubled, from $91 billion to $166 billion. In four years industrial production doubled and agricultural production increased by 20 percent. Entirely new industries, like synthetic rubber, nonexistent in 1940, were fully productive before 1945, and the war also dramatically boosted the electronics and other developing industries. The Manhattan Project, the program to produce the atomic bomb, may be the clearest example of the beneficial effect of the planned economy. Thousands of Americans worked in the three entirely new (and secret) cities, where laboratories, factories, workshops, homes, and stores were erected for the atomic program. Other scientists were mobilized to aid in the production of new weapons, the refinement of existing weapons, and the development of medicines, seeking any advantage that could be used against the enemy. Resources were directed to areas deemed vital to the war effort, accelerating research and development as well as expanding production.

While expanded production and, ultimately, victory were the results, the war effort also produced an unintended, or unanticipated, impetus toward greater social equality. The demands of increased production forced social and racial prejudices to yield somewhat. Women went to work in increasing numbers, frequently to the consternation of those who were convinced that women were inherently incapable of such labor. As many African Americans moved to the industrial cities to claim war-related jobs or served in the military (albeit a segregated military with its upper ranks and skilled positions still closed to them), President Roosevelt pledged there would be no racial discrimination in war-related industry. The federal government established the Fair Employment Practices Commission to enforce mandatory nondiscrimination clauses in all federal war-related contracts. However, the legal stipulations were widely evaded and the commission had limited authority. The war also accelerated regional development. The South, for example, which had been predominantly rural and agrarian, underwent a spurt of urbanization and industrialization as war-related industries offering good wages enticed people to move to cities like Atlanta where they found jobs in factories.

Propaganda bears consideration as another manifestation of the American war effort. The Office of War Information, a federal agency, oversaw official campaigns designed to weaken enemy morale or to stir Americans to greater exertion. "Rosie the Riveter," the prototypical woman worker, appeared on posters encouraging (or cajoling) other women to join the work force. The military enlisted Hollywood in the propaganda effort. Frank Capra, noted for his prewar madcap romantic comedies, directed *Why We Fight*, a series of films shown to draftees; they so successfully explained the war that they were later released to civilian audiences as well. Not all military-Hollywood partnerships had such happy results, however. John Huston produced a film on the Aleutian Islands that was so grim that the military locked it away for years. Many prominent entertainers donned uniforms and served on active duty, appeared in army training films, or played in army bands.

Entertainers also took up the war propaganda theme without government funding or even much prompting. Donald Duck, Bugs Bunny, and other cartoon characters easily overwhelmed the Nazis or the Japanese in their animated films. Spike Jones and His City Slickers mocked the Nazis when they sang "Der Fuehrer's Face" which ended with a raspberry "right in der Fuehrer's face." Popular songs featured lyrics on the trials of separated lovers and other situations common to a nation at war.

In addition, dozens of feature films also focused on the war theme. *Casablanca* (1942), a classic American romantic drama, epitomized unofficial propaganda. An allegory of America's evolution from neutrality to belligerence, the film promised victory ("Welcome back to the fight. This time I know our side will win.") when no victories were in sight and reinforced the American sense that there are only two sides to any question, the right side and the wrong side. Rick Blaine, played by Humphrey Bogart, represented the United States. Early in the film, he voiced his cynical "I stick out my neck for no man" philosophy, which yielded to belligerency by the end of the film (Rick proclaimed, "The problems of three little people don't amount to a hill of beans in this crazy, mixed up world. . . . I've got a job to do"). Encumbered by allies who were dismissable twits, the Nazis appeared as brutal and duplicitous villains, and, yet, hardly invincible. *Casablanca* suggested the existence of a continent-wide, well-organized, and active resistance, a fantasy in 1942, and asserted that dozens of opponents to Nazi domination were ready to replace those killed. Rather optimistically, one character proclaimed that even the Nazis could not kill that quickly. Rick's Cafe Americain served as a prototypical American union of peoples, a variation on the melting pot myth; Russians, French, English, Bulgarians, and assorted other unidentified characters roamed the sets, speaking nicely-accented English, and upholding standards of civility, for the most part. Contemporary viewers enjoying the film's timeless romantic storyline should not miss its propaganda component.

As the economic, scientific, and entertainment communities were organized to serve the war effort, mobilization efforts were extended to communities across the country. Boy Scouts collected tin and scrap metal. Women's clubs sponsored drives to gather other essential materials for the war effort. Civic groups sold war bonds. Whether these local efforts had any appreciable impact can be debated, but, once war was declared, national, state, and local campaigns sought to enlist the energies along with the hearts and minds of the citizenry. The result was that, by May 1945 when Germany capitulated, and by mid-August, when the Japanese emperor announced surrender to his people by radio, America's war economy was booming.

The greater authority that coordinated these remarkable achievements also had its dark side. Shortly after Pearl Harbor, some 110,000 Japanese Americans from the Pacific coast states were subjected to forced removal to detention (or "relocation") camps. Wartime fears of their disloyalty were so great that legal challenges to this indiscriminate violation of fundamental legal protection failed; and the Japanese Americans, in spite of the absence of espionage or sabotage, remained behind fences and barbed wire for the duration. In addition to the unjust incarceration, they lost their homes, businesses and farms, and other possessions. For decades after the war, officials responsible for this gross violation of the fundamental rights of citizenship defended their actions as necessary and prudent. Finally, in 1988, the U.S. Congress issued a formal apology and authorized modest financial compensation. This tardy admission of error could not assuage the stain because, in spite of appeals from Japan and the fact of detention, these Americans had remained consistently loyal to their new homeland during the war.

Pandora's box had been opened; would the officials wisely wield their increased authority? In every society there is a tension between liberty and authority; expansion of one must come at the expense of the other. The possibility of abuse of authority in the pursuit of a noble cause remains real as demonstrated by the case of the Japanese Americans. Obviously, the war did not transform the United States into a Nazi-style dictatorship, but diminished liberty—even when taken by a friendly authority—remains diminished liberty.

The American experience was unlike the experience of any other people. The homeland remained safe. American goods and personnel went to war, but most Americans learned about the war through the newspapers, newsreels, or *Life* magazine. Enemy airplanes did not drop their loads upon American cities, parents did not send their children to safety in the countryside, and no one faced occupying authorities. The war was fought far from their towns, shores, and homes, which allowed Americans to view their fight as one for values like freedom and justice while the Soviets and others fought for survival. These divergent types of war experiences left far different legacies.

Near the end of the war, the journalist Walter Lippmann proclaimed the advent of the American Century, encapsulating the high expectations of Americans and their new sense of pride, place, and prosperity. With a reinforced conviction of their distinctiveness, Americans believed that all dilemmas could be resolved and, given sufficient will and resources, with dispatch. Nothing could hinder American desire as the rightness or even righteousness of their cause was self-evident. With the American monopoly on the atomic bomb expected to last well into the foreseeable future, what power could deny American will or threaten its security?

The impact of the war continued to be discernable long after the shooting ended. World War II was the good war, the clear-cut struggle between good and evil, almost like a Western standoff, fostering the image of the American reluctant to fight but able to fight to the finish if necessary. World War II became even more popular in the light of the frustrating limited conflicts later in Korea and Vietnam. At a distance, the war, the good war, was easily romanticized in novels, films, and television series. For all the romanticizing, however, the memory of how this incredible conflagration began produced a sort of Munich-Pearl Harbor trauma affecting American foreign policy for decades. Fear of negotiation that might result in appeasement similar to that at Munich before World War II, along with the fear of sudden attack, played on the American mind-set throughout the Cold War.

The war clearly altered the American role in world politics. American economic and military power translated into unprecedented political power, which, in turn, led to the assumption of a range of responsibilities far beyond what could have been imagined in 1940. American power and wealth stood in stark contrast to the poverty and destruction in the war zones. American largesse was counted upon to restore prosperity, and the Marshall Plan and other aid programs were extended to both allies and defeated enemies. After the war, the United States played leading roles in the newly-formed United Nations organization, the International Monetary Fund, and a plethora of other forums.

Tensions between the United States and the Soviet Union—what came to be known as the Cold War—played a major role in the American assumption of commitments around the world. Fearful that the Red Army was poised to roll across Western Europe and then perhaps down Main Street, USA, American leaders offered the assurance of security through the Truman Doctrine, the general policy of containment, and, eventually, a wide range of regional organizations, like the North Atlantic Treaty Organization (NATO), and bilateral commitments. Soviet influence increased dramatically as the Red Army drove Hitler's forces out of eastern Europe; but, for all their bluster and their determination to allow no other influences into their recently acquired sphere of influence, the Soviets lacked the will and the ability to engage in a military battle with the United States. The Soviets refused to knuckle under to American power, though, even in the face of the bomb, and they successfully tested their own atomic bomb in 1949, touching off a fear approaching hysteria in the United States, based in part on the assumption that such an evil system could never have accomplished this feat on its own. Americans turned on other Americans with a fear of pervasive, but hidden, Communist forces—a "Red Scare"—fighting the Cold War domestically as well as internationally as communism appeared to be on the march everywhere in the late 1940s.

Other new and unforeseen constraints on American power also emerged in the postwar period. The United States had limited influence in the newly emerging nations around the world. The world war undermined Western authority throughout Africa and Asia. In the fifteen years after the war, dozens of former colonies separated themselves from their Western masters, evincing a determination to secure their independence even in the face of overwhelming power. The newly independent states could risk American disapproval because the disparity between their very limited power and the unlimited power of the United States frequently rendered many American weapons unusable. Several skilled statesmen adeptly played off the Americans against the Soviets and vice versa. Americans were quite frustrated, having power that could be used only sparingly, if at all. So the American Century turned out to be less idyllic than Lippmann and others had anticipated.

As World War II becomes more and more the province of scholars, several controversies centering on the atomic bomb and the origins of the Cold War have emerged. Although the question of the use of the atomic bomb is not surprising, the relative silence over the broader issue of bombing of urban areas is. (In this total war the traditional distinction between soldiers and civilians, or noncombatants, had evaporated.) Every side in World War II engaged in the indiscriminate killing of thousands of noncombatants by dropping high explosives and incendiary bombs on urban areas; this provoked relatively little indignation or condemnation.

The atomic bomb turned out to be a weapon of a different kind rather than simply a bomb with a bigger blast. The atomic bomb controversy centers around questions of race, utility, and intention. Some have pondered whether the Americans would have dropped the bomb on the Germans if a working bomb had existed in early 1945. This question reflects the development of the politics of race in the postwar world where the long record of Western violence against peoples of color is vigorously decried. Although hypothetical questions cannot be definitively answered, it is difficult to believe that the same authorities who did not shrink from the 1943 firebombing of Hamburg would have hesitated to use atomic bombs on any enemy.

By the end of July 1945, the deterioration of Japan's war-making ability and the extension of tentative peace feelers indicated that the end was not far off. Was the bombing of Hiroshima and Nagasaki necessary? After the initial demonstration, did the second bomb have to be used? Could a less deadly demonstration have been arranged to impress Japanese authorities? The record indicates that the political and military authorities never considered not using the atomic bomb, which was seen as just a bigger and more lethal bomb than the ones that had rained down on Japanese cities for months. The qualitative distinction between conventional bombs and nuclear bombs did not exist in August 1945. This distinction gradually developed as the long-term effects of radiation and other distinctive attributes of nuclear weaponry came to light. Even so, the American authorities were willing to sacrifice countless Japanese lives to avoid an invasion of Japan, which could have produced a million American casualties. From this point of view, the two bombs served their intended purpose: the hastening of the end of the war. But from another point of view, the controversy over nuclear weapons raises the fundamental question of the propriety of indiscriminate attacks on noncombatants regardless of the type of weapon. If one can legitimately question the bombing of Hiroshima and Nagasaki, then one should also question bombing Berlin, Tokyo, Dresden, London, and Warsaw.

An offshoot to this controversy questions whom the detonation was intended to impress. This argument asserts that Japan was so clearly defeated that the bombs must have served another purpose, such as to warn the Soviet Union of the new American power. Some scholars have suggested that President Harry S Truman and his advisors engaged in a showdown mentality when they used the bomb to try to force the Soviets to be more receptive to American desires. Here the record is more murky, and adherents on all sides of the question can find evidence to support their viewpoints. There is also the attendant risk of allowing subsequent developments and knowledge to color one's reading of earlier events. Whether or not the detonation of the two bombs was intended to intimidate the Soviets, American politicians did expect to have their way as the only nuclear power.

Another controversy arising from the study of World War II asks who started the Cold War. For most of the Cold War era this was a very political question as the answer devolved from where one stood in the political arena. Simplistically, the political answer on both sides was that the other side bore all of the responsibility. As time passes, passions cool, and archives open—especially now that researchers are gaining access to Soviet documents, which have been unavailable until very recently; the definitive account of the origins of the Cold War remains to be written.

However, those who profess surprise that the Grand Coalition broke apart fail to recognize, first, that the coalition was a highly artificial creation drawn together only by a common enemy, an enemy that no longer existed by mid-1945, and, second, overlook the strains within the coalition from the very start. The record is replete with actions or postures taken by representatives of each side in the growing divide, taken wittingly or unwittingly, that cumulatively increased tensions. Actions taken by both the Soviet Union and the United States contributed to the other's suspicions and insecurities, producing a rupture where each projected the worst onto the other, while loudly proclaiming its own virtues. More than likely, there will be few innocents when this account is written.

Moreover, one must point out that something akin to the Cold War existed prior to World War II. A battle of ideologies came into existence when the Bolsheviks seized power in 1917. The first American Red Scare came immediately after World War I, and the U.S. government refused to recognize the legitimacy of the new Soviet government until 1933. Throughout the interwar era few Western powers made any effort to disguise their hostility toward the Soviet Union, sparking Soviet fears that the capitalist states would pull their economies out of the Great Depression by assaulting the USSR. One could even suggest that the origins of the Cold War began with the publication of *The Communist Manifesto* (1848) and the subsequent formation of revolutionary and counterrevolutionary organizations.

Thus, the Cold War may be no more than a new term for a state of affairs that had existed in many parts of the West for close to a century.

By 1945, this dispute was being played in the center ring; the two superpowers, each with its own agenda, had replaced the traditional Great
Powers of Europe. Into the vacuum of a devastated world these powers
stepped to offer their distinct systems. How could there be any result
other than tension and rivalry?

   In conclusion, World War II accelerated the emergence of the United
States as a world power. The American political alternative and its geographical separation from Europe had fostered a sense of exceptionalism;
and, by the middle of the twentieth century, the United States, further
distinguished from the rest of the world by its unprecedented wealth
and power, had lost its reticence about using its power and wealth beyond the Western Hemisphere. The drive for efficiency and production
also challenged, with limited success, widespread notions of the inherent
superiorities or inferiorities of groups of people. The authorities unin-
tentionally unleashed a rationality that eroded the social supports for
discrimination on the basis of race or gender. Even without World War
II, more than likely these developments would have materialized, but
the war had a greenhouse effect: inside, flowers blossomed with remarkable intensity, while the harsh climate outside choked other blooms.

SELECTED BIBLIOGRAPHY

Alperovitz, Gar. *Atomic Diplomacy: Hiroshima and Nagasaki.* New York: Simon and
       Shuster, 1965. Argues that the atomic bombs were used more to impress
       the Soviets than to end the war with Japan.
Borg, Dorothy, and Okamato Shumpei, eds. *Pearl Harbor as History: Japanese-
       American Relations, 1931–1941.* New York: Columbia University Press,
       1973. This collection of essays focuses on the rivalry and growing strain
       between the United States and Japan in the decade before the war.
Calcavoressi, Peter, and Guy Wint. *Total War: The Story of World War II.* New
       York: Pantheon Books, 1972. Describes the military and political events in
       both the Asian and European theaters of war.
Clausen, Henry C., and Bruce Lee. *Pearl Harbor: Final Judgement.* New York:
       Crown, 1992. Clausen, who conducted a wartime secret study of the attack
       on Pearl Harbor, lays out a thorough account of responsibility for this
       debacle and evaluates the strengths and weaknesses in other accounts of
       Pearl Harbor.
Dalfiume, Richard M. *Desegregation of the Armed Forces: Fighting on Two Fronts,
       1939–1953.* Columbia: University of Missouri Press, 1960. A good account
       of the efforts to end the military policy of racial discrimination.
Dallek, Robert. *Franklin D. Roosevelt and American Foreign Policy, 1932–1945.* New

York: Oxford University Press, 1979. A sweeping survey of the foreign policy of President Roosevelt and the factors that influenced its formulation and execution.

Daniels, Roger. *Concentration Camps USA: Japanese Americans and World War II.* New York: Holt, Rinehart, Winston, 1971. A full description of the Japanese relocation policy.

Divine, Robert A. *The Reluctant Belligerent: American Entry into World War II.* New York: Wiley, 1965. One of the better accounts of the American entry into the war.

Dower, John W. *War without Mercy: Race and Power in the Pacific War.* New York: Pantheon Books, 1986. A very important book on war in which the author compares racist ideology employed by the Japanese and by the Americans and argues that these beliefs contributed to the particular brutality of the war in the Pacific.

Effects of Strategic Bombing in the German War Economy. Washington: U.S. Strategic Bombing Survey, 1945. An assessment of where and to what extent the American bombing effort effectively contributed to the war, which concludes that the disruption of the German transportation system was its most significant impact.

Fussell, Paul. *Wartime: Understanding and Behavior in the Second World War.* New York: Oxford University Press, 1989. In this follow-up to his highly acclaimed study on the First World War, Fussell continues his examination of the peculiar culture of war.

Groueff, Stephanie. *Manhattan Project: The Untold Story of the Making of the Atomic Bomb.* Boston: Little, Brown, 1967. The author relates the remarkable story of the development of the weapon that ended the war in the Pacific.

Herken, Gregg. *The Winning Weapon: The Atomic Bomb in the Cold War 1945–1950.* New York: Alfred A. Knopf, 1980. After a brief section on the bomb's development, Herken argues that the atomic powers sought to use their monopoly on the bomb as a tool in the Cold War.

Laqueur, Walter. *The Terrible Secret.* Boston: Little, Brown, 1980. Demonstrates that Allied leaders were well informed during the war about the extent of the Nazi efforts to exterminate the Jews.

Morse, Arthur D. *While Six Million Died: A Chronicle of American Apathy.* New York: Random House, 1967. An account of American indifference to the plight of European Jewry.

Ruchames, Louis. *Race, Jobs, and Politics: The Story of the FEPC.* New York: Columbia University Press, 1953. The saga of the federal efforts to ensure fair employment practices.

Schroeder, Paul W. *The Axis Alliance and Japanese-American Relations, 1941.* Ithaca, NY: Cornell University Press, 1958. This diplomatic study of the maneuverings prior to Pearl Harbor is also interesting for its observations on the Tokyo War Crimes trial.

Terkel, Studs. *"The Good War": An Oral History of World War II.* New York: Pantheon Books, 1984. A variety of Americans tell stories of their experiences on the battlefront as well as the home fronts.

Toland, John. *The Rising Sun: The Decline and Fall of the Japanese Empire, 1936–1945.* New York: Random House, 1970. A fine popular history of the period.
Willmott, H. P. *The Great Crusade: A New Complete History of the Second World War.* London: M. Joseph, 1989. A very good single-volume survey of the war on all fronts, which offers considerable interpretation as well as narrative.

5

The Cold War, c. 1946–1991

INTRODUCTION

The Cold War may be defined as a period of tense, and occasionally hostile, relations between two heavily armed camps: the United States and its allies and the Soviet Union and its allies. It began shortly after the end of World War II and ended with the collapse of the Soviet Union in 1991. Although the two rivals had not enjoyed a pleasant diplomatic relationship before the war, a series of events between 1945 and 1947 brought the reality of the Cold War to the forefront of international affairs.

In east-central Europe, the persistent occupation of the Soviet army, coupled with the blatant political control assumed by Moscow, brought a quick end to the promise of democratic elections agreed to in the Declaration of Liberated Europe (1945). By 1947, U.S. leaders had to deal with subservient Communist governments in Poland, Hungary, Romania, and Bulgaria; by 1949, Czechoslovakia and the nominally independent East Germany were in the Communist bloc. In occupied Germany, squabbling and lack of cooperation among the commanders of the occupation zones developed within months after the end of the war. Those in the western zones came to realize that if the Soviets were allowed to remove an unlimited amount of industrial equipment from their zones,

Few Americans epitomized the confrontational side of the Cold War better than Secretary of State John Foster Dulles, shown here with President Dwight D. Eisenhower. (Reproduced from the Collections of the Library of Congress)

economic recovery would be impossible. Thus, barriers were set up, interzonal communication broke down, and the evolution of West Germany and East Germany as independent countries began.

Another dispute arose in the United Nations (UN) over the question of the control of atomic energy. Bernard Baruch, an American delegate, proposed turning over U.S. atomic secrets to an international authority connected with the UN, but not until an arrangement had been made that would provide for the proper control of atomic energy and not until the permanent members of the UN Security Council had waived their veto power on this issue. The USSR did not agree, asserting that the United States ought to surrender its atomic secrets before any kind of international agreement was signed. The United States found this unacceptable and resumed testing atomic bombs, while the Soviets continued their own development of an atomic weapon.

In early 1946, a controversy in Iran was another signal of the coming of the Cold War. The Soviets had stationed troops in Iran during the war to protect Iranian oil fields from the Germans. After the German surrender, the Soviets balked at withdrawing the troops, and it was not until considerable pressure from both the UN and a U.S.-backed Iranian government that Moscow finally removed its forces. President Harry S Truman later said that this incident convinced him and others in Washington that the USSR was not trustworthy.

Meanwhile, the rhetoric of the Cold War was heating up. In February 1946, Joseph Stalin, the Soviet premier, gave a speech in Moscow in which he warned of the inevitability of war between capitalism and communism. This was followed a month later by Winston Churchill's famous speech at the dedication of Westminster College in Missouri. There the former British prime minister painted a vivid verbal picture of millions of people trapped behind an "iron curtain" that had descended over east-central Europe.

A year after the end of the war, nearly all of the western European nations were suffering from grave economic problems, which were having an impact on politics. France and Italy had strong indigenous Communist and Socialist parties, which threatened to increase even further their influence by exploiting the economic crisis; Britain, under the socialist policies of the Labour party, was so beset by economic difficulties that it announced it could no longer lend financial support to Greece and Turkey. This announcement came at a particularly difficult time, as the Greek government was confronting an insurrection by Communist-led rebels, and Turkey was under great pressure from the Soviet Union for free access through Turkish waters to the Mediterranean.

In March 1947, a concerned President Truman responded to this crisis by asking Congress for $400 million to prop up Greece and Turkey. In what has become known as the Truman Doctrine, he declared that the United States should be ready to support free people threatened by internal subversion or external aggression. Congress, in a fine show of bipartisanship, voted by wide margins to give the president what he wanted, marking the first time the United States had involved itself so deeply in European affairs in a time of official peace. At this time, the Truman Doctrine was limited to Greece and Turkey and to monetary assistance. This would soon change as the Cold War developed.

In the summer of 1947, the respected foreign policy journal *Foreign Affairs* published an article, "The Sources of Soviet Conduct," in which the author, George Kennan (identified as "Mr. X" in the journal), laid out what became the policy of "containment." Kennan, a Soviet expert in the State Department, wrote that the United States should contain Soviet expansionism in the hope that eventually the Soviet system would collapse or evolve in such a way as to be more accommodating. As Kennan described it, containment was to be nonmilitary in nature and confined to Europe (and perhaps the Middle East). Although it would, in practice, be much altered from Kennan's original idea, containment became the cornerstone of U.S. foreign policy for most of the Cold War era.

The first practical application of containment was the Marshall Plan. Named for Secretary of State George Marshall, this was a massive economic aid program designed to spur European economic recovery and, in so doing, remove the threat of Communist political ascendancy. Although the Soviet Union and its satellites (as the countries in east-central Europe were often called) were invited to participate, they chose not to, and Marshall Plan aid went to western Europe. Between 1948 and 1952, some $13.1 billion was directed to Europe, with Great Britain, France, West Germany, and Italy receiving about $8.8 billion of that amount. The program was remarkably successful and was a major influence in the growth of European economic integration seen in the Common Market and, later, the European Community.

The Soviet response to the Marshall Plan was unexpectedly hostile. In early 1948, when Czechoslovakia indicated its interest in associating with the West, Soviet forces moved into Prague and brutally forced the Czechs into line. Western leaders were shocked by the suspicious death of Jan

Masaryk, the pro-Western Czech leader. In June 1948, the Soviets blocked land access to Berlin, the jointly-occupied former capital of Germany that lay within the Soviet zone. Rather than forcing a confrontation on land, Truman responded with the Berlin Airlift, in which food, fuel, and medicine needed by the Berliners was delivered by a flotilla of aircraft in a remarkable and inspiring feat of logistics. After eleven months, the blockade was lifted.

The Czech takeover and the Berlin blockade convinced Western leaders that the situation was dangerous enough to warrant a military alliance, and in April 1949, the North Atlantic Treaty Organization (NATO) was formed, consisting of eleven European nations, the United States, and Canada. Later, other nations joined NATO, and in 1955, the Soviet bloc responded with the Warsaw Pact, a similar kind of alliance.

In the fall of 1949, the scene of the Cold War shifted to the Far East with the victory of the Chinese Communist forces under Mao Zedong in a civil war against the pro-Western Nationalist army of Chiang Kai-shek. Although the United States had sent large amounts of aid to the Nationalists, they were simply too corrupt and inefficient to prevail in their struggle with the disciplined Communists and were forced to flee to the island of Formosa. This "loss of China" to the Communists sent shock waves through the U.S. political arena and caused serious difficulties for the Truman administration, which had to take the blame.

Less than a year later, the Korean War broke out with Communist North Korea's invasion of pro-Western South Korea. The North Koreans seemed to represent another act of aggression by the monolithic forces of communism; their action provoked Truman to respond with military force (conveniently done under the UN flag, which was made possible by a Soviet boycott of the UN at that time). The Korean War showed that the military side of the Cold War could be fought in "limited" warfare that need not escalate into World War III; and, in that respect, it was a forerunner to the U.S. war in Vietnam and the Soviet war in Afghanistan.

The "loss" of China and, to a lesser extent, the Korean War helped fuel a kind of domestic Cold War in which Americans became stridently patriotic and, at the same time, highly suspicious of the loyalty of their friends and neighbors. Initiated by a well-publicized Congressional hearing about Communist influence in Hollywood, and the investigation of Alger Hiss, a high-ranking State Department official accused of passing secret information to the Communists, the nation's anti-Communist fears were exploited by Senator Joseph McCarthy, a Republican from Wisconsin, who sought to capitalize on the issue to assure his reelection. McCarthy's followers believed his assertions that the State Department and much of the rest of the government were infested with Communists. The conviction of Julius and Ethel Rosenberg in 1950 for passing atomic secrets to the Soviet Union served only to confirm the fear that McCarthy was exploiting, and their execution in 1953 was generally approved. Popular culture reflected this fear in dozens of anti-Communist movies, television shows, magazine articles, and books; and private vigilante groups enforced blacklists on prominent entertainers. By 1954, however, McCarthy had fallen from favor, and the tide of McCarthyism, as the movement was called, began to ebb.

One reason for that was the easing of global Cold War fears. The Korean War finally wound down in 1953, the same year that Stalin died and Dwight D. Eisenhower was inaugurated as president. The confluence of these events brought a lull to Cold War tensions for a number of years, although Eisenhower's Secretary of State, John Foster Dulles, worked hard to globalize containment by forging military alliances and bilateral security treaties that, by the end of the decade, literally surrounded the Soviet Union and China.

In 1958, Cold War tensions rose again as separate events in Germany and the Middle East grabbed headlines. In the Middle East, Western powers had been badly discredited in the wake of the 1956 Suez crisis, in which Britain and France joined with Israel to create a military situation whereby Britain and France could regain control of the Suez Canal. Their plans failed, and the waterway remained under the control of Egypt, whose independent-minded leader, Gamal Abdel Nasser, had nationalized it. Nasser, who had steered his country in what was perceived to be a leftist direction since his accession to power in 1952, was representative of a new brand of Middle East leadership that U.S. policy makers saw as a Communist threat. Consequently, when Lebanon teetered on the brink of political chaos in 1958, the Eisenhower administration dispatched 14,000 troops to show the flag and discourage a possible Communist takeover.

In Germany, trouble flared again over the status of Berlin. Nikita Khrushchev, who had emerged as the successor to Stalin, announced that he would sign a separate peace treaty with East Germany, which would give the East Germans control over access routes to West Berlin. The United States saw this as a test of Western support of Berlin, and Eisenhower tried to persuade the Soviets to negotiate the Berlin situation. A foreign ministers' meeting in 1959 deadlocked, and a proposed summit conference between Eisenhower and Khrushchev in 1960 was scuttled when it was revealed that the United States had been regularly using U-2 planes to carry out surveillance on the USSR.

The Berlin crisis simmered for several months until Khrushchev announced the end of 1961 as a deadline for the treaty signing as well as a major increase in Soviet military spending. The new U.S. president, John F. Kennedy, responded in kind, requesting $3.2 billion more for the U.S. military and the authority to call up military reserve forces. Frightened Americans built bomb shelters in their back yards and debated the question of whether they could shoot neighbors who tried to force their way in.

After some rhetorical bluster on both sides, the crisis suddenly and unexpectedly ended with the building of the Berlin Wall, which physically divided the German city, in August 1961. The Kennedy administration made no significant response to the wall, and tensions eased. In December, Khrushchev announced that there was no need to rush on the Soviet-East German treaty.

Meanwhile, another, potentially more serious confrontation was brewing over Cuba. Fidel Castro, a charismatic nationalist leader, had taken control of the Cuban government in 1959 and had quickly formed close relationships with nations in the Communist bloc. In April 1961, a disastrous attempt by U.S.-trained Cuban exiles to invade Cuba and overthrow Castro only served to drive the Cuban leader closer to Moscow. In the summer of 1962, rumors surfaced that Soviet missiles were being placed in Cuba and aimed at targets in the United States. Aerial photographs from U-2 planes confirmed these rumors, and the administration imposed a naval quarantine, or blockade, on traffic to Cuba. President Kennedy demanded that the missiles in Cuba be removed, and after a few days of great tension, Khrushchev agreed to remove the missiles in return for a U.S. pledge not to invade Cuba. Both sides recognized that this had, indeed, been a serious crisis; and by the end of 1963, a "hot line" telephone system linked Washington and Moscow, and a treaty banning the testing of nuclear devices everywhere except underground had been signed.

Once again, the Cold War's tensions abated somewhat, as the United States became embroiled in Vietnam in the 1960s in another exercise of containment through the process of limited war. In the 1970s, President Richard M. Nixon and his national security adviser, Henry Kissinger, developed a policy known as "detente" with the Soviet Union, in which each side worked to find those areas (science, culture, trade) in which they could agree and left disputed areas alone. From this period came profitable grain sales for American farmers, joint space missions, and fruitful arms limitations talks.

In December 1979, however, the Soviet Union invaded Afghanistan, a country on its southern border, in what appeared to Americans as a clear act of aggression. President Jimmy Carter, taken aback by this turn of events and fearful of growing Soviet influence in the Persian Gulf region, responded by withdrawing SALT II, an arms limitation agreement that had been signed in 1979, from the Senate, which was considering its ratification, suspending grain sales to the Soviet Union, and announcing that the United States would boycott the 1980 summer Olympics scheduled to be held in Moscow. None of these actions deterred the Soviet Union from its Afghan adventure, and the situation had not changed when Ronald Reagan assumed the presidency in early 1981.

Reagan, whose conservative political principles were well-known, immediately took a hard line toward the Soviet Union and communism in general, terming the USSR an "evil empire" and organizing a Nicaraguan exile military force to try to overthrow a pro-Soviet regime that had come to power in Managua in 1979. He increased U.S. military spending, deployed medium-range nuclear missiles in Europe, and continued to be harshly critical of Moscow in his speeches. While some limited progress on arms talks occurred, much of this was obscured by the president's embrace of the Strategic Defense Initiative (SDI), a complex nuclear defense system designed to protect the United States against incoming nuclear missiles. Although most scientists pronounced SDI unworkable, and the press mocked it as "Star Wars," the administration allocated a great deal of money to research and probably forced the Soviets to reallocate some of their resources.

After several years of unstable leadership in Moscow, Mikhail Gorbachev assumed power in 1985 and set a new tone for U.S.-Soviet relations. Gorbachev, interested in trying to revive the failing Soviet economy, pulled back on a number of Soviet military initiatives and was much more open in his posture toward the West. Reagan, too, seemed to change his attitude toward the USSR following his reelection in 1984, and, as a consequence, he and Gorbachev had annual summit meetings each year between 1985 and 1988. Out of these meetings evolved a new cordiality between the two superpowers, as well as some practical accomplishments, notably the Intermediate Nuclear Force (INF) treaty (1987), in which each side agreed to remove its medium-range missiles from Europe. In addition, Gorbachev terminated the Soviet war in Afghanistan and reduced support for friendly regimes in Cuba, Angola, and Nicaragua.

By 1989, Gorbachev's efforts to restructure the Soviet economy had revealed the fatal weakness of the Soviet system. As the Soviet leader was forced to reduce the size of the Red Army, it became clear that dissident elements in the old satellite countries might at last be able to have their way. With the tacit encouragement of President George Bush's administration, reform elements in Poland and Hungary brought about new constitutions. The Berlin Wall was dismantled, and the process of German reunification began; and, with more difficulty, Communist regimes were overturned in Czechoslovakia, Romania, and Bulgaria. In 1990 and 1991, the Soviet Union itself disintegrated into sixteen states, Russia being far and away the largest. In the wake of that trauma, Gorbachev was replaced by Boris Yeltsin as the leader of Russia. Throughout all of this turmoil in the former Soviet bloc, the United States followed a policy that supported the notion of reform and the legitimacy of the new states, including Russia. Without a rival, the United States would no longer be engaged in a Cold War.

INTERPRETIVE ESSAY
David Mayers

The term Cold War is loosely applied to identify the era of intensive Soviet-U.S. rivalry. It began as the Anglo-Soviet–U.S. alliance, forged in war against Nazi Germany, and fell apart between 1945 and 1946. The retreat of Soviet power from Eastern Europe in 1989 and the political implosion of the USSR in 1991 marked the end of the Cold War as popularly defined.

In this span of forty-five years, relations between the two great powers alternated between sharp tension and detente. In an analytical sense, three separate Cold Wars can be distinguished. The first began in earnest with the falling out of the victors over the spoils of defeated Germany and Japan, Churchill's "iron curtain" speech, Stalin's pronouncement that the world was divided into two irreconcilable camps, the Truman Doctrine, and the Marshall Plan. Following in rapid succession, events afterward strained Soviet-U.S. relations nearly to the point of rupture and war. These included the Berlin crisis in 1948, when a Soviet-imposed blockade of the city threatened to deprive it of access and goods from the West. An Anglo-U.S. airlift and implied resort to war (should the Soviets disrupt the air bridge) successfully countered the Communist action—though Berlin remained for decades a flash point in the East-West contest. Also in 1948, a coup by Czech radicals (with Soviet backing) brought Communists to power in Prague. That same year, Yugoslavia bolted from the Soviet fold, sustaining its independence henceforth by economic and security arrangements with the West. A year later, NATO was founded with the express purpose of deterring Soviet aggression against non-Communist Europe. In 1949, the Soviets also exploded their first atomic bomb, thereby ending the U.S. monopoly on such weaponry. President Truman responded to Soviet acquisition of the bomb by approving plans that accelerated the arms race: an even more destructive weapon, namely the fusion, or hydrogen, bomb, should be developed.

In the Far East, meanwhile, Mao's triumph in China and alignment with the Soviet Union suggested to observers (on both sides of the ideological divide) that the Asian balance of power had shifted against the United States and its allies. Confirmation of this thesis was said to be evident in the North Korean invasion of South Korea in June 1950. The idea was that Stalin and his Chinese comrades felt so emboldened that they inspired the North Koreans to unify their country on Communist terms; the West presumably was on the defensive and could not respond effectively.

In 1953 the first Cold War began to thaw. Joseph Stalin, who was held responsible by many Americans for causing postwar tensions, died in March. His successor, Georgi Malenkov, charted a "new course" and affirmed the need for Soviet-U.S. coexistence. He emphasized, too, the desirability of increased East-West trade and other types of economic cooperation. In 1953 the Korean War ended in compromise and an armistice—which despite ups and downs since has nevertheless held. The next year, in Geneva, representatives from East and West negotiated a settlement to end the war between the French and nationalist forces in Vietnam. And in 1955, Soviet and U.S. leaders convened the first postwar summit conference, aimed at resolving, or at least discussing, the main problems between them: the division of Germany, the strategic arms race, and Soviet hegemony in Eastern Europe. Notwithstanding crises in 1956—Soviet suppression of the Hungarian Revolution, and the Suez Crisis—relations between the two powers did not deteriorate appreciably. This condition obtained in part because of Nikita Khrushchev's anti-Stalin campaign and his embracing of the idea of competitive, but peaceful, coexistence.

The second Cold War started in 1958, when Khrushchev delivered his ultimatum over Berlin. This revived Cold War culminated in 1962, with the Cuban missile crisis and near brush with nuclear conflict. Signs of improvement were apparent as early as 1963, when the limited test ban treaty was signed. Thereafter, despite differences between Moscow and Washington over the Vietnam War and the 1968 Warsaw Pact invasion of Czechoslovakia, arms control was an object of Soviet and U.S. concentration. By 1972, Soviet-U.S. detente was under way, its cornerstone being strategic arms control, exemplified by the signing of SALT I by Richard M. Nixon and Leonid Brezhnev.

Detente started to fray in the mid-1970s as critics in both countries charged that the adversary was enjoying unilateral advantages—in Middle East diplomacy, arms production, and maneuvers for influence in Africa and Latin America. Following the Soviet invasion of Afghanistan in 1979, the U.S. Senate suspended its deliberation on SALT II, and the treaty went unratified. Detente had become a dead letter and remained so throughout the first Reagan administration. A wheat embargo, the Olympics boycott, an accelerated arms race, and inflated rhetoric were symbols and substance of yet another round of the U.S. Cold War effort. Talk of an "evil empire" everywhere on the offensive and research on a comprehensive defense shield (SDI) were aspects of U.S. policy in this third Cold War. Only as the USSR lurched to its demise—first under a reformist government headed by Mikhail Gorbachev, and then in accordance with the logic of a failed economy—did the competitive-cooperative cycle in Soviet-U.S. history cease.

A standard question about the first (or classical) Cold War concerns its origins: Is it properly traced to 1918, when the Americans (along with the French, British, and Japanese) intervened in the Russian civil war on the anti-Bolshevik side? This action was ineffective and feeble. Additionally, it was hobbled by an absence of clear goals or of coordination among the intervening powers—to say nothing of poor cooperation with sundry anti-Bolshevik Russian forces. Still, the Soviet regime concluded—understandably from its viewpoint—that the capitalist West, including the United States, had sought to kill the workers' revolution in its infancy.

In the aftermath of World War I, V. I. Lenin's Comintern, an organization devoted to the revolutionary transformation of world politics, pitted itself against the liberalism of President Woodrow Wilson and U.S.

attempts to reform world politics. In the United States, the postwar Red Scare widened the gulf between the two countries. Formal relations between them were not established until Franklin D. Roosevelt became president in 1933.

The Cold War is aptly characterized by Leon Trotsky's phrase, originally used to describe relations between Bolshevik Russia and Imperial Germany in 1918: "Neither war nor peace." Beyond this, professional historians have produced three conflicting schools of interpretation.

The one best known to American audiences might be labeled the "orthodox." From this point of view, the USSR bore major responsibility for beginning the Cold War. Contrary to the joint declaration on liberated territories and in defiance of promises made at Yalta, Stalin pursued an aggressive policy in Europe. It started with Soviet domination of Poland and continued in attempts to stir trouble in Greece, Italy, and France through local Communist parties. The Soviets also waged unfriendly diplomacy against Turkey and Iran. By 1949, the Soviets had, with the single exception of Yugoslavia, placed puppet regimes throughout east-central Europe. Within this zone the liquidation of people who would not comply with Stalinist dictates proceeded apace with the imposition of the Soviet version of socialism. Overall, the Soviet Union was militant and aggressive. American policies against the Soviets were essentially reactive, or defensive, as implied in the word "containment."

According to the orthodox analysis, one key to Soviet conduct in the late 1940s was Stalin's personality which was usually described as paranoid, willful, and cunning. The ravages of old age, together with the moral corrosiveness of absolute power—and a keen sense of his country's vulnerability—made Stalin and his government more fearsome and suspicious than any other, at any time in Soviet history.

Communist doctrine is also said to have animated Soviet foreign policy. It aimed at world revolution and conquest by Marxist-Leninism. And it was firmly planted under Soviet leadership: the Chinese (and others) could only play a supporting role to the USSR's lead. Moscow was, and remained to the end, the source of revolutionary ideas and the undisputed head of the proletarian movement.

Except for a forceful U.S. response in the late 1940s, Soviet armies would have occupied all of western Europe right up to the English Channel. Even though the Marshall Plan and the founding of NATO confined Soviet influence in Europe to the poorer areas, the United States was unable to reverse Stalin's manipulation of so-called free elections in Eastern Europe. There he methodically enthroned his stooges. A Stalinist imperium replaced the Nazi empire in east-central Europe, and the peoples therein continued to live under a brutal brand of foreign subjugation.

A second interpretation of the Cold War, the "revisionist," is a mirror image of the orthodox. It runs roughly like this: the United States, not the USSR, was mainly responsible for the disintegration of the Grand Alliance. The U.S. government acted on behalf of private capital—investment firms, heavy industry, agro-business conglomerates, companies engaged in exploiting natural resources.

In the war's aftermath, capitalism's ambition was to reestablish U.S.-European trade. A revived European economy could absorb surplus U.S. products and capital, thereby staving off in the United States a return to the prewar condition of depression. The U.S. government was also eager to promote an Open Door Policy in Eastern Europe. By penetrating that area economically and politically, the United States could force east-central Europe to revert to its earlier status as a zone of exploitation. In future years, in exchange for their raw materials and agricultural goods, the East Europeans could again purchase French, British, and (above all) American finished products.

Unfortunately, U.S. preoccupation with avoiding economic dislocation at home—which drove this frantic effort to rehabilitate Europe economically and to make it a dependent partner—grated on Soviet sensibilities; Moscow balked as the United States tried to obtain a position of privilege in east-central Europe. Such a position would have been extremely trying—geopolitically speaking—for the USSR. By way of analogy, one has only to imagine the uproar in the United States, if the Soviet Union (or any other great state) had tried to establish for itself a zone of dominance in Canada or Mexico.

Revisionist scholars also stress what can be termed as shabby U.S. treatment of the USSR during World War II. For example, they point out, work on the atomic bomb was strictly a British-U.S. affair. Soviet leaders were never told about this Anglo-American project until after it was an accomplished fact. Nor were the Soviets ever seriously consulted about the weapon's deployment against the common foe. Not until after the experimental explosion at Alamogordo, New Mexico, during the Potsdam Conference (1945), did a confident Harry Truman inform Stalin of the bomb's existence. Such remarkable unilateral conduct by the United States was contrary to diplomacy's most elementary rule: allies, if they are going to remain as such, confer over issues of mutual concern. Were the Americans acting in bad faith by trying to keep the Soviets in the dark?

Some revisionists contend that the United States used the atomic bombs against Japan in 1945 for one basic reason: to remind Stalin of the odds facing him should he choose to defy American wishes in the postwar world. To phrase it bluntly, the bombing of Hiroshima and Nagasaki constituted the first attempt to press Stalin for concessions in east-central Europe and was a warning that, after the war, Soviet misconduct (as defined by the West) could be severely punished. Thus, the fateful events of August 1945 are properly understood not as the final act in World War II but as the horrific opening of the Cold War.

Another indication of America's lack of good faith, according to revisionists, is Truman's abrupt cancellation of Lend-Lease aid to the Soviets just after V-E Day. This event occurred at a time when the USSR was still reeling from the effects of a gruesome war against Germany and was dutifully preparing to join the campaign against Japan.

There is also the revisionist slant on the slowness with which the Anglo-Americans opened a second front. While they dabbled about in secondary theaters—in North Africa and Italy—the Soviet Union was bled white and its economy savaged. Did Western leaders, with an eye to the future, ideologically suspicious of the Soviets and economically at odds with them, choose not to relieve German pressure on the eastern front until late in the war? To support this thesis, revisionists cite statements by Churchill and Truman suggesting that they were content to see Germany and Russia whack each other to pieces. By the time hostilities ended, the Soviet Union confronted daunting tasks of reconstruction. Drought and famine during 1946 and 1947 in the Ukraine, the disproportionately high number of old people and youngsters in the labor force, and the numerical imbalance between men and women of child-rearing age (52 million women versus 31 million men) were the most visible signs of national plight. Expanses of western Russia and the Ukraine, fought over by German and Soviet armies, were denuded of habitation and agricultural life. Stalin made his subjects salvage these areas, while reestablishing industrial production and repairing the physical foundations of such cities as Leningrad, Kiev, and Stalingrad. This work of restoration had to be shouldered by a population simultaneously grieving for its war dead and improvising for millions more left maimed.

Surely, these grim facts of Soviet life in 1945 comforted U.S. policy planners as they contemplated future relations with Moscow. To what degree, and for what Machiavellian reasons, had the Americans delayed the invasion of Europe? To what degree were they satisfied to see the Soviet Union grievously wounded? From consequences—namely Soviet damage sustained and delays in opening the second front—some scholars have ascribed cynical motives to U.S. wartime policy.

A third interpretation of the Cold War places postwar Soviet-U.S. rivalry within the context of traditional European power politics. This "postrevisionist" viewpoint attributes fault to both sides. But the allocating of blame and praise is not its primary concern. Most postrevisionists allow that the Cold War was not inevitable. But they also make the point that, given the nature of international relations, it is hard to see just how the Cold War might have been avoided.

To begin with, say postrevisionists, it must be understood that the Soviet-American wartime partnership was based solely on the mutual desire to defeat Nazi Germany. As such, the alliance was a marriage of convenience. Suspicions rooted in ideological antipathy and historical conflict underlay Washington's necessary cooperation with Moscow. It could not obviate for the Soviets, no matter how expedient or effective in wartime, instances of Western hostility (that is, Allied intervention during the Russian civil war). Nor could the alliance erase from Western memories examples of Soviet misconduct—be it Comintern meddling in labor organizations or Stalin's cooperation with Hitler in the Nazi-Soviet Nonaggression Pact (1939).

Given this unhappy record of prewar relations, it was not surprising that the Grand Alliance collapsed with the end of its *raison d'être:* defeat of the Axis powers. Further, in the postwar period, the nature of Soviet-American antagonism, previously never a threat to global peace, had altered. Indeed, the international distribution of power had been transformed.

The war had devastated Europe and the local states could no longer maintain the traditional balance of forces. Germany was ruined and occupied. France was politically uncertain and demoralized after long years of Nazi occupation. An enfeebled Great Britain had begun to liquidate its empire.

After the war, the Soviet regime, to avoid future disasters, sought assiduously to assure external security. For Stalin, idealistic principles of world peace put forth in the United Nations Charter could not substitute for friendly governments—that is to say Soviet-controlled governments—on Russia's vulnerable western frontier. During the interwar period, all of the border states had been hostile toward the Soviet Union and some—Hungary and Romania, for example—had cooperated with Hitler in the 1941 invasion. In addition, Stalin was suspicious of the American-designed, universally-pretentious collective security system: the United Nations. He viewed it as a mere tool of U.S. diplomacy in much the way that the League of Nations had previously functioned as an Anglo-French instrument. In the meantime, he forced subservient regimes upon those east-central European states occupied by the Red Army. Perceived Soviet security needs, requiring specific regional arrangement, resulted hence in a new Communist cordon sanitaire.

As for the United States, the Truman administration did not react as decisively or as adroitly to the Grand Alliance's collapse as Churchill would have liked. Yet by early 1947, the Americans had abandoned the chimera of Soviet-U.S. peacetime partnership and assumed the role traditionally played by Great Britain. Europe's strategic balance, threatened by the Soviet Union, was maintained by U.S. counterweight.

By 1949, then, clashing concepts of security and national interest had displaced wartime hopes for a durable Allied concert. An historically unique, politically symmetrical division of Europe had taken root. The several lesser states on either side of the continental divide coalesced around a power center and adopted—or had imposed on them—its form of social-political organization. Militarization of the bipolar scheme ensued. Confrontation in Europe expanded into Soviet-U.S. rivalry over other parts of the world, notably China, Korea, and the Middle East.

To summarize postrevisionism: World War II destroyed the traditional balance of power in Europe. The two extra-European powers, the United States and the Soviet Union, filled the resulting power vacuum. They established a new balance of power system marked by clearly delineated spheres of influence and rival alliance systems, NATO and (after 1955) the Warsaw Pact.

The Soviet-U.S. contest, enduring from 1946 to 1991, ended on terms favorable to the West. Yet it would be rash to overlook the vexing problems that beset U.S. Cold War policy. How might they have been better handled?

It is fair to say that the premises underlying policy between 1946 and 1953 were sound. The USSR did pose a threat—not an overwhelming one, but a grave one all the same—to U.S. strategic, economic, and political interests in Europe and, to a lesser degree, in Asia. American policy, mixing diplomatic and economic means (notably the Marshall Plan) with military means (such as NATO and the intervention in Korea) prevented the expansion of Soviet influence into vital areas.

But U.S. policy also had its defects. Prominent among them was the tendency by Washington policymakers to overestimate the military capabilities of the Soviet Union: there was undue alarm about a potential Soviet march to the English Channel, for example. This concern was understandable, given the rapid demobilization of Western military forces and unpreparedness in the few U.S. units on the Continent in the years immediately after World War II. Nonetheless, as the U.S. embassy in Moscow reported and as common sense should have indicated, the extensive damage inflicted on the Soviet Union during the war had impaired its ability to pursue a militarily aggressive policy. During the German-Soviet war, upwards of 10 percent of the Soviet population had perished. Some 20 to 27 million people had died—to say nothing of those left underfed and inadequately sheltered. The damage done to Soviet agricultural production and industry was also vast. Consequently, Soviet reconstruction was a monumental effort. It and the consolidation of Communist power in east-central Europe consumed Soviet attention and devoured scarce resources. To ease the manpower shortage in the factories and collective farms, Soviet armed forces were reduced from a wartime high of 12 million to less than three million by 1948. The surviving force was itself thinly spread from the Soviet Far East to garrisons in Stalin's recently acquired east-central European empire.

A deeper appreciation of the USSR's actual strength and of Stalin's fears about U.S. power—manifest in a superproductive, unscathed economy—could have resulted in more forceful U.S. responses to such issues as German reunification or the Communist coup in Czechoslovakia.

Additional problems during this period included the misplaced emphasis by various people (such as Secretary of Defense James Forrestal) on Marxist ideology as a determinant of Soviet foreign policy. During Stalin's waning years, the Soviet Union was a place of unrelieved terror, but it was not one in which the categories of Marxism mattered. Most true believers, such as Nikolai Bukharin, had perished in that earlier orgy of violence and party purge in the 1930s. In their place stood Stalin, arguably the most ruthless realist in European history, but whatever he was, Stalin and his world view had little to do with Marx. In other words, Communist ideology was no longer a source of inspiration for external policy, though it remained a powerful sanction to enforce conformity at home.

But none of these items constituted the major flaw with U.S. Cold War policy. Indeed, the chief problem was not of a strategic or tactical nature. Rather, what was disturbing—in retrospect—was Washington's method of waging the Cold War on the home front and in the popular mind as it listened from abroad.

Policy was justified by an excessive, ideologically-saturated rhetoric. The verbal overkill, as practiced by the executive branch and then adopted by legislators and pundits, gained an independent momentum. It helped create a domestic atmosphere that eventually hobbled policy-makers as they sought to advance U.S. interests according to a realistic assessment of international power. In other words, Cold War mythology created political problems for the mythmakers and hampered them in achieving their objectives, such as pursuing a policy to weaken Chinese and Soviet commitments to each other in the 1950s. Furthermore, the long-term consequences of selling the Cold War at home helped damage American self-esteem during the Vietnam War disillusionment, thereby contributing to an unhealthy season of doubt in the United States about foreign policy purpose and raising doubts among allies about the stead-fastness of people in Washington.

Behind the rhetoric used in the period 1946 through 1953 was the public's propensity to have its foreign aspirations conform to a moralistic framework, peculiarly understood in the United States. Truman became convinced in the winter of 1946-1947 that a dispassionate analysis of Europe's vulnerability to the Soviet Union was inadequate. Such an analysis could not persuade Congress (or the public) to support a policy reorientation as significant as that embodied by the Truman Doctrine and the Marshall Plan. A January 1947 poll indicated that 40 percent of the U.S. public thought Stalin could still be trusted. Almost 75 percent believed the United States was as much to blame for global problems as the Soviet Union. Unless something drastic was done, popular support would lag behind policies aimed against the Soviets. Beginning in March 1947, with the Truman Doctrine speech, the administration publicly equated the policy of checking Soviet power with preventing Communist expansion in general.

Synonymous as the Soviet Union and communism were, so also were they identified with benighted forces in conflict with the United States. Opposition to Soviet power was justified to the public as necessary if freedom and liberty were to prevail. In effect, U.S. interests were associated with enlightened forces everywhere struggling for democracy. In a world where the stakes were absolute and the enemy's nefarious designs sharply contrasted with U.S. aims, the Soviet side was dogmatic and tyrannical, the American tolerant and democratic. Moreover, said

Truman, U.S. policy should support peoples everywhere that resisted Communist subjugation.

Thus was refuted the alternative wisdom of John Quincy Adams. Adams, who served as both secretary of state and president in the early nineteenth century, had warned Americans of his generation against policies of intervention that would subtly corrupt the democratic spirit of the United States or lead it to rely heavily upon the instruments of force. The sensibility of the Monroe Doctrine, which, in 1823, had declared U.S. hegemony in Latin America, won out with Truman. It was writ large and now applied to the world.

Similar analyses soon were forthcoming from other officials, who condemned the Soviet adversary as the successor evil to Hitlerite Germany. Meanwhile, they affirmed the American belief that, in Woodrow Wilson's words, the United States is the "most unselfish nation in history." In the ensuing debate, critics as diverse as Walter Lippmann, Hans J. Morgenthau, and Henry A. Wallace argued against policies likely either to weaken the United States by overextending its resources or to provoke war with the Soviet Union. Lippmann blasted "containment" as a "strategic monstrosity." Even the influential theologian Reinhold Niebuhr, a staunch supporter of U.S. policy at the time, warned against the willfulness of national pride, blind to the dangers of imperial purpose.

Some officials, including George Marshall, Charles E. Bohlen, and George Kennan, also feared difficulties related to Truman's public explanation of international problems. After all, Marshall communicated to him, wasn't there too much flamboyant anticommunism in the speech? The reply came back from Truman that, from all his contacts with the Senate, it was clear that this was the only way (the way of the hard sell) in which enabling legislation could be passed.

Thus still-prevalent isolationist sentiments were overcome, as were Congress's fiscal conservatism and residual American sympathies for the Soviet Union. However, the concerns of the critics proved well-founded. The emotional portrayal of policy combined with three features in postwar America: namely, unfulfilled expectations for global harmony, unanticipated international setbacks, and electoral politics. Together, these elements led to exaggerated fears of internal subversion and betrayal.

Primitive thought during the Cold War was not the exclusive province of the Joseph McCarthy wing of the Republican Party; but the Wisconsin senator and his associates were vivid examples of it. By 1950, these members of the GOP, frustrated over years of Democratic rule, allied themselves with southern Democrats to exploit widespread fears and frustrations. America's foreign setbacks, as exemplified in Berlin and elsewhere in Europe, were attributed by these people to an administration "soft on communism" and infiltrated by Soviet spies and fellow travelers.

The House Committee on Un-American Activities proclaimed in 1948 that all Communists within U.S. borders must be rendered politically and economically impotent. In the attempt to purge government of subversive agents, few, if any, Soviet spies were exposed; but slander and innuendo were hurled against a number of public servants and private citizens by sanctimonious politicians, often motivated by personal ambition as much as by devotion to the common good.

To a degree, Truman's domestic policies were influenced by the prevalent anticommunism. The Loyalty Order in 1947, which resulted in the processing of several hundred cases of purported betrayal and bad security risks, was promulgated partly with an eye to the upcoming presidential election and to demonstrate the president's toughness. A number of competent and dedicated people in the State Department were dismissed—by Truman's own later admission—"on the flimsiest charges."

These and similar episodes add poignancy to Kennan's injunction: In the protracted struggle against the Soviet Union, Americans must have courage and self-confidence enough to cling to their own methods and conceptions of human society. Though Truman's self-survival strategy compromised traditions of fairness and due legal process, his maneuvers did not blunt the fury of enemies eager to discredit his leadership.

Unlike the administration's successful European policy which thwarted Communist expansion and provided the resources and incentives for recovery, the Far Eastern record was eminently open to criticism. Indeed, few U.S. misadventures have caused greater debate than the "loss of China." Critics included respectable people like Senators Robert A. Taft and William Knowland, as well as McCarthy. They blamed China's subjugation by Mao Zedong on the leftist orientation of the State Department and White House. By allegedly "selling out" China, "red" Dean Acheson and his presidential dupe had jeopardized U.S. security and peace. Even soldier-statesman George Marshall was villified and implicated in the "conspiracy" of delivering China to Mao Zedong.

Political pressures and popular doubts aroused by McCarthy forced Acheson to undertake a good-will tour of the United States in an attempt to convince his countrymen that he was not corrupt, opposed communism, and did not hire traitors. In large measure, Truman's support of his secretary prevented his congressional opponents from forcing him to resign. Less prominent officials, though equally innocent, were not as fortunate. Charges of subversion and disloyalty were leveled against most, of the China specialists in the Foreign Service. By 1953, only two of more than twenty such persons possessing hard-earned knowledge of China remained in the government's employ. At a time when events required sensitivity to Chinese matters, the division of Far Eastern Affairs had been purged of its experts. The people best able to design a wedge to split the Sino-Soviet alliance were simply missing from government councils. In fact, the overall impact of McCarthyism on the Foreign Service was devastating. During the Eisenhower administration (and to his anguish), the internal security system was expanded and became less restrained.

Breathless anticommunism encouraged the country to ally itself with some authoritarian regimes whose only virtue was their noisy opposition to communism. The United States was criticized in Europe, among other places, for hypocrisy in supporting undemocratic regimes and was identified with and blamed for their successes. During the protest era of the 1960s, many Americans used this contradiction to heap abuse on the government. In doing so, they obscured this austere truth: a country need not be a paragon of American democratic virtue to be an international partner for the United States. In other words, the philosophical weakness inherent in demonizing enemies and idealizing allies was allowed to work mischief. The truth is simpler: the United States, like any country, has neither permanent friends nor permanent enemies. It merely has interests. This understanding does not allow for the adolescent mentality that sees a world populated only by angels and devils, rather than one inhabited by imperfect, frightened people trying to preserve their security and that of their children. Much domestic controversy could have been avoided had American policy not been phrased in such excessive terms in 1947.

Not surprisingly, given the ideological cast of American foreign policy and its crusading impulse during the Cold War, the debate over Vietnam was impassioned. Many critics indulged in a national self-lacerating discussion. They concluded that American history and contemporary society were tainted with an original defect—be it racism or capitalism or sexism—that explained the perpetration of American "crimes" in Vietnam.

However exaggerated this reaction to the Vietnam War and unsatis-factory the atonement of sins, there is no doubt that the war prompted widespread dissatisfaction with the scale, behavior, and thrust of U.S. global involvement. In effect, the war destroyed the consensus that had supported foreign policy since 1947. During the 1970s, the principles in the Nixon Doctrine and periodic congressional attempts to withdraw U.S. forces from Europe indicated Washington's new perception of the public's capacity to sustain a global involvement.

Admittedly, it would not have been easy to instruct the public of the virtues of moderation and the necessity of counterbalancing Soviet power back in 1970. To begin with, wartime propaganda depicting the Soviet Union as a heroic fellow democracy would have to be overcome. Yet despite what Acheson and others thought, the public is not so obtuse as to be incapable of appreciating the main lines of international politics. If the public had been coolly informed of the magnitude of the Soviet threat, very likely a general consensus would have emerged anyway to support the policy of containment. American policy, however, should not have been staked to an ideological-moral root susceptible to the vi-cissitudes of the public mood. This is not to say that the ideological aspect of Soviet-American rivalry could have been ignored, but neither should it have been overly dramatized. There did not, in other words, have to be a call to crusade, a tempting but irresponsible appeal to the religious revival aspects in American political culture.

The likelihood that the public would have accepted a policy modestly stated and in which the sacrifices were potentially great—such as keep-ing a military force in Europe and possibly fighting limited wars for limited objectives—and the gains seemingly incremental was at best problematic. Indeed, for the public to unburden itself of Wilsonian pre-cepts would have been as significant a revolution in American policy thinking as was the decision to participate intimately in the postwar affairs of Europe. Clearly, though, in 1947, Americans accepted a new direction in foreign policy. Perhaps, they could have accepted more.

In any case, if a similarly phrased assessment of international problems as above had been accepted, some of the major difficulties in U.S. Cold War policy would have been avoided. At the minimum, a more serious effort should have been made to educate the public on the nature of international affairs. Generally, Americans have a sophisticated under-standing of domestic politics and seek pragmatic solutions to problems. If the international dilemmas in 1947 had been carefully explained and the policy options explored—namely, do nothing, attack the Soviet

Union, or strike a balance between bellicosity and peace as the United States did—the public probably still would have supported its patent best interests.

To conclude, a necessary contradiction does not exist between a democracy pursuing realistic-pragmatic politics abroad and maintaining its open institutions at home. If leaders are to remain faithful to their special responsibility—maintaining the democratic integrity of the United States—then they must honestly confront the nation with the broad policy choices (while letting people with specialized expertise sort through the complexities of any given policy).

The official formulation of America's international situation in the late 1940s was exaggerated and a disservice to truth. Also a foreign policy presented as indiscriminately anti-Communist clouded the fact that the USSR was the real danger (not some nineteenth century utopian idea) and paved the way for intervention against numerous national revolutions—themselves invariably cloaked by radical rhetoric and symbols, but hardly instruments of Soviet power. Both hostility toward a nationalist revolution and deception of the public culminated in the Vietnam War. By the end of it, the public had been misled about various wartime activities and goals, thereby helping to bring about an unprecedented lack of popular confidence in U.S. institutions and purpose, which, in turn, meant that a war won on the field and in the air became politically a lost cause.

SELECTED BIBLIOGRAPHY

Acheson, Dean. *Present at the Creation*. New York: W.W. Norton, 1969. The autobiography of one of the principal architects of early Cold War policy.

Alperovitz, Gar. *Atomic Diplomacy: Hiroshima and Potsdam*. New York: Vintage Books, 1967. Argues that the atomic bomb was used on Hiroshima to intimidate the Soviet Union.

Bohlen, Charles. *Witness to History, 1929–1969*. New York: W.W. Norton, 1973. Bohlen, a State Department career officer, was one of the authors of the Marshall Plan and, later, ambassador to the Soviet Union.

Carothers, Thomas. *In the Name of Democracy: U.S. Policy toward Latin America in the Reagan Years*. Berkeley: University of California Press, 1991. A readable account of the Reagan administration's efforts to fight the Cold War in Latin America.

Fischer, Louis. *The Road to Yalta: Soviet Foreign Relations, 1941–45*. New York: Harper & Row, 1972. Blames the Cold War on desires for Soviet expansionism unchecked by Western powers.

Gaddis, John Lewis. *The United States and the End of the Cold War*. New York:

Oxford University Press, 1992. A good survey of the latter years of the Cold War.

———. *The United States and the Origins of the Cold War, 1941–1947.* New York: Columbia University Press, 1972. A balanced account, tracing the roots of the Cold War back through World War II.

Gardner, Lloyd. *Architects of Illusion: Men and Ideas in American Foreign Policy.* Chicago: Quadrangle Books, 1970. Gardner concludes that the Cold War was shaped by American policymakers who misunderstood the Soviet Union.

George, Alexander, and Richard Smoke. *Deterrence in American Foreign Policy: Theory and Practice.* New York: Columbia University Press, 1974. Important analysis of the impact of nuclear weaponry on foreign policy during the Cold War.

Hogan, Michael. *The Marshall Plan: America, Britain and the Reconstruction of Western Europe, 1947–1952.* Cambridge: Cambridge University Press, 1987. A basic account of the U.S. economic program to restore Europe's shattered economies.

Hyland, William G. *The Cold War Is Over.* New York: Random House, 1990. Early study of the end of the Cold War by the editor of *Foreign Affairs.*

Isaacson, Walter, and Evan Thomas. *The Wise Men: Six Friends and the World They Made.* New York: Simon and Schuster, 1986. A collective biographical study of six key Cold War figures: Dean Acheson, Charles Bohlen, Averell Harriman, George Kennan, Robert Lovett, and John McCloy.

Kennan, George. *Memoirs, 1925–1950.* Boston: Little, Brown, 1967; and *Memoirs: 1950–1963.* New York: Pantheon Books, 1983. Kennan, who formulated the policy of containment, was at the center of early Cold War policymaking.

LaFeber, Walter. *America, Russia, and the Cold War, 1945–1992.* New York: McGraw-Hill, 1993. Now in its seventh edition, this is a standard and succinct account.

Leffler, Melvyn. *A Preponderance of Power: National Security, the Truman Administration, and the Cold War.* Stanford, CA: Stanford University Press, 1992. Another recent analysis of the origins of the Cold War.

Mastny, Vojtech. *Russia's Road to the Cold War: Diplomacy, Warfare, and the Politics of Communism, 1941–1945.* New York: Columbia University Press, 1979. Study of Soviet objectives during both World War II and the postwar years.

Mayers, David. *George Kennan and the Dilemmas of US Foreign Policy.* New York: Oxford University Press, 1988. A thorough study of Kennan's career and thought.

Szulc, Tad. *The Illusion of Peace: Foreign Policy in the Nixon Years.* New York: Viking, 1978. Critical study of foreign policymaking and policymakers in the Nixon administration.

Ulam, Adam. *Expansion and Coexistence: Soviet Foreign Policy, 1917–1973.* 2d. edition. New York: Holt, Rinehart, Winston, 1974. Basic study of Soviet policy from the Russian Revolution to the 1970s.

Williams, William A. *The Tragedy of American Diplomacy.* New York: Dell, 1962. The fundamental revisionist study, attributing most American foreign policy actions to economic motives.

6 —————————————————————————

The Development of Atomic Energy, 1945–1995

INTRODUCTION

The ability to harness and utilize atomic energy for military and peaceful purposes was a by-product of World War II. In August 1939, the eminent physicist Albert Einstein wrote to President Franklin D. Roosevelt that a bomb fueled by the energy released when the nucleus of a uranium atom was split—a process known as nuclear fission—was theoretically possible. Acting at least partly out of fear that German scientists might be working on the same theory, Roosevelt authorized the Manhattan Project, which began in 1940 to develop such an atomic bomb.

In December 1942, at the University of Chicago, scientists built the first nuclear "pile," an arrangement whereby the nuclear reaction brought on by fission could be controlled. Over the next two and a half years, some $2 billion was spent to build plants and assemble the material needed to construct an actual bomb. Much of the work was done in a remote laboratory at Los Alamos, New Mexico, under the guidance of Robert Oppenheimer and a team of brilliant scientists, some of whom had fled from Hitler's Germany in the 1930s. On July 17, 1945, near Alamogordo, New Mexico, Oppenheimer's team successfully detonated an atomic bomb, or A-bomb, as it came to be known.

President Harry S Truman, in office only since April, after Roosevelt's

The development of more powerful nuclear weapons was an important element in the early years of the Cold War. Here U.S. troops witness a hydrogen bomb test in Nevada. (Reproduced from the Collections of the Library of Congress)

death, decided to use the atomic bomb against Japan in order to shorten the war in the Pacific. The best intelligence estimates suggested that in order to force Japan into an unconditional surrender, the war would have to be carried to Japan's home islands and might last until 1947 and cost another one million lives. Truman hoped that the bombs dropped on Hiroshima and Nagasaki on August 6 and 9 would bring about a Japanese surrender; they did, and the United States entered the postwar world with an atomic monopoly.

As the Cold War between the United States and the Soviet Union developed in the months following the Japanese surrender, there was much debate about the future of atomic weaponry. At the United Nations (UN), Bernard Baruch, an American delegate, introduced what became known as the "Baruch Plan" for the control of atomic energy. He urged the UN to create an international agency to control all atomic weapons. Member nations would pledge not to build atomic bombs, and the agency would be empowered to carry out inspections and impose sanctions on any nations violating their pledge. The United States would voluntarily give up its atomic weapons to the agency once it was established. The Soviet Union, however, rejected the Baruch Plan, calling it an American "trick" to maintain an atomic monopoly. Moreover, said the Soviets, the proposed inspections were designed to reveal Soviet military secrets. Their alternative was to demand that the United States destroy its atomic arsenal before an international agency was created. The United States refused to do this, and, knowing that the Soviets were working on their own atomic weapons, continued the research, development, and testing of more powerful atomic bombs.

In the United States, atomic development was done under the authority of the Atomic Energy Commission (AEC), which had been created in the McMahon Act (or Atomic Energy Act) of 1946. The AEC, which came into existence in 1947, in its early years was concerned about military uses of atomic energy. It was overseen by the Joint Congressional Committee on Atomic Energy (JCAE). In 1974, the Energy Research and Development Administration (ERDA) and the Nuclear Regulatory Commission (NRC) replaced the AEC in the federal bureaucracy.

A great deal of atomic testing was done in these years, but one U.S. test cycle, Operation Sandstone, paved the way for the mass production of atomic bombs. As a result, the American arsenal contained over one thousand such bombs by 1953. By this time, atomic weapons had become the central element in U.S. defense policy. Meanwhile, the Soviet Union successfully tested an atomic bomb in September 1949 and became the second member in the "nuclear club." This event, combined with other Cold War conflicts, heightened tensions in the United States, contributed to the rise of a virulent anti-Communist movement in the United States known as McCarthyism, and prompted the Truman administration to push forward the development of the hydrogen bomb, or H-bomb, a weapon many times more powerful than an A-bomb.

With the administration of President Dwight D. Eisenhower, who took office in 1953, nuclear weapons became important not only because of their awesome power, which was seen as a deterrent to potential enemies, but also because of their relative economy, as it was clearly cheaper to kill thousands of people in one bomb blast than in traditional combat. Committed to economy in government, the administration continued atomic testing, and the army worked on small nuclear weapons that could be used in battlefield situations, often sending troops to observe tests at close range or to undertake maneuvers in areas where tests had recently occurred.

As the Eisenhower administration increased its reliance on atomic weapons, however, it also remained active on the diplomatic front. In a speech at the United Nations in December 1953, President Eisenhower laid out his "Atoms for Peace" proposal. This involved the creation of an International Atomic Energy Agency, to which the United States and other nuclear powers would contribute fissionable materials, which the agency would then allocate to others having plans to use it for peaceful purposes. Cold War tensions, however, were still too high, and the Soviet Union was not trustful enough of the United States to concur. In 1955, Eisenhower proposed an "Open Skies" agreement, which would involve a U.S.-Soviet exchange of military establishment site plans and aerial inspections of one nation by the other. Again, the Soviets were not interested. Later in the 1950s, as medical research revealed more health risks associated with nuclear fallout (the residue remaining in the atmosphere following a nuclear test), the two atomic powers engaged in some discussion about banning atmospheric testing. But the U-2 incident (1960), in which an American surveillance plane was shot down over the Soviet Union, worsened relations and ended the negotiations. All that was accomplished was a 1959 treaty banning military bases and nuclear waste disposal in Antarctica.

The Cuban Missile Crisis (1962) brought the world close to a nuclear war and stimulated renewed discussion about the dangers of atomic warfare. The most direct result of the crisis was the Partial Nuclear Test Ban Treaty (1963), in which the United States and the Soviet Union agreed to discontinue nuclear testing on the ground, under water, or in the atmosphere. Only underground tests were permitted. Later in the decade, treaties were signed banning testing in outer space and making Latin America a nuclear-free zone.

In 1968, the Nuclear Non-Proliferation Treaty attempted to maintain non-nuclear status for as many countries as possible. Nuclear power signatories to the treaty pledged not to divulge their nuclear secrets to other countries; non-nuclear nations promised to refrain from developing military nuclear capability. By the early 1990s, over 125 nations had signed the treaty, but a number of nuclear powers and potential nuclear powers, including France, the People's Republic of China, Libya, Pakistan, Israel, South Korea, and Brazil had not.

Beginning around 1971, relations between the United States and the Soviet Union improved in a policy known as "detente," in which each power informally sought to find areas of agreement and to minimize conflict in areas of disagreement. One consequence of detente was a new round of arms limitation negotiations known as SALT (Strategic Arms Limitation Talks). The first treaty to result from these talks was SALT I (1972), which included an ABM (Anti-Ballistic Missile) Treaty, limiting to two the number of sites that could be protected by defensive missiles, and an interim agreement on the limitation of strategic offensive arms. Both nations ratified SALT I; and negotiations continued on SALT II, which was finally signed in 1979, providing for overall ceilings on the number of different kinds of missile launchers and heavy bombers as well as limits on the testing of newly developed missiles. SALT II was a far more complex treaty than its predecessor, and the U.S. Senate never ratified it because relations with Moscow deteriorated rapidly after the Soviet invasion of Afghanistan in December 1979 and the election of Ronald Reagan the next year.

Under Reagan, who once characterized the Soviet Union as an "evil empire," the United States underwent a significant military buildup, including the initiation of development work on the Strategic Defense Initiative, an ambitious space-based nuclear defense system. By 1985, with the ability to negotiate from a position of greater strength, Reagan began serious discussions with the new Soviet leader, Mikhail Gorbachev, on START (Strategic Arms Reduction Talks), based on the premise that reducing the number of nuclear weapons was preferable to limiting their growth.

The first practical result of these talks was the Intermediate Nuclear Force (INF) treaty (1987), which eliminated American and Soviet medium-range (300 to 3000 miles) missiles from Europe, a total of about 4 percent of the nuclear capability of each side. The INF treaty was, however, significant for two other features. First, it legitimized the principle of asymetrical reduction, in that the Soviet Union was obliged to destroy about four times the number of missiles as the United States. Second, the treaty called for unprecedentedly intrusive inspection procedures. Each side was permitted to send teams of experts to the nuclear sites of the other side to observe firsthand the dismantling or destruction of the medium-range missiles. But political turmoil in the Soviet Union and changes of administration in the United States precluded the signing of other arms reduction treaties.

The diversion of nuclear power for peaceful purposes began in the United States in 1954 with the passage of the Atomic Energy Act, which enabled private contractors to build reactors for the nuclear-fueled production of electricity under license from the Atomic Energy Commission. The passage of this act represented a political victory for Lewis Strauss, the chairman of the Atomic Energy Commission, over congressional Democrats who argued that the government should control the development of a civilian nuclear energy program. In 1957, the Price-Anderson Act made nuclear power development economically feasible by limiting the liability of commercial utilities to $560 million in case of a nuclear accident. The first nuclear generating station was opened in Shippingport, Pennsylvania, in 1957, after Admiral Hyman Rickover, who in 1954 had overseen the construction and launching of the U.S.S. *Nautilus,* the first nuclear powered submarine, supplied the plant with a reactor from a never-built nuclear aircraft carrier.

Little further development took place during the 1950s, however, because of the cheap cost of both domestic and imported oil and the abundant supplies of natural gas and coal in the United States. But the successful operation at Shippingport eventually opened the door for other utilities to build nuclear power plants. Between 1965 and 1967 alone, utilities ordered fifty plants from the four nuclear reactor manufacturers. The size of the reactors grew as well, from the 60 megawatts of the Rickover reactor to 1000 megawatts by the 1980s.

In the 1970s, the glow began to tarnish, despite the continued growth of the industry during the decade. Interest rates rose, increasing the cost of construction, while the cost of electricity declined, reducing income and ultimately squeezing profits. The question of nuclear waste disposal, inadequately anticipated, arose and became a political controversy at both the state and national level. And, in 1979, a serious nuclear accident at the Three Mile Island station in Pennsylvania renewed fears about the safety of nuclear power.

In March 1979, a reactor overheated at Three Mile Island, causing a rise in steam pressure. A valve designed to relieve pressure opened, as it was supposed to, but then did not close when the pressure dropped. As a consequence, thousands of gallons of radioactive water spilled out, exposing the nuclear core and almost bringing about a disastrous "meltdown." Some 100,000 people were evacuated from nearby homes, and it was weeks before radiation levels fell enough for investigators to enter and assess the damage. The incident contributed to a growing antinuclear movement in the country, which caused plans for some plants to be shelved and construction on other plants to be halted. In 1990, the United States had 111 operating nuclear reactors supplying about 22 percent of domestic energy needs; however, very few additional ones were being constructed or even planned.

INTERPRETIVE ESSAY
James W. Kunetka

Few events in modern history have shaped both a nation and a world as swiftly and profoundly as the discovery and exploration of atomic energy. While the first third of the twentieth century was spent examining the nature of the atom and its structure, the key breakthrough was made in 1939 by German scientists led by Werner Heisenberg. They discovered nuclear fission, the elemental process by which atoms split and release tremendous energy. The implications of fission were immediate: fissioning atoms, if moderated and controlled, could theoretically generate cheap and virtually inexhaustible energy. Such a force could generate electricity or propel ships; but the same fission process could also be made to run out of control deliberately and thereby produce a powerful explosion. It was the United States during World War II that applied the fission discovery to the development of a new and powerful weapon, the atomic bomb. This effort was conducted in secret and was code-named the Manhattan Project. The creation of these weapons not only left the United States the dominant world power at the end of the war, but also initiated profound social, political, and economic changes that helped shape the rest of the century.

Perhaps the most immediate and dramatic result of atomic weapons was a change in the nature of warfare. Now it was possible for a single bomb to do the same damage to cities, industrial centers, and military installations that before had taken hundreds or even thousands of bombs to achieve. During the war, for example, Allied raids on Japan and Germany frequently utilized a thousand bombers; a few raids massed two thousand. But the one atomic bomb carried by a single bomber and dropped on Hiroshima destroyed almost 70 percent of the city and killed perhaps as many as 100,000 residents.

Early atomic weapons were large and cumbersome, but scientists were already devising ways in which they could be made smaller and at the same time more powerful. And, as production in the huge plants that produced uranium and plutonium gained momentum, the actual cost of each atomic weapon declined. Very quickly, they became cost effective in terms of damage versus cost to produce and deliver. It was also clear that different types of atomic bombs could be designed and built that would serve different purposes. Small bombs, for example, could be fired as artillery shells for limited, tactical purposes in the field, or attached to rockets and delivered great distances as strategic weapons. The German V-2 rocket, used at the end of World War II, had demonstrated that warfare by long distance was not only possible but also inevitable.

More importantly, scientists already knew, in 1945, that even more powerful atomic weapons were theoretically possible. While the bombs that devastated Hiroshima and Nagasaki utilized the "fission process," future weapons might well utilize another nuclear process called "fusion." By fusing light and heavy elements, scientists could duplicate the process that fuels the sun and thereby produce explosions of even more destructive power. Such weapons would come to be known as thermonuclear, or hydrogen, bombs.

At the end of the war, the United States was the only nation to possess atomic bombs; this made it the world's preeminent military power. The nations of Europe lay devastated from six years of war and, for the moment at least, possessed neither the resources nor the technology to produce atomic weapons. Great Britain was the exception in that it had worked closely with the United States during the war to develop the bomb and knew its secrets. The British, however, did not possess the economic resources to embark upon a vast rearmament program that included atomic bombs. The Soviet Union, although struggling to recover from its wartime losses, now occupied vast territories outside its own borders and had several million men under arms. It had pursued its own limited program to develop an atomic bomb throughout the war and was aided by information transmitted from the United States by spies placed deep within the Manhattan Project. The USSR, with its strategic position, wartime conquests, and substantial natural resources, quickly emerged as the second great superpower. Knowing that this position would be guaranteed by an arsenal of atomic bombs, soviet leader Joseph Stalin made development of the new weapon the highest national priority. There was little doubt among American scientists and some political leaders that the Soviets would eventually succeed, although few believed that they would do so before the middle or late 1950s. The United States and the world were therefore surprised when the Soviets detonated their first atomic bomb in September 1949. The global balance of power was now clearly divided between East and West.

The role of nuclear weapons in the diplomatic and strategic planning of the postwar world grew steadily. Both superpowers threw enormous resources behind the development of larger and more powerful weapons, both fission and fusion. Early atomic bombs were in the 18–20 kiloton range, which means that they produced explosions equivalent to eighteen to twenty thousand tons of conventional explosives like TNT. Very quickly, fission weapons were over 100 kilotons and fusion or hydrogen weapons were over one megaton, or equivalent to a thousand thousand tons of TNT. By 1960, both nations possessed thermonuclear bombs that were thousands of times more powerful than those dropped on Japan. Scientists were also able to make these weapons smaller and adaptable to different kinds of delivery systems. At first, atomic bombs were developed for delivery by aircraft, but very quickly they were modified for use as warheads on intercontinental ballistic missiles, known as ICBMs.

Military strategy in both countries continued to evolve, largely because of changes in weaponry. Any major war directly between the United States and the Soviet Union would almost certainly mean the use of atomic weapons. The sheer power of such weapons, however, meant that both sides would suffer devastating destruction and loss of life. As both sides built weapons and increased their ability to deliver them accurately, the implications of any direct war between the two superpowers became even more frightening. The United States always maintained that its atomic arsenal was purely defensive and would never be used in a "first strike" against its enemies. The Soviet Union essentially maintained the same posture. Therefore, a strategy of Mutually Assured Destruction, or MAD, evolved wherein the destructive power of both sides was considered so great that neither side would deliberately seek direct confrontation. One difficultly with MAD, however, lay in the possibility of a "preemptive" strike by either side. Such a move would be a sudden, massive attack with the single purpose of destroying as much of the enemy's military capability as possible, but in full knowledge of having to absorb a limited retaliatory attack in the process. Such a possibility fueled the continuing arms race until well into the 1980s, largely through the research and development of more effective weapons.

Both sides also diversified their delivery systems. The use of missiles was significant because a single rocket could carry multiple warheads and be fired great distances from silos or off-shore submarines. Consequently, both the United States and USSR evolved military strategies that relied on a "triad" of aircraft, ground-based missiles, and submarine-launched missiles. All these systems delivered nuclear warheads, and by the end of the Cold War both sides had amassed staggering arsenals: in 1994, for example, the United States stockpile was approximately 15,000 warheads; and the former Soviet Union's, 29,000. The total equivalent destructive megatonnage for the United States alone was 2,375,300 tons of TNT.

In the early 1980s, President Ronald Reagan proposed a defensive concept called the Strategic Defense Initiative, or "Star Wars," a nickname based on the popular film series. Star Wars called for a technologically advanced panoply of earth and sky-borne devices that could detect and destroy incoming enemy missiles. Circling high above the United States in orbit would be a series of satellite detectors that would spot any unusual or unexpected objects, differentiating between a missile and space debris, for example. Having identified which were enemy warheads, a series of innovative weapons would be unleashed to destroy them. These weapons included, among others, electromagnetic rail guns, powerful lasers, and mines designed to destroy a warhead by releasing thousands of pieces of shrapnel. Even more exotic responses were imagined, such as using small nuclear explosions to generate high-energy X rays.

As imaginative as Star Wars was, it was plagued with both design problems and certain limitations imposed by the technology itself. The system would only work if it correctly identified enemy warheads with sufficient speed and accuracy. In addition, all elements depended upon precise coordination, including the development of a foolproof computer utilizing extremely complex programs. Although some components, like the rail gun, proved quite promising, most other weapons produced only mixed results. There were other problems as well. Theoretically, the Soviets could defeat the system in part by simply firing more and more missiles, many with dummy warheads designed to confuse the detectors. This seemed to insure that at least a small percentage of incoming missiles would hit their targets. Perhaps the greatest problem was the simple fact that any large system, with hundreds of complicated, interdependent components, could never be fully tested beforehand. That meant that the only sure test of the system would be during an actual enemy attack when problems or defects could not be corrected.

After five or six years, the Star Wars effort began to flounder under disappointing results and increased criticism from both scientists and members of Congress. Opposition gained momentum, and Congress began to reduce funding. By the middle 1990s, the United States had retreated from serious commitment to the program. Fortunately, a renewal of diplomatic efforts during the previous two decades began to pay off and led to a series of arms limitation and reduction treaties.

One of the earliest diplomatic successes was the Limited Test Ban Treaty of 1963 which forbade above-ground testing. The 1968 Nuclear Non-Proliferation Treaty required signees to withhold sharing nuclear technology and weapons with non-nuclear nations. The Strategic Arms Limitation Treaties (SALT I and SALT II) of 1972 and 1979 limited anti-ballistic missile sites as well as the growth of strategic arms arsenals. The Intermediate Nuclear Force (INF) treaty of 1987 actually eliminated some medium-range missiles and introduced on-site inspections. In 1963, a special telephone/telegraph "hot line" was created between the American president and the Soviet premier as a way of facilitating discussions and forestalling precipitous action.

The emergence of a rough parity between the United States and the Soviet Union, as reflected in the MAD doctrine, meant that aggressive actions between the superpowers were more likely to be played out through other nations and with conventional weapons. Historians of the Cold War period believe that the Korean and Vietnam wars were examples of war by proxy, that is, confrontations between East and West that avoided the use of nuclear weapons and involved third-party nations.

Atomic energy's peaceful potential, however, was just as real and far less threatening. Controlled fission, for example, is a source of low-cost energy. Scientists as early as 1942 were able to control the fission process in an arrangement known as an atomic "pile," or more simply, a reactor. The nature of fission is such that by controlling the process, it is possible to keep a chain reaction just below the level where it moves from "critical" to "supercritical." This is done by absorbing or impeding neutrons, small uncharged particles that are part of every nucleus and responsible for the fission process. At this level, intense radioactivity and heat are produced. The heat is the key factor in generating power, however, as it is used to turn water into steam, which in turn propels a turbine that generates electricity. Over the years, a variety of reactors have been designed that have as their primary purpose the generation of electricity. Some of these designs have proven to be more efficient and safer than others. In the mid-1990s, there were over a hundred operating nuclear generating plants in the United States, although they provided less than 25 percent of the nation's total electrical output. In contrast, France had embarked several decades earlier on the construction of a national array of reactors that may eventually provide almost 100 percent of the nation's electrical needs. Almost all Western countries have one or more reactors, as do many less developed countries, such as North and South Korea, India, Pakistan, and Egypt.

There is considerable controversy over the role and efficacy of nuclear power. Proponents point to the fact that once operational, plants generate enormous quantities of power at very little cost; in addition, they maintain that these plants operate with far less danger to the environment than conventional plants that use either petroleum or coal and generate sulfur dioxide and other air-borne pollutants. In addition, proponents argue that nuclear energy lessens a nation's dependency on the importation of oil, gas, and coal.

Opponents, however, have equally strong arguments, largely about the short-and long-term safety of nuclear plants. They point to the accidents at Three Mile Island in this country and to Chernobyl in the USSR as examples of what can go wrong. At Three Mile Island, radioactivity was accidentally released into the atmosphere, and although no one was hurt, the incident galvanized public awareness of reactor risks. At Chernobyl, a reactor suffered a disastrous "meltdown," which caused a non-nuclear explosion that cracked the reactor's protective steel and concrete casing. Radioactivity at dangerously high levels was suddenly released, which not only heavily contaminated hundreds of square miles in the immediate area but also was carried by winds into Europe and eventually through high altitude jet streams all over the world. Hundreds have died from the short-term effects of this radiation, and many scientists believe that thousands of others will experience medical problems and shortened lives because of the exposure. Chernobyl remains the worst nuclear accident in history. In general, critics of nuclear energy fear that many, if not all, existing plants represent dangerous technologies and that the potential for a catastrophic accident, especially in countries with questionable safeguards, is quite high.

Another major problem concerns nuclear waste. All reactors, whether designed to generate electricity or to produce material for bombs, generate considerable by-products. Uranium transmutes into plutonium and a variety of other elements, most of which have what scientists call long radioactive "half-lives." This means that the radioactivity generated by these elements remains active for long periods, in some cases for hundreds or thousands of years. The problem becomes one of storage and disposal. Radioactive materials can be either solid or liquid; many are corrosive and can be stored only in special containers. At present, there is no fool-proof system for long-term storage other than the destruction of the material itself. This difficulty has led the federal government to utilize a number of temporary storage measures, many of which pose increasing danger as they age and decay. One long-term plan calls for storage in deep underground vaults where seismic activity poses no earthquake threat. Some scientists have even suggested firing radioactive waste into the sun with rockets where the material would burn up harmlessly.

Critics also argue that nuclear plants are prime targets for terrorists who could either destroy a reactor and thereby release radioactivity, or steal weapons-grade plutonium and uranium for use in an atomic bomb. This last concern appears to have more relevance today than ever before. There are several major designs for nuclear reactors, but most use uranium as their fuel. Uranium, specifically an isotope called uranium 238, is utilized because it is comparatively easy to refine from uranium ore. In the reactor, as the fission process continues, the uranium breaks down into several other elements, including plutonium 239, which is the key ingredient of atomic bombs. And while a rare form of uranium called 235 can be used in a weapon, plutonium is the inexpensive by-product of reactor operation that is the most frequently used element in weapons. Indeed, reactor production is the primary means by which plutonium has been produced for this nation's vast stockpile.

Over the course of the last fifty years, a considerable amount of plutonium has been produced as a by-product of reactors. Inevitably, there exists the possibility for loss and theft unless considerable care is taken to safeguard all by-products. The Nuclear Non-Proliferation Treaty of 1968 specifically calls for technologically advanced nations to withhold sharing both nuclear technology and materials. This agreement has worked to a large extent, but the world community is now faced with controlling ever-increasing quantities of materials like plutonium. Total, authenticated accounting is difficult at best and may ultimately prove impossible. Moreover, the recent breakup of the Soviet Union has raised new concerns that either weapons technology will be sold illegally or that nuclear materials, specifically plutonium, will find their way into the arms market. It is even possible that a weapon itself will become available. And it is also true that nations with existing reactors can turn to the production of weapons-grade plutonium. At various times, for example, both Iraq and North Korea have been suspected of using their reactors to produce plutonium. In the late 1980s, Israel conducted an air strike against Iraq's nuclear reactor because of the fear that it would be used to produce plutonium for this illegal purpose.

Weapons technology is now sufficiently advanced wherein fission weapons can be broken down into several small components that can be easily transported in a suitcase. This makes them highly desirable as a weapon for terrorists. A small bomb, for example, utilizing less than twenty pounds of weapons-grade plutonium, would be sufficient to destroy the greater part of any major city. The threat posed by such a device is a real possibility unless all nations with the appropriate technology agree to scrupulous controls.

Fortunately, not all the benefits of atomic energy are so dangerous. Many side products of fission, called isotopes, are critical elements in the treatment of human diseases and provide helpful aids to scientific researchers in many different fields, from agriculture to the manufacture of steel. X rays are universally used in the diagnosis of medical conditions and diseases. Other forms of radiation treat cancers and are widely used in research, development, and manufacturing. Small reactors power satellites in space and propel submarines and aircraft carriers.

The social implications of atomic energy are also diverse. The sudden announcement by President Harry S Truman of the atomic bombings of Japan was viewed at the time with almost universal acclaim. Public opinion surveys in 1945 showed an 85 percent approval rating among Americans; Europeans responded similarly. And most people at the time credited use of the atomic bomb with the final collapse of Japan and the end of the war. There is general agreement today that the bomb saved both American and Japanese lives by forestalling a direct Allied attack on the Japanese home islands. Some critics at the time, however, believed that use of the bomb was unnecessary and immoral. Interestingly, this argument has resurfaced today. Opponents of the bomb argue that Japan was near collapse and point to diplomatic overtures by that nation to negotiate a surrender. Moreover, these critics maintain that the United States was aware of these circumstances but nonetheless insisted on total, unconditional surrender. They also suggest that there was an element of racism toward the Japanese that permeated American considerations.

Most historians disagree, however, which suggests that one must study the decision to drop the bomb in the context of the times, not with information or hindsight gained since the war. They point to the massing of both armies and material in Japan itself in the spring and summer of 1945 as evidence of that nation's preparations for defending itself. They also suggest that the fierce fighting in Okinawa, an island close to Japan, is the best evidence of the Japanese will to resist. Over 100,000 Japanese were killed in the battle for Okinawa and thousands of others died in suicide "Kamikazi" attacks. And although the numbers vary, a variety of military studies in 1945 predicted total losses for both sides in an assault on Japan to be high, perhaps as many as one million deaths, with an even greater number of wounded.

In 1945, however, atomic energy was widely viewed as one of the most important scientific breakthroughs in the history of humankind. Popular reaction was immediate and widespread. The scientists who developed the atomic bomb became overnight heroes. For example, J. Robert Oppenheimer, who led the laboratory that actually designed the bomb during the war, because a household name and was featured on the cover of *Time* magazine as the "Father of the Atomic Bomb." Popular culture instantly absorbed the new weapon into its mainstream. Suddenly, there were Atomic Motels, children's books on atomic energy, foods and games with atomic motifs, and even a nationwide craze to discover uranium that was reminiscent of the gold rushes of the last century. The famous toy maker, A. C. Gilbert, best known for trains and erector sets, even produced a child's Geiger counter during the early 1950s.

In the United States, a curious cultural and social bifurcation resulted. On the one hand, individuals could clearly see the promise of atomic energy in their lives. It provided life-saving possibilities in medicine and supplied some cities with low-cost electricity. On the other hand, especially with the emergence of the Soviet Union as a nuclear power, people now had to live with the prospect of nuclear annihilation. And the tensions between East and West, which constituted the Cold War, seemed to have no end. No matter how many or what kind of weapons one side possessed, the other side always seemed to catch up. The arms race would continue for nearly half a century and consume perhaps 25 percent of total government spending on all activities on both sides.

Popular culture now had to face the dark side of atomic energy as well. The United States had been spared physical destruction during World War II, and civil defense measures, except rudimentary ones on the East and West coasts, were nonexistent. With the Soviet atomic bomb, however, there was now the possibility of a direct attack. Every major population center and military installation was a potential target. Civilian defense suddenly grew as a serious enterprise. Until the late 1950s, any major nuclear attack by the Soviets would likely be by airplane. This was thought to afford the country as much as eight or ten hours warning time, sufficient, it was believed, to order hasty exits of all major American cities and military targets. As the means of delivery changed from airplanes to missiles and the window of warning narrowed from hours to minutes, however, the value of civilian defense lessened considerably. The government undertook to ensure its own survivability. Military command centers were placed deep underground or inside mountains; Congress and key government officials had a similar bunker outside Washington, D.C.; and the means of continuing war after an attack was assured through multiple command structures and elaborate communication systems. The public was left to its own devices.

Ironically, it was believed for a while that some significant percentage of the population could survive a nuclear attack. Home and public basements were considered suitable as bomb shelters. The government undertook to store food, water, and medical provisions in many public buildings in all urban centers. Children were taught to "duck and cover" at the sound of an air-raid siren. A number of cities conducted annual mock evacuations. Increasing evidence suggested, however, that as weapons grew in number and destructive power, civilian defense activities like evacuations would be chaotic and ineffectual: Los Angeles would inevitably be jammed with escaping cars, and there was simply insufficient transportation available in New York City for all of its residents.

The problem of survival is compounded by the radiation effects of a nuclear explosion. Surviving a bomb's blast would be possible in shelters deep enough underground or in buildings far enough away from Ground Zero, the center of the explosion. But radiation would not only spread over a much larger area but also would linger for weeks, months, even years, affecting the human body, water and food supplies, cloth-ing—essentially everything it touched.

Concerns over nuclear war were not limited to the United States. The Soviet Union established its own civilian defense program, complete with the construction of large underground shelters for civilians. All western European nations had some version of civilian defense, includ-ing the Swiss, who built enough protective shelters to accommodate their entire population.

Novels and motion pictures of the time capitalized on public fears of nuclear war. Films like *On the Beach* and *Fail Safe* portrayed an "end of the world" scenario as well as the consequences of an "accidental" attack on the Soviet Union. Similar themes were played out in novels like *Alas Babylon* and *WarDay.*

Despite growing public concern, Americans nonetheless consistently supported government spending on defense. Politicians, in fact, were often able to win election by promising even stronger defense policies. Democrat John F. Kennedy received support in 1960 by alleging, among other things, that the Republicans had permitted a missile "gap" to occur between U.S. and Soviet military arsenals. Twenty years later, Republi-can Ronald Reagan received strong public support for a renewed defense program, argued largely on the basis that the United States under the Democrats had fallen dangerously behind the Soviets.

Support for defense spending became a "litmus test" of sorts for in-dividuals, both public and private. Politicians rarely ran on platforms that encouraged reduced spending or, rarer still, that suggested a major reexamination of defense policy. Time and again, political candidates lost elections when their voting publics believed them to be weak on defense or soft on communism. This unhealthy condition reached its peak during the 1950s when Republican Senator Joseph McCarthy became the most visible symbol of a nation gripped by anti-Communist hysteria. He rose quickly to fame by promising to ferret out and reveal Communists in all branches of the government, from the State Department to the U.S. Army. His attacks were unfounded, however, and he was eventually discredited and censured by the Senate. His name, however, is linked indelibly to a period of political persecution called McCarthyism.

One victim of this time was J. Robert Oppenheimer, the director of the wartime laboratory that had developed the first atomic bombs. Oppen-heimer quickly rose to prominence as one of the most influential au-thorities on atomic energy. He served on a number of important government committees and frequently testified before Congress. During the late 1940s and early 1950s, he questioned whether this country really needed the thermonuclear weapons it appeared resolved to develop. He argued that conventional fission weapons could be made as large as required, but, more importantly, that pursuing thermonuclear weapons would only force the Soviets to do the same, thus perpetuating the arms race and bringing the world closer to nuclear confrontation. In 1953, during the height of the McCarthy period, Oppenheimer was brought before a secret board which found him a "security risk." They removed his access to all classified weapons work, even though he himself was largely responsible for much of their past success.

The race for thermonuclear weapons was accelerated, and scientists tried to create an atmosphere of emergency akin to that underlying the original Manhattan Project. The Los Alamos, New Mexico, laboratory, which had developed the first atomic bombs and was working furiously on thermonuclear ones, was considered insufficient so a second research center was created, Lawrence-Livermore, in California. Edward Teller, director of the new center, like Oppenheimer, had his portrait on the cover of *Time*. He was billed as the "Father of the H-Bomb."

It took the negotiation of arms reduction treaties between the United States and the USSR finally to slow down the arms race. The process was also helped by the collapse of the Soviet Union in the late 1980s and by an evolution of public attitudes toward atomic energy. Certain aspects were now deeply ingrained in society. Radiation treatment for cancer and other diseases was commonplace; the use of reactors to generate electrical power was widespread. Many of America's aircraft carriers and submarines were nuclear powered. Nevertheless, the great promise of atomic energy was now known to be offset by its concomitant dangers. While society readily accepted the use of atomic energy in medicine and industry, it pulled back from building new nuclear power plants and slowly began to assess the legacy of the Cold War.

There are still thousands of aging weapons, both in the United States and in the former Soviet Union, more than enough to destroy the world several times over. There are tons of nuclear waste materials waiting for proper disposal. There is a vast military and industrial complex that must somehow transfer its skills and experiences to peaceful purposes. And there is still the need for the nation to remain a strong military power. Perhaps only now, with the end of the Cold War and the emergence of new national priorities, can society more objectively assess what role atomic energy will play in its social, cultural, and economic lives.

SELECTED BIBLIOGRAPHY

Alperovitz, Gar. *Atomic Diplomacy: Hiroshima and Potsdam.* New York: Simon and Shuster, 1965. Controversial reevaluation of the conventional assumptions, hesitations, and decisions that determined the use of the first atomic bombs against Japan.

Boyer, Paul. *By the Bomb's Early Light: American Thought and Culture at the Dawn of the Atomic Age.* New York: Pantheon Books, 1985. Multifaceted study of the role of the atomic bomb in shaping American culture and thought in the late 1940s and early 1950s.

Bundy, McGeorge. *Danger and Survival: Choices about the Bomb in the First Fifty Years.* New York: Random House, 1988. Political history of the atomic bomb, from the discovery of fission in 1939 through the 1980s.

Campbell, Christopher. *Nuclear Weapons Fact Book.* Novato, CA: Presidio Press, 1984. Popular illustrated description of nuclear weapons of all nations.

Clark, Ronald W. *The Greatest Power on Earth.* New York: Harper & Row, 1980. Narrative on the interplay of science, politics, and technology in the discovery and development of nuclear fission in this century.

Cochran, Thomas B., William M. Arkin, and Milton M. Hoenig. *Nuclear Weapons Databook. Vol. 1, U.S. Nuclear Forces and Capabilities.* Cambridge, MA: Ballinger Publishing Company, 1984. Comprehensive study of U.S. nuclear weapons, their history and diversity, with photographs and tables.

Dyson, Freeman. *Weapons and Hope.* New York: Harper & Row, 1984. Philosophical discussion of nuclear weapons and society.

Ehrlich, Paul R., Carl Sagan, Donald Kennedy, and Walter Orr Roberts. *The Cold and the Dark: The World after Nuclear War.* New York: W. W. Norton, 1984. Groundbreaking discussion of "nuclear winter," the worldwide collapse of climate and life systems following a nuclear war.

Freedman, Lawrence. *The Evolution of Nuclear Strategy.* New York: St. Martin's Press, 1981. History of nuclear strategy and the technological and strategic forces that shaped it.

Grodzins, Morton and Eugene Rabinowitch, editors. *The Atomic Age: Articles from the* Bulletin of the Atomic Scientists, *1945–1962.* New York: Simon and Shuster, 1963. Collection of articles on a wide variety of topics relating to atomic energy, including weapons, arms control, disarmament, peaceful developments, and international cooperation in nuclear science.

Groves, Leslie R. *Now It Can Be Told: The Story of the Manhattan Project.* New York: Harper & Row, 1962. Personal account of the wartime Manhattan Project from the man who directed it.

Halperin, Morton H. *Nuclear Fallacy: Dispelling the Myth of Nuclear Strategy.* Cambridge, MA: Ballinger Publishing Company, 1987. Critical discussion of the role of nuclear weapons and military strategy.

Hansen, Chuck. *U.S. Nuclear Weapons: The Secret History.* New York: Orion Books, 1988. Encyclopedic illustrated history of every nuclear warhead built by the United States since 1945.

Herken, Gregg. *The Winning Weapon: The Atomic Bomb in the Cold War, 1945–50.*

New York: Alfred A. Knopf, 1980. History of the atomic bomb and post-war diplomacy.

Hewlett, Richard G., and Oscar E. Anderson, Jr. *The New World, 1939/1946. Vol. 1: A History of the United States Atomic Energy Commission.* University Park: Pennsylvania State University Press, 1969. Most comprehensive history of the government's role in the development of nuclear weapons, written with access to classified documents.

Hewlett, Richard G., and Francis Duncan. *Atomic Shield, 1947/1952. Vol. 2: A History of the United States Atomic Energy Commission.* University Park: Pennsylvania State University Press, 1969. See description above.

Holloway, David. *The Soviet Union and the Arms Race.* New Haven, CT: Yale University Press, 1983. Discussion of the Soviet Union, its nuclear weapons program, and its role in the world arms race.

Katz, Arthur M. *Life after Nuclear War.* Cambridge, MA: Ballinger Publishing Company, 1982. Sobering analysis of the physical, economic, and social impacts of a nuclear attack on the United States.

Kevles, Daniel J. *The Physicists.* New York: Vintage Books, 1971. Broad history of prominent scientists in this century, particularly those involved with nuclear physics and weapons.

Kunetka, James W. *City of Fire: Los Alamos and the Atomic Age, 1943–1945.* Albuquerque: University of New Mexico Press, 1979. Readable history of the development of the first atomic bombs at Los Alamos during World War II.

———. *Oppenheimer: The Years of Risk.* Englewood Cliffs, NJ: Prentice-Hall, 1982. Biography of Robert Oppenheimer, focusing on his wartime directorship of Los Alamos and his subsequent rise and fall from public service.

Rhodes, Richard. *The Making of the Atomic Bomb.* New York: Simon and Shuster, 1986. Popular comprehensive history of the Manhattan Project and the development of the atomic bomb.

Sherwin, Martin J. *A World Destroyed: The Atomic Bomb and the Grand Alliance.* New York: Alfred A. Knopf, 1975. History of the diplomatic role of the atomic bomb in World War II.

York, Herbert F. *The Advisors: Oppenheimer, Teller, and the Superbomb.* San Francisco: W. H. Freeman and Company, 1976. An insider's history of the development of the first hydrogen bomb and the controversial roles played by Oppenheimer and Teller.

7

The Rise of Television, c. 1948–1995

INTRODUCTION

Experimentation with the wireless transmission of pictures began in both the United States and Great Britain in the 1920s, shortly after radio, or the wireless transmission of sound, became commercially feasible. The development of television, as it was called from the beginning, was slowed by the economic depression of the 1930s, but the British public was able to see the 1937 coronation of King George VI on television and could enjoy regular commercial programming by 1938.

In the United States, the development of television was somewhat slower, perhaps because of the continuing success of radio and the fact that the producers of radio shows were also involved in the development of television. Television was promoted at the 1939 New York World's Fair, where the opening ceremonies were telecast; and the first sets were sold to the public that year. However, there was little to watch. A college baseball game was shown that summer; but with only one camera, situated along the third base line, viewers missed most of the action. Other programs included fashion shows, wrestling and boxing matches, and planes landing at the local airport.

World War II virtually halted the further development of commercial television, but the late 1940s saw a spectacular explosion of the business.

Television's popularity skyrocketed in the 1950s. Here a Louisville, Kentucky family enjoys a special Christmas present. (Photographic Archives, University of Louisville, Caufield and Shook Collection)

Americans bought 7,000 sets in 1946, and, as television stations were established in more cities, sales went up to 172,000 in 1948 and 5 million in 1950. By 1960, some 79 million television sets were in use, and well over 90 percent of American families had become television viewers.

By 1948, there were over one hundred stations on the air, and transmission problems were occurring because of crowding on the Very High Frequency (VHF) band (channels 2 through 13) allotted to television, which caused stations to interfere with one another's signals. The Federal Communications Commission (FCC), the agency responsible for regulating broadcasting, put a four-year freeze on the issuance of new licenses for stations until the development of stations on the Ultra High Frequency (UHF) band (channels 14 through 88) could take place. However, stations that received licenses to broadcast on the UHF band were at a distinct disadvantage, as most receivers were not capable of tuning them in without a special attachment, and because the picture quality was generally inferior. As a consequence, the major networks dominated the VHF band, while smaller, independent stations and educational stations were relegated to the higher channel numbers.

Despite the fact that technicolor had invaded Hollywood during the 1930s, all commercial television before 1960 was in black and white. The Columbia Broadcasting System (CBS), one of the large radio networks that had moved quickly into television, developed a method of broadcasting programs in color of excellent quality soon after the war, but its system was incompatible with existing television sets. Meanwhile, Radio Corporation of America (RCA), a major rival of CBS, developed its own version of color broadcasting that could be received by existing sets, but the quality of the image was poor. The FCC approved the RCA system, but it took more than a decade for the system to be improved enough to appeal to consumers.

Initially, television promoters hoped that television, with its superior technology, could result in a great cultural uplifting of the American public. But they were crushingly disappointed; Americans were not much interested in watching culturally uplifting shows, and if they would not watch, sponsors would not be willing to underwrite the cost of the shows. It was not long before television adopted the programming format successfully used on radio, with fifteen-, thirty-, or sixty-minute blocks of time featuring drama, mystery, comedy, western, and variety shows. It was simply radio with pictures. Apart from a few shows presenting original dramatic productions of high quality, most programs appealed to popular taste and shied away from any material that was intellectually challenging or controversial.

Alternative, public noncommercial television began as National Educational Television (NET) in 1952, funded by a combination of government money, corporate grants, and private donations. In 1967, Congress created the Public Broadcasting System (PBS), a national network of educational television stations, but only a tiny fraction of viewers—3 or 4 percent—regularly watch its programs.

Cable television, sometimes called community antenna television (CATV), was created in the 1950s to bring television reception to rural areas located far from cities. By the 1960s, CATV began to be seen as an opportunity for additional stations to come on the air and give viewers more choices. The FCC was reluctant to sanction the use of CATV in this way, for fear of ruining UHF stations economically. In 1972, however, the commission allowed satellites to serve cable television operators. Cable service to consumers began in 1976 and proved very effective in delivering a wide range of stations and improved reception to those who had a satellite "dish." Later, service became available in many locations by the installation of a cable to anyone with a television receiver. In 1965, CATV served only 2.4 percent of sets; this figure steadily increased to 60 percent in 1995.

Another invention, the video cassette recorder (VCR), introduced about 1980, gave viewers new options of recording their favorite shows to see at a more convenient time or renting tapes of prerecorded movies or other features, such as aerobic exercise routines. Despite the fact that by 1992, about 77 percent of television owners also had a VCR, there is no evidence that VCRs have made significant inroads into the popularity of regular television broadcasting, although the combination of cable television and VCRs has reduced the dominance of network television.

The film industry has had an uneasy relationship with television over the years. In the late 1940s, television contributed to the decline in the frequency with which people attended the movies, although labor problems, the end of the studios' dominance of theater chains, and revelations about Communist influence in the industry were also factors. Many in Hollywood ignored television, thinking it to be little more than a cute toy showing nothing but bad comedians and dreadful films from the 1930s. Moreover, the movies had survived radio. Some movie producers experimented with "theater television," in which television shows were shown on movie screens in theaters—a kind of early "pay-TV." But the costs were high, audiences were small, and the experiment was soon abandoned.

Some studios attempted to buy television stations or even networks, such as ABC or Dumont, two smaller operations that were struggling to compete with CBS and the National Broadcasting Company (NBC), owned by RCA. But none was able to work out a deal, and the FCC was unsympathetic, generally favoring those individuals with radio experience in its granting of licenses. Partly as a consequence of not being able to join the television industry, some major movie studios decided to fight television by refusing to sell the rights to better films, to use their facilities for television production, or to allow their stars to appear on television (unless it was to promote their latest films). By the 1960s, however, the studios had relented, finding greater profit in selling, for ever-increasing fees, the rights to broadcast recent movies on television.

The decade of the 1970s saw the high point of television's dominance over American culture. Despite the ban on tobacco advertising in 1971, revenues from television commercials reached all-time highs; increased advertising fees ended the practice, originated with radio, of a program having just one sponsor.

The success of network television led to new departures in programming, with an emphasis on political and social relevancy. This was seen in shows such as "All in the Family," featuring a bigoted white male as head of the family, "The Mary Tyler Moore Show," about an unmarried career woman, and "M*A*S*H," a socially relevant comedy set in the Korean War. As Hollywood films began to be more sexually explicit, television responded with shows such as "Charlie's Angels," ostensibly a detective show but clearly designed to reveal the physical attributes of its three attractive lead actresses. The sometimes controversial subject matter of shows like these caused the FCC to declare the first hour of the evening as "family viewing hour" in 1975. In 1976, however, the courts declared the FCC decision to be a violation of the networks' First Amendment rights. Nevertheless, the networks moved their more explicit shows to later prime-time slots.

By the early 1980s, competition from independent stations and cable pushed the networks into a further programming shift, featuring harder, more realistic dramatic shows, such as "Hill Street Blues," about daily life in an urban police precinct, and stronger comedies, such as "The Cosby Show," starring the African-American comedian, Bill Cosby, as the head of a middle-class family, and "Cheers," set in a convivial Boston bar. These well-written, popular shows were accompanied in the 1980s by a general relaxation of traditional taboos on sex and violence, both in series shows and in made-for-television movies.

Since its inception, television has also been an important influence in the world of news and current events. In its earliest days, television producers filled up unsold air time with live broadcasts of news events, such as sessions of the United Nations. The congressional investigations of Estes Kefauver into organized crime in 1951 and of Joseph McCarthy into communism in the army in 1954 achieved much more notoriety for the two senators by virtue of being telecast. Coverage of national political conventions, campaigns, and elections began in 1948; a televised speech in 1952 by Republican vice-presidential candidate Richard M. Nixon, defending himself against allegations that he had misused campaign funds, saved his place on the ticket and, in all probability, his political career.

In the 1960s, with the advent of more portable cameras and satellite transmission, television began to witness historical events and bring them live to America's viewers. Network television news departments covered the aftermath of the assassination of President John F. Kennedy in 1963, the events of the civil rights movement of the 1960s, and much of the tragedy of the Vietnam War. In 1968, noted newscaster Walter Cronkite's on-air declaration that the war was a terrible mistake had a significant effect on public opinion about the war. Similarly, revelations during the televised Watergate hearings in 1973 about what President Richard M. Nixon and his chief aides knew about that scandal helped create the public attitudes that brought on Nixon's resignation the following year.

In 1968, the news program "60 Minutes" was launched, featuring the investigative reporting of Mike Wallace and a number of other notable CBS television journalists. A television "magazine," "60 Minutes" was given a prime-time slot following professional football on Sunday evenings; for nearly thirty years, it has been among the most popular programs on the air. In recent years, it has spawned a number of imitators, further attesting to its appeal.

Sport has long been an important element in American popular culture, and the twentieth century has seen increasing emphasis on spectator sports—a phenomenon made for television. Virtually every sport has been televised at one time or another; indeed, there are cable television channels that are devoted entirely to sports programming. Some sports, in particular, have benefited greatly from television. Professional football is easier (and more comfortable) to watch on television than at a stadium, especially since the introduction of videotaped "instant replay" in 1964; and, as a consequence, football now rivals baseball as the most popular sport in the United States. The telecasting of tennis and golf greatly enhanced the popularity of those sports, not so much because they provide good television action, but, rather, because television has brought to the public some very appealing heroes from these sports, like Chris Evert and Arnold Palmer.

Perhaps even more importantly, television has injected a massive financial input into sport through the fees paid by the networks for the rights to broadcast games, tournaments, or matches. The escalation of these fees has been staggering in the last twenty years and has led to huge increases in player salaries or prizes, depending on the sport, as well as substantial expansion of those sports where there is league play, such as professional baseball, football, basketball, and hockey. In return, the networks have demanded changes in the way games are played. For instance, important contests like baseball's World Series are now played mostly at night, and "television time-out" has become standard in football and basketball games in order to increase the number of commercials that can be aired. All of this has pushed sport, both financially and artistically, in the direction of pure entertainment.

Over the last fifty years, television has moved from the status of a toy with a flickering image to a powerful and influential communications medium that commands an important place in the lives of most Americans. As early as 1960, surveys showed that the average American watched television 44 hours per week, and over the years, that figure has not changed much. Although technology will continue to change the way television functions in our lives, perhaps moving next into some kind of interactive mode, it is clear that the development and diffusion of television has been an event of great significance in our century.

INTERPRETIVE ESSAY
James E. St. Clair

In 1927, 21-year-old Philo T. Farnsworth, one of the key inventors of American television technology, successfully transmitted his first pictures, one of which was a dollar sign. His selection of this graphic, while it was most likely unwitting, could not have been more appropriate because the symbol of money best represents the television industry in the United States. Commercial television, since its beginnings at mid-century, has been such an extraordinary money-making machine that media magnate Lord Thomson once equated owning a television station with having a license to print money.

Television's mint-like status stems from its unmatched ability to attract and sustain mass audiences for advertisers, who spend about $35 billion annually on national and local TV to sell their goods and services. No other merchandising method is as efficient in reaching out and touching 93 million U.S. homes every day. Television wins hands down compared to other media in terms of the advertising industry's standard gauge of wise spending known as CPM (cost per thousand), or how much money it takes to reach one thousand people. Because of television's potential to influence the public's buying habits, it changed the way mass consumer products such as cars, soap, chewing gum, toilet paper, bug spray, soft drinks and beer are sold in this country.

Of course, television changed much more. Practically overnight, television revolutionized the way Americans used their free time. As soon as a station signed on in a city, people spent less time going to movies, eating out, frequenting the corner bar, checking books out of the library, and listening to radio. By demonstrating early in its history that it had the magnetic power to draw hordes of people to a flickering screen and the hypnotic power to keep them there for hours, television's primary function as mass merchant was all but sealed.

It took a tiny lipstick company named Hazel Bishop to show corporate America what could be done by exploiting such a captive audience. When it began using TV commercials in 1950, Hazel Bishop had been generating only $50,000 in annual sales. In two years, company sales rocketed to $4.5 million a year and continued skyward. This happened at a time when television was available in only 10 percent of American households; in 1995 its reach was nearly complete at 98 percent. The Hazel Bishop story caused a stampede to television, as other companies, hoping to duplicate such astonishing growth, clamored to buy TV commercials. As media critic Ben H. Bagdikian has observed, "Television was never the same thereafter" (Bagdikian 1992, 140).

TV networks, trying to corral all the business suddenly surging their way, ended the practice of single-sponsor programs. More money was to be made by carving up commercial time into shorter spots that could be sold to many advertisers. This change not only ushered in a golden age of profitability for the industry, it also profoundly affected what was shown on commercial television. According to Bagdikian, networks began developing new programs that created a "buying mood" for the 30-second, or shorter, commercials, which are laden with emotional appeal, but contain little product information. Thus, most programs inconsistent with the happily-ever-after pitch of commercials—dramas and documentaries, for example—were ditched. In their place came fantasy and lighthearted fare that blended in perfectly with the sponsors' promises of brighter teeth, spotless commodes, no more ring around the collar, and sweet-smelling armpits.

Naturally, not all serious programming disappeared from network television, but the race was on to develop and air shows that would draw the largest audiences for advertisers. Ratings, or how many viewers tune in, became the litmus test for most programs, even news and public affairs, because the bigger the audience the higher the charge to advertisers. For example, corporations were willing to pay ABC $1 million for thirty seconds of commercial time during the 1995 Super Bowl so they could reach an audience of more than 130 million.

Out of this obsession for ratings and wealth grew the concept known as Least Objectionable Programming (LOP), which means that what a broadcaster airs doesn't necessarily have to be good, just less objectionable than other shows on at the same time. LOP capitalizes on the knowledge that Americans just watch television regardless of what is on, which simplifies matters for TV programmers. They only compete with one another, not with other activities that could be consuming the public's time, such as reading, attending school board meetings, or going to plays.

When Newton Minow, chairman of the Federal Communications Commission (FCC), the agency charged with requiring broadcasters to use the public airwaves responsibly, surveyed what the LOP approach had wrought for the nation, he was dismayed. In his first public address as head of the FCC in 1961, he declared television a "vast wasteland." He made this famous pronouncement in a speech to TV executives, whom he blistered for squandering their public trust: "I believe in the people's good sense and good taste, and I am not convinced that the people's taste is as low as some of you assume" (Minow 1964, 52). If TV officials watched a day's worth of their own programming, they would see, Minow said, a procession of "game shows, violence, audience participation shows, formula comedies about totally unbelievable families, blood and thunder, mayhem, violence, sadism, murder, Western badmen, Western good men, private eyes, gangsters, more violence and cartoons. And, endlessly, commercials—many screaming, cajoling and offending. And most of all, boredom." He then asked, "Is there one person in this room who claims that broadcasting can't do better?" When he revisited the "vast wasteland" thirty years later, Minow was even more distraught. "In 1961, I worried that my children would not benefit much from television, but in 1991, I worry that my grandchildren will actually be harmed by it," he said (reported in the *Louisville Courier-Journal,* December 22, 1991).

In defending what they air, broadcasters usually counter such criticism by saying that television must be fulfilling its legal obligations to serve the public's interests or else millions would be tuning out instead of tuning in everyday. TV executive Robert Sarnoff, son of legendary broadcast pioneer David Sarnoff, once remarked that the "ultimate decisions on what the public sees can come only from the public itself, as long as it is free to watch or not to watch as it pleases" (MacDonald 1990, 221).

Clearly, the public chooses to watch. This indisputable fidelity to television may or may not be a validation of responsible broadcasting, but statistics on the viewing habits of Americans affirm that television, in the short span of fifty years, has become the nation's premier preoccupation. According to Nielsen Media Research, which has studied the industry since 1950, Americans have their televisions on an average of about seven hours a day. More than 100 million viewers are usually watching during prime time, the slot from 8 P.M. until 11 P.M. With the advent of public broadcasting and cable television, people have more choices than ever, although more than 70 percent of prime time viewing goes to the networks (ABC, CBS, NBC and Fox). Watching television, including cable, takes up four hours and nine minutes a day for the average adult American. Only sleep and work consume more time. Teenagers, by the time they have finished high school, will have spent more time in front of the television than in the classroom.

This monopoly on the public's time and attention, in turn, has profoundly affected American culture and society. Television has altered the intellect, behavior, and values of individuals; the conduct of elections and governmental policy—both domestic and foreign; and the nature of other major U.S. mass media.

In his provocative book *Amusing Ourselves to Death,* Neil Postman dissects the impact of television's meteoric rise to its position as preeminent entertainer and prime news and information source. He echoes media scholar Marshall McLuhan's notion that the "medium is the message"; that is, how we get our knowledge determines what we know. McLuhan described television as a *cool* medium because it requires little effort or intellectual involvement. The print media of books, magazines, and newspapers, on the other hand, are *hot* media, McLuhan said, because they involve their users so intimately and require a high degree of concentration and thought.

America, Postman writes, was a far different place when *hot* media instead of *cool* dominated. During the eighteenth and nineteenth centuries, which Postman calls the Age of Exposition, the printed word held sway, creating a nation of readers who possessed a sophisticated literacy. Accordingly, most Americans engaged in informed and intelligent discourse and were active and purposeful participants in matters of public importance. They viewed the world, Postman writes, as a "serious, coherent place, capable of management by reason, and of improvement by logical and relevant criticism" (Postman 1985, 62).

By contrast, Postman argues, that the Age of Television has transformed American society into one vast arena for show business, where politics, religion, business, education, law, and other important social matters are offered as entertainment, which is television's natural format for the way it represents all experiences. "The problem," Postman writes, "is not that television presents us with entertaining subject matter but that all subject matter is presented as entertaining" (Postman 1985, 87).

Under this circumstance, Postman adds, Americans are the best entertained, but perhaps the least well-informed people in the Western world. He warns that when a society becomes "distracted by trivia, when cultural life is redefined as a perpetual round of entertainments, when serious public conversation becomes a form of baby-talk, when, in short, a people become an audience and their public business a vaudeville act, then a nation finds itself at risk" (Postman 1985, 156).

A vast majority of Americans have come to rely on television for most of their information about national and international events, a development that is unsettling even to those in the TV news business. Cable News Network (CNN) anchor Bernard Shaw says the fact that "75 percent of the public gets their information from television means that 75 percent of Americans are underinformed. You must read newspapers, you must read magazines, you must read books. The essence of journalism is the printed word" (Reported in the *Louisville Courier-Journal*, February 16, 1994). Similarly, Av Westin, a veteran broadcast journalist who has served in top positions at CBS News and ABC News, is disturbed that so many rely on television as their primary source of information. Unless people read, "they are going to be uninformed," Westin says. "You can't substitute a headline for a full account. We are *always* leaving things out" (Lowe 1981, 114).

Televised news, although not without value, has an undeserved reputation for credibility, in part because of the notion that seeing is believing. The constraints of technology and time, however, insure that television's version of reality will be greatly skewed. Completeness, complexities, and subtleties are impossible when the camera captures only those scenes from an event that have the greatest visual impact and when news reports must be edited to fill eighty or ninety seconds of air time.

These limitations on presenting what approximates accurate accounts of the day's news are compounded by television's neverending search for profits, which means news shows tend to air the stories that draw the largest audiences for advertisers, not necessarily those that inform viewers about critical issues or developments. By the mid-1990s, the audience-generating and money-producing needs of local and network news producers seemed best served by filling the airwaves with reports on crime and violence, lurid sex, and celebrity scandals. This trend toward televised titillation is most pronounced on the networks' prime-time news magazine programs that have proliferated in response to the stiff competition from "reality-based" cop shows and the TV tabloids such as "A Current Affair," "Hard Copy," and "Inside Edition." Network offerings, including "Dateline NBC," "Day One," and "48 Hours," are similarly sensational, devoting their fair share to tales of the blood-and-guts variety. Commenting on why such stories are so prominent on these shows, Katie Couric of NBC said, "Let's face it, the ratings have a lot to do with it" (reported in an article by Howard Kurtz in the *Washington Post National Weekly*, March 21–27, 1994, 11).

While crime and violence may be good for television's bottom line, there is growing concern about what the daily doses of televised mayhem—through both news and entertainment programming—are doing to society, particularly to children. Few dispute that television is a violent place, but being able to link TV violence with real-life violence is more problematic, although there are research findings that do.

A study commissioned by *TV Guide* examined the content of ten channels—network affiliates, independents, and cable—for eighteen hours during a typical television day. The cumulative 180 hours of programming, including news, fictional shows, cartoons, movies, and commercials, contained nearly 2,000 individual acts of violence, leading the study's authors to conclude that violence is a major part of TV programming and is being presented in greater volume by an increasing number of sources. Another study, this one a five-year probe into the role of television in society by a task force of the American Psychological Association, estimated that children will see 8,000 murders and 100,000 other acts of violence on television before finishing elementary school. The task force report concluded that television can foster aggressive behavior and values favoring aggression in some children. Those especially susceptible to effects from televised violence are the youngest viewers, up to age ten, who have trouble distinguishing between what is real and what is not on television and children whose home and community environments already are saturated with violence.

Television's influence on children, of course, is by no means limited to the issue of violence, nor are these other effects restricted by age or socioeconomic status. Television and the constant stream of commercials, in fact, may be far more effective than schools in educating the nation's youth. Certainly, young people spend considerably more time soaking in lessons from the TV screen than in the classroom: 900 hours a year in classrooms compared with 1,200 to 1,800 hours a year watching television, according to Benjamin R. Barber, a political scientist at Rutgers University. In an article on education published in *Harper's* magazine in November 1993, he asks, "From which are they likely to learn more?" The main lesson learned, Barber argues, is that America preaches a different message than it practices. The sermon to youth may be get a good education, but the point they see on television "is to start pulling down the big bucks." The potent role models on television are not the educated and dedicated, but the clever corporate takeover artist and the man "with a rubber arm and an empty head who can throw a ball at 95 miles per hour pulling down millions of dollars a year." Barber believes that schools can and should lead, "but when they confront a society that in every instance tells a story exactly opposite to the one they are supposed to be teaching, their job becomes impossible."

It was perhaps inevitable that television, the most powerful communication instrument ever devised for selling images and ideas, would become a dominant force in how political candidates are elected and how public officials govern. This has been especially true in presidential politics since 1952.

That was the year General Dwight D. Eisenhower and Richard M. Nixon, the Republican presidential and vice-presidential candidates, demonstrated how important televised commercials and news coverage were to national electioneering. The campaign for Eisenhower, the likable World War II hero whom everybody called "Ike," was carefully crafted by an advertising agency to present him as the embodiment of a sincere, honest, and trustworthy public servant. His personal appearances of twenty minutes each were tightly scripted into three acts for maximum dramatic effect: the hero arrives, makes his remarks, and then departs, thunderous applause at each stage. The campaign was also notable for the numerous 20-second TV commercials each of which began with an announcer saying, "Eisenhower answers the nation." These spots, which cost $1.5 million, saturated the airwaves during the last two weeks of the campaign. While these brief commercials scarcely could be informative, they served the purpose of reinforcing Ike's image as the decent, caring guy-next-door.

It was Nixon's use of television in the campaign, however, that stole the show in 1952. In danger of being dumped from the ticket after it was revealed that a group of wealthy California supporters had established a $18,000 private fund for his use, Nixon went on the air and delivered his famous "Checkers" speech to a television audience of 25 million. To defend himself against charges of corruption, he detailed every aspect of his financial history and claimed that money from the private fund had been used only for political expenses, not personal. As part of this accounting, Nixon mentioned that his daughters had been given a black and white spotted dog, which they named Checkers. Nixon's performance, which had been stage-managed by an advertising agency, was a hit with viewers, who responded with calls, telegrams, and letters of support; and Eisenhower kept him as his running mate.

When Nixon, after serving eight years as Eisenhower's vice president, became his party's presidential candidate in 1960, television again played a major role in deciding his political future. But this time he was not so fortunate. The pivotal events of the 1960 contest between Nixon and John F. Kennedy were the four televised debates, the first one in particular because it so convincingly illustrated television's power in presidential campaigning. Many of those who heard the debate on radio thought the candidates were fairly equal in their effectiveness, or even that Nixon had the edge. But it was how the TV audience of 75 million responded that really mattered. Here, it was no contest: telegenic Kennedy had clearly "won." This debate was not decided so much by what the candidates said, which was typical campaign rhetoric, but rather by how they looked. Just back from campaigning in California, Kennedy appeared tanned, robust, and athletic. He was confident and witty and answered questions with ease. Nixon, by contrast, recently had been hospitalized and was still suffering from a virus. He was pale and haggard and seemed tense in his responses.

Kennedy, who was elected president by the slimmest of margins, left no doubt about the importance of television to his success: "We wouldn't have had a prayer without that gadget" (quoted in Barnouw 1990, 277). And neither would all future presidential aspirants, including, ironically, Richard Nixon.

When he ran for the presidency again in 1968, there was a "new" Nixon, this one much more schooled in how to use television to control his image and message. Nixon's campaign strategy, which is detailed in Joe McGinniss' best-selling book, *The Selling of the President 1968*, was formulated by a team of media advisers experienced in advertising, public relations, and TV production. According to McGinniss, who was permitted by the Nixon camp to observe this group in action, it was as "if they were building not a President but an Astrodome, where the wind would never blow, the temperature never rise or fall, and the ball never bounce erratically on the artificial grass" (McGinnis 1969, 39). From this approach came the staged question-and-answer sessions with TV-studio audiences that appeared on television as spontaneous, but actually were tightly controlled. Only those partial to Nixon were in the audience; call-in questions were rewritten by Nixon staffers; Nixon read his answers from cards; and those in the audience were instructed to applaud Nixon's answers enthusiastically. Commenting on this concept that he had helped create, Nixon adviser Roger Ailes, a former TV producer, said, "This is it. This is the way they'll be elected forevermore. The next guys up will have to be performers" (quoted in McGinnis 1969, 155).

Indeed, the 1968 Nixon campaign did forever change the face of presidential politicking: The role of media advisers, especially those, like Ailes, who know how to manipulate television for maximum effect, now often eclipses that of political professionals and party organizations; the amount of money spent in presidential primaries and elections, much of it for TV commercials, has grown to hundreds of millions of dollars; candidate appearances are staged to get the most favorable TV coverage; and speeches are written in sound bites, the "read my lips" catch phrases that make the 6 o'clock news.

Television and media advisers, likewise, have transformed how presidents govern once in office. Presidents need public support to carry out their policies, and one of the most effective ways of generating that support is by shaping the major source of information for most Americans: television.

The modern-day president who fared best under the constant glare of TV lights was actor-turned-politician Ronald Reagan. At ease in front of cameras and adept at learning his lines, Reagan expertly used television to gain wide support for his administration and its policies, although what appeared on the screen did not always match reality. For example, Reagan's version of what happened during the October 1983 invasion of Grenada, which news media were initially barred from covering, turned out to be riddled with error. But by the time the misinformation was corrected, it was too late; the public's attention was elsewhere. All most people remembered about Grenada was their president on television telling them that U.S. troops had arrived "just in time" to save the American civilians there. The Reagan administration's strategy of controlling information and using television paid big dividends. Reagan's standing in public opinion polls increased, and Grenada was part of the "bringing back America" theme used in his successful reelection campaign in 1984.

This lesson of media control for political gain was applied by Reagan's successor, George Bush, first in Panama and then on a grander scale during the 1991 Persian Gulf War. Again, news media access in both operations was restricted so that what the American public learned, largely from television, was the Bush administration's account of developments. As with Grenada, however, the administration's version of events in Panama and the Persian Gulf later turned out to be inaccurate in many respects.

For example, the United States government inflated the number of Panamanian soldiers killed and downplayed the number of civilian casualties. Later it was revealed that the civilian toll exceeded the military toll by a 4-to-1 margin. Jesse Jackson, in a column about the failures of news reporting from Panama, wrote that the "media surrendered its watchdog role, choosing during the crucial first days after the invasion to play mindless cheerleader for the U.S. government" (reported in the *Evansville Courier*, June 7, 1990). In their coverage of the Persian Gulf war, the American media, hindered by battlefield censorship, again performed more like a lapdog than watchdog. Televison was filled with pictures of the precise "smart bombs," but many of these wonders of technology missed their targets, something the American public never saw. Nor did the public learn about Iraqi soldiers being bulldozed alive in their trenches by American forces until long after the war.

Such effective stage-managing of the war won praise from Michael Deaver, one of Reagan's top image-makers. He asserted: "Television is where 80 percent of the people get their information," and what was done to control that information during the Gulf war "couldn't have been better" (quoted in Mowlana, Hamid, Gerbner and Schiller 1992, 23).

Television's impact on other major U.S. media was felt most imme-

diately by movies, radio, and large-circulation, general-interest magazines; but, in time, all three have devised successful survival strategies.
The print media of newspapers and book publishing, while they too have
attempted to cope with the effects of television, may be in a struggle
they cannot win.

The first medium to suffer the consequences of television was the film
industry. In 1946, movies were America's primary means of escapism,
with theater attendance reaching 90 million weekly. Less than ten years
later, ticket sales had dropped to 46 million a week and continued plum-
meting. Although movie attendance in the mid-1990s was down to about
16 million a week, Hollywood was basking in the glow of new-found
wealth due in part to its reconciliation with television. Since making
peace, not war, against television, the film industry has reaped riches
from the additional sources of revenue provided by television. Once a
new movie has run its course at the box office, it starts recycling through
potentially lucrative television "after-markets" which include home vid-
eos, premium cable channels, pay-per-view, cable superstations, networks and their affiliates, and independent stations. Not only has the
film industry benefited from sales to these sources, Hollywood also has
become the main production center for most of TV programming.

An accommodation of a different type helped the radio and magazine
industries survive and prosper in the wake of television. In the early
1950s, radio appeared all but dead because it lost the mainstay of its
talent and entertainment programming—soap operas, quiz shows, comedies, westerns, and cops & robbers—to the more exciting visual medium of television. Large-circulation, general-interest magazines were in
trouble as well when advertisers quickly discovered television was a
better way to reach a mass audience. *Collier's* was the first national magazine to fold, followed in subsequent years by *The Saturday Evening Post,
Look,* and the weekly version of *Life.*

In time, both the radio and magazine industries adapted to the new
competitive challenge of television by adopting essentially the same
strategy. Unable to compete with television in providing advertisers
huge numbers of potential customers, radio and magazines did the exact
opposite: through specialized content, they offer advertisers small,
sharply defined audiences so that commercial messages have a better
chance of hitting the intended consumer target. For radio, adopting specialization meant replacing the network programming that went to television with more recorded music. Through a concept known as
"narrowcasting," radio stations play a particular type of music that ap-

peals to a specialized audience that can be identified by age, gender, and other demographic characteristics. Narrowcasting appeals to advertisers because it permits them to be more precise in formulating and placing their commercials.

Specialized magazines work in much the same way. By focusing on single-subject material, whether it has to do with a profession, hobby, or leisure-time activity, a magazine attracts a certain reader. In turn, advertisers needing to reach this targeted market spend their money with the magazine.

While both industries have suffered periodic economic slumps, they, like the movie business, discovered not only that it is possible to co-exist with the behemoth television but that prosperity is even attainable. Far from disappearing, radio is the country's most ubiquitous medium: the average household has between five and six radio receivers, almost all cars have them, and the average American over the age of twelve spends about three hours a day with the sounds of radio. There are more than 10,000 radio stations in the United States today, up from about 3,000 in 1950 when television began making its presence felt. During the ten-year period, 1980 to 1990, industry revenues went from $3.7 billion to more than $10 billion, a 270 percent increase.

The age of specialization in the magazine business created a boom that has given U.S. readers a choice of about 12,000 different titles. Today, there is a magazine for just about every occupation, age group, entertainment interest, hobby, or leisure pursuit imaginable. The industry is often turbulent, as competition for advertising dollars forces hundreds of magazines out of business each year. Still, despite the risks and financial gyrations, magazines continue being launched at the rate of about five hundred a year as publishers seek to cash in on emerging niche markets created by the constantly changing nature of society and culture.

By some key measures, newspapers and books also appear to have withstood the onslaught of television. Newspapers, for example, continue to collect more advertising revenue and employ more people than any other mass medium. The nation's 1,586 daily newspapers circulate to more than 60 million people, and 8,000 weekly papers reach 45 million readers. The U.S. book industry, ostensibly just as robust, is a $20 billion business that consists of 12,000 publishers producing 50,000 new titles annually and more than 25,000 stores selling millions of books a year.

However rosy the present may seem to be, these print media face an uncertain future because of one condition that is perhaps insurmountable: America is no longer a nation of readers. The evidence of this is apparent in newspaper-readership statistics, which plot a steady decline in the percentage of Americans who read a newspaper every day. In 1967, for example, the figure was 73 percent; 25 years later, less than 50 percent of Americans read a paper daily, and the percentage continues to fall. Of greatest concern to the newspaper industry is its failure to attract younger readers. Daily newspaper readership among those 18- to 29-years-old has been cut in half, from nearly 60 percent in 1967 to less than 30 percent in 1995. This trend led one newspaper editor to remark that "our readers are going to die and we won't have any to replace them" (*Media/Impact Update* 2 [1]:1).

Without readers, of course, newspapers themselves die. And hundreds have since 1950, when there were about 1,775 daily newspapers compared with fewer than 1,600 today. This decline of more than 10 percent in the number of newspapers occurred during a period when the U.S. population grew by 65 percent. Most of the failures have been afternoon newspapers, also called PMs, which are more likely to go out of business than morning papers, or AMs, because of competition from television. Television dominates America's evenings, and, by delivering the latest news, it can make the news content in afternoon papers appear stale and irrelevant.

As newspapers continue to fail and daily circulation continues to fall, the industry is seeking solutions to prevent all newspapers from appearing to be stale and irrelevant. Leading the way are two of the biggest newspaper corporations, Gannett and Knight-Ridder. Gannett, which owns about eighty-five daily newspapers along with many other media properties, boldly confronted the competition from television in 1982, when it began publishing *USA Today*, which is commonly referred to as the first newspaper designed for a generation raised on television. Because of its lively and upbeat tone, abbreviated stories, splashy color, charts, and "factoids" (quick bites of information), it also has been likened to fast food and derisively called "McPaper." Still, *USA Today* is credited with at least forcing the industry to examine how it packages and presents the news. Many daily newspapers have followed *USA Today's* lead in better front-page design, shorter stories, liberal use of color, informational graphics, and colorful weather maps. Whether *USA Today* will be able to lead daily newspapers out of the wilderness to the promised land is debatable; but the paper does claim a higher percentage of readers in the critical 18 to 29 age group than the industry average.

Meanwhile, Knight-Ridder, which owns about thirty dailies, revamped its daily paper in Boca Raton, Florida, *The News*, in an effort to capture readers ages 25 to 43. Along with more color and graphics, came stories and features determined to be of prime interest to those in this age group: issues of health, child care, personal finance, and lifestyle. The changes at *The News* did spur slight circulation gains, but Knight-Ridder said the importance of the 25/43 Project was to make its other papers more attuned to readers' interests.

The book publishing industry confronts the same gigantic television-induced hurdle as newspapers: a dwindling supply of readers. True, every year millions of books are sold, and millions more are checked out of libraries and borrowed from friends. However, vast numbers of Americans, even those who are literate, read no books at all. During any given year, less than half of U.S. adults buy at least one book. A survey in early 1994 revealed that there are 40 million illiterate or barely literate adults in America and that the literacy of young adults is rapidly declining.

Like newspaper publishers, book publishers, too, are looking to computer technology and electronic publishing as part of their survival tactics. Already, many school libraries have electronic encyclopedias on compact disks that give students instant access to articles, illustrations, photographs, and even brief animations. They also have interactive capabilities, allowing users, for example, to pick a country on a map, zoom in for more detail, and then retrieve an article for further information. The novel on computer also is at hand. In the electronic version of *Jurassic Park*, for example, readers could call up scientific information or view animated scenes of dinosaurs.

Regardless of what alterations newspapers, books, and other major media make, however, they are destined to remain subservient to television. Moreover, their subordinate roles could erode even further by the year 2000 as high-definition TV (HDTV) and fiber optics usher in a revolutionary era for television viewers. HDTV, a large-screen television that offers true-to-life pictures and compact disk-quality sound, is at the center of the revolution. It will be the terminal for a 500-channel interactive electronic highway that is paved with a dazzling array of entertainment options, computing capabilities, and information sources. The full impact of this brave new world of television is difficult to project, but if the past is any gauge, the effects on American culture and society will be just as monumental as those of the first Age of Television.

SELECTED BIBLIOGRAPHY

Auletta, Ken. *Three Blind Mice: How the TV Networks Lost Their Way.* New York: Random House, 1991. Reveals how the big three networks—ABC, CBS, and NBC—tumbled from dominance in the face of cable, VCRs, and Fox.

Bagdikian, Ben H. *The Media Monopoly.* 4th ed. Boston: Beacon Press, 1992. Provides convincing evidence of the increased concentration of mass media ownership in the United States and the dangers that result when just a few large corporations control all major outlets of news and entertainment.

Barnouw, Erik. *Tube of Plenty: The Evolution of American Television.* 2d rev. ed. New York: Oxford University Press, 1990. A compact history of the emergence of television as a dominant force in American life and of the influence of American TV throughout the world.

Clark, Charles S. "TV Violence." *CO Researcher,* March 26, 1993, 267–87. A comprehensive examination of the debate over the effects of violence on television.

Comstock, George. *Television in America.* 2d ed. Newbury Park, CA: Sage Publications, 1991. Describes the growth of television and analyzes how political, social, and economic forces have shaped the medium.

Friendly, Fred W. *Due to Circumstances beyond Our Control . . .* New York: Random House, 1967. A pioneering broadcast journalist's account of the constant tension at CBS News between airing quality news programming and making as much money as possible.

Gomery, Douglas, Todd Gitlin, and Frank D. McConnell. "Television and American Culture." *The Wilson Quarterly,* Autumn 1993, 40–65. Three critics analyze how television has forever changed American society and culture.

Lowe, Carl, ed., *Television and American Culture.* New York: The H.W. Wilson Company, 1981. A collection of brief articles that examines such critical issues as television's effect on children and education; how politicians and evangelists use the medium; and how TV news changes viewers' perspectives on world events.

MacDonald, J. Fred. *One Nation under Television.* New York: Pantheon Books, 1990. A study of the development of television networks and how they maintained a stranglehold on the industry until the 1980s, when technology helped usher in a new video order.

Mander, Jerry. *Four Arguments for the Elimination of Television.* New York: Quill, 1978. Confessions of a former advertising executive who saw the true light of television and became alarmed by its insidious nature.

McGinniss, Joe. *The Selling of the President 1968.* New York: Trident Press, 1969. An insider chronicles how Richard Nixon and his team of young media-savvy advisers manipulated TV images and messages in winning the 1968 presidential election.

Mowlana, Hamid, George Gerbner, and Herbert I. Schiller, eds. *Triumph of the Image.* Boulder, CO.: Westview Press, 1992. The studies in this book conclude that television was a prime culprit in misleading America and the rest of the world about the realities of the Persian Gulf War.

Minow, Newton N. *Equal Time: The Private Broadcaster and the Public Interest.*

Edited by Lawrence Laurent. New York: Atheneum, 1964. The speeches of the chairman of the Federal Communications Commission under President Kennedy, including the famous "vast wasteland" address he made to the National Association of Broadcasters in 1961.

Palmer, Edward L. *Television and America's Children: A Crisis of Neglect.* New York and Oxford: Oxford University Press, 1988. Explains the failure of American television to offer quality programming for children and provides possible solutions.

Postman, Neil. *Amusing Ourselves to Death.* New York: Penguin Books, 1985. A provocative tale of how television has sapped the intellectual strength of American society.

Sperber, A. M. *Murrow: His Life and Times.* New York: Bantam Books, 1987. The definitive biography of America's most revered broadcast journalist, Edward R. Murrow.

8

The Civil Rights Movement, c. 1954–Present

INTRODUCTION

The modern civil rights movement in the United States may be said to have begun in 1935, when the National Association for the Advancement of Colored People (NAACP) began a concerted effort to end racial segregation, which had been made part of the American social fabric in the landmark case of *Plessy* v. *Ferguson* in 1896. That case had sanctified racial segregation as long as "separate but equal" facilities were provided for blacks. Led by Charles Houston, a professor at Howard University, and Thurgood Marshall, a young lawyer, the NAACP decided to start its campaign with higher education and, specifically, law schools.

In many states, there was only one law school, open to white students only, and black students seeking a law degree had to go elsewhere for their education. This put them at a significant disadvantage if they wanted to return to their home state to practice law. In *Murray* v. *Maryland*, a suit was brought against the University of Maryland law school, where a black applicant had been denied admission and where there was no black law school. Maryland offered financial aid to black students to help them go out of state for their education; but Houston and Marshall, arguing the case to a successful conclusion, said that this did not constitute equality. In 1938, a similar case was won in Missouri; these

The Civil Rights Act of 1964 put an end to segregated public accommodations such as this movie theater. (Photographic Archives, University of Louisville, Roy Stryker Collection)

victories suggested that segregation at other levels of schooling might also yield to legal decision.

Although World War II slowed the legal struggle, the NAACP created the Legal Defense Fund in 1946 to continue its campaign against segregation. Marshall, now legal counsel for the NAACP, filed suit against the University of Texas law school, which had offered to teach the plaintiff separately in three small rooms with part-time faculty. Although this clearly was not equal to the education white students received, the lower court ruled against the black student; however, in 1950, the case reached the Supreme Court, where the decision was reversed. A similar case concerning the University of Oklahoma graduate school of education was also decided in favor of the black plaintiff, but in both cases the Court was careful to limit its ruling to graduate schools and not overturn the fundamental law of *Plessy.*

During the early 1950s, the NAACP developed the strategy that would prevail in the 1954 landmark case of *Brown* v. *Board of Education of Topeka.* It was their contention that black children were irreparably damaged, psychologically, socially, and financially, by having to attend segregated schools. After losing a case against the public school system in South Carolina, the NAACP prevailed in the *Brown* case, one of the first major decisions in which Earl Warren, the new chief justice, took part. During the fifteen years that Warren headed the Court, civil rights advocates generally received a sympathetic hearing, and the Court was important in pushing forward the civil rights movement.

The civil rights movement entered a more activist phase in December 1955 with the Montgomery (Alabama) bus boycott. Under the inspirational leadership of Martin Luther King, Jr., then a young divinity school graduate pastoring a church in the city, the boycott was intended to end segregation on the city buses. By walking to work or using car pools, Montgomery's blacks avoided the buses for a year before the Supreme Court declared the segregated seating ordinance unconstitutional. This boycott, moreover, thrust King into a major leadership role in the civil rights movement, where he remained until his assassination in 1968.

Compliance with the *Brown* decision desegregating schools was remarkably slow throughout most of the South. School boards, supported by local public opinion, found ways to circumvent the Court's ruling, and the Eisenhower administration did very little to speed the process. In 1957, however, the president was stirred to action when the governor of Arkansas Orval Faubus refused to provide protection for nine black students who, by court order, were entering Little Rock Central High

School. Threats of violence against the students forced the president to order one thousand paratroopers to Little Rock to ensure their safety. Armed guards patrolled the school the entire year, and many southerners believed that a second Reconstruction, with federal occupation troops, was at hand.

In the election of 1960, neither Republican Richard M. Nixon nor Democrat John F. Kennedy was an ardent champion of civil rights, although Kennedy's efforts to win Martin Luther King's release from an Atlanta jail just days before the election was helpful in his quest for black votes. Once elected, however, Kennedy sent no civil rights legislation to Congress in 1961 or 1962, for fear that congressional resistance would lead to the defeat of other domestic programs. Kennedy's cautious attitude was not shared by the movement's leaders. In 1961, busloads of white and black protestors attempted to integrate bus and train stations serving interstate travel. The "Freedom Riders," as they were called, received no protection from local police and were often beaten by residents who resented the activities of the "outside agitators." In September 1961, the Interstate Commerce Commission ordered the desegregation of bus and train station facilities.

In 1962, a black student, James Meredith, attempted to gain admission to the University of Mississippi. The presence of federal marshals on campus, sent there to ensure Meredith's peaceful enrollment, led to a two-day riot in which two died and nearly four hundred were injured. Meredith eventually graduated from the university, and the Kennedy administration was persuaded that strong national leadership in civil rights was needed.

The following year, the pace of the nonviolent civil rights movement accelerated with a series of marches in the South. Well-publicized, these marches often led to violent confrontations with local police, which, when shown on television, generated considerable sympathy for the protestors. The Kennedy administration, meanwhile, sent a major civil rights bill to Congress that included protection for voting rights, access for all to public accommodations, equal employment opportunity, and the creation of Community Relations Services to allow problems to be worked out on a local level.

In August 1963, a "march on Washington" brought over 200,000 people to the Lincoln Memorial to hear speeches by King and most of the other prominent civil rights leaders and their congressional supporters. Although many had predicted that the event would turn violent, it did not; and its success was helpful in moving the civil rights bill through Congress.

After Kennedy's assassination in November 1963, Lyndon Johnson, the new president, used his political skills to overcome southern resistance to civil rights legislation; and the Civil Rights Act of 1964 became law in July. This landmark act outlawed segregation in public accommodations, created an Equal Employment Opportunity Commission, and also contained a provision prohibiting discrimination on the basis of gender. The following year, Congress passed the Voting Rights Act, which banned literacy tests as a qualification for voting and provided federal marshals to register voters in those counties, principally in the South, where fewer than half the adult population had voted in 1964. Finally, the Civil Rights Act of 1968 banned discrimination in the sale or rental of most housing in the United States.

While President Johnson and Congress were creating a body of civil rights legislation in the mid-1960s, the movement itself turned ugly. Urban riots each summer between 1964 and 1967 left the black districts of many cities burned out and demoralized. Further, the growing dilemma of "white flight," the move of whites from the city to the more affluent suburbs, led to a sharp decline in city tax revenues and a consequent lessening of city services to those who remained. The frustration of blacks who lived in the "ghetto" often spilled over into violence, sometimes stemming from a relatively minor incident that was blown up out of all rational proportion. These were not "race riots" in the classic sense of the word; they were riots pitting blacks against police or national guardsmen, with the violence and destruction taking place in their own neighborhoods and business districts. The rhetoric of this new militancy was provided by new radical black organizations, such as the Black Muslims, the Black Panthers, and the Student Nonviolent Coordinating Committee (SNCC), and their leaders, who often advocated racial separation rather than integration, radical economics, and, occasionally, revolutionary tactics.

One effect of this was the so-called "white backlash," a lessening of white sympathy for the black movement seen in opposition to civil rights demonstrations and increasing resistance to civil rights legislation in Congress. The passage of the 1968 Civil Rights Act may have been due to the publication that year of the Kerner Commission Report, which concluded that conditions for urban blacks were deplorable, and to the assassination of Martin Luther King. The election of Richard M. Nixon, no friend of civil rights, in November 1968, signalled the end of the most active phase of the civil rights movement.

The Nixon administration, which had come to office with a great deal of support from southern whites, worked to delay school integration and to appoint conservative justices to the Supreme Court. Despite the efforts of the administration, the Court left desegregation laws in place and ruled that "forced" busing was an acceptable technique to bring about school integration. Subsequent Republican administrations, headed by Ronald Reagan and George Bush, similarly resisted new advances in civil rights but were unable to roll back the gains that had been won in the 1950s and 1960s.

After years of relative inactivity, the women's movement, or feminism, emerged in the 1960s as a by-product of the larger civil rights movement. An increase in the number of working women, combined with the involvement of many women in the civil rights struggle, led to the awareness that women in American society were faced with many forms of legal, economic, social, and cultural discrimination.

In 1963, Betty Friedan published *The Feminine Mystique,* a best-selling book asserting that women were discontented because housewivery was boring and the home was no more than "a comfortable concentration camp." The only remedy, wrote Friedan, was meaningful work outside the home. Friedan's book raised the consciousness of many women about their status and helped lead to the creation of the National Organization of Women (NOW) in 1966. This mainstream organization lobbied Congress for legislation that would end women's inferior status.

Central to the efforts of NOW and of other concerned women was the Equal Rights Amendment (ERA), which would have forbidden any kind of discrimination on the basis of gender. Originally written by the suffragist Alice Paul in 1923, the ERA was finally passed by Congress in 1972 and sent to the states for ratification. A long and bitter struggle ensued for ten years before the amendment fell short by three states of the number needed for ratification. Opposition to the ERA came from conservative organizations and from some working women who felt that the amendment would take away from women certain "privileges" that they enjoyed, such as protective laws in the workplace and exemption from the military draft. Although the federal ERA failed, many states passed their own equal rights legislation, which did remove many discriminatory legal features against women. In addition, the Supreme Court aided the feminist cause with a number of decisions, including, for example, *Drewery's Ltd* v. *Barnes* (1972), which provided that an employer must set the same retirement age for women as for men.

The most controversial Supreme Court decision affecting women, however, was *Roe* v. *Wade (1973),* which declared unconstitutional many state laws prohibiting or severely limiting abortion. Feminists regarded it as a legitimization of a woman's reproductive rights, including the right to choose whether or not to terminate an unwanted pregnancy. Those who opposed the decision, including the national Right-to-Life organization, the Catholic Church, and many fundamentalist Protestant denominations, saw abortion as a form of murder; since 1973 they have waged an intense battle to get the decision overturned and the practice of legal abortion ended in the United States.

In the 1970s, the women's rights movement was strongly influenced by radical feminist organizations, which challenged the traditional family structure and other institutions in America that they felt were male-dominated. Their abrasive tactics created a backlash, similar to that in the black civil rights movement, and a lessening of sympathy for women's issues. This backlash continued during the 1980s, with the rise of conservative Christian-based political organizations, which espoused traditional family values, and the influence of the Reagan and Bush administrations, neither of which was interested in promoting the feminist agenda.

By the 1990s, both blacks and women could point to some significant gains as a result of the civil rights movement. More blacks and women were serving in political offices, from the Congress down to the local level. Many discriminatory laws had been repealed, and public attitudes seemed to be more accepting of racial and sexual equality.

INTERPRETIVE ESSAY
Thomas Clarkin

The civil rights movement grew out of the struggle of black Americans to regain constitutional rights long denied them. Using the nation's courts, political pressure, and active protest, blacks brought an end to decades of legal discrimination. Other Americans have since adopted the movement's strategies to secure similar rights. Although the civil rights movement had many successes, it also raised questions about economic inequalities and racial identity that have not yet been resolved.

Within fifteen years after the end of Reconstruction in 1877, the legislatures of the southern states began enacting laws designed to curtail the freedom that blacks had recently won. Known as "Jim Crow" laws, these regulations called for racially segregated facilities. In 1896, the United States Supreme Court's ruling in *Plessy* v. *Ferguson* upheld the doctrine of "separate but equal": segregated facilities did not violate the constitutional rights of blacks as long as the separate facilities were equal to those used by whites. Southern states quickly enacted hundreds of Jim Crow laws, and separate restaurants, bathrooms, and water fountains all became part of the southern way of life. While separate facilities became the norm, the notion of equality was discarded. Facilities provided for blacks generally were inferior to those for whites. Southern legislatures were unwilling to spend money on blacks, and their schools and neighborhoods received little funding.

Black Americans lost ground in other areas, too. In 1898 the Supreme Court upheld a Mississippi law requiring voters to pass a literacy test, which served to disenfranchise many blacks and poor whites. Other states required poll taxes, which most blacks could not afford. The number of black voters dropped dramatically in the South. As blacks lost their right to vote, the national political parties ignored their concerns. Violence against blacks often went unpunished, and lynchings were common throughout the South. With few educational or employment opportunities, most blacks were trapped in poverty from which they had little hope of escaping.

Black leaders struggled to respond to the crisis. Booker T. Washington advocated a gradual approach to acquiring civil rights. He believed that blacks should avoid political battles and, instead, concentrate on improving themselves through education and hard work. Washington's Tuskegee Institute offered blacks training in various trades. Other blacks spurned Washington's advice, accusing him of accepting segregation and white domination. W.E.B. Du Bois also recognized the value of education but called upon blacks to become doctors and lawyers. Du Bois rejected Washington's gradual approach and called for political agitation.

Whatever means they espoused, most black leaders found that their cause generated little concern on the part of white America. Southerners were satisfied with their way of life, and many northerners considered race to be a southern problem. Many Americans, including presidents Theodore Roosevelt and Woodrow Wilson, accepted "scientific" theories that proved blacks were naturally inferior to whites. National politicians saw no gain in assisting blacks who could not vote at the risk of alienating racist whites who could. Lacking financial resources and political power, civil rights leaders made little headway during the first three decades of the twentieth century.

At this time, hundreds of thousands of blacks were leaving the South. World War I had created a demand for laborers in northern industries, and southern blacks moved to cities such as New York, Detroit, and Chicago in hope of finding work. Called the "great migration" by historians, this trend continued for several decades. Although still victims of discrimination and racism, blacks in the North enjoyed greater prosperity. A new sense of cultural identity developed, and black music and literature flourished in the 1920s. Most important, blacks in the North were able to vote, which allowed them over time to develop the political clout they needed to advance their cause.

Black Americans had a difficult time during the Great Depression of the 1930s. Whites were usually the first hired for the few jobs that were available. Several New Deal initiatives had the unintended effect of limiting opportunities for blacks. Unwilling to alienate southern congressmen whose support was crucial for New Deal programs, President Franklin Roosevelt offered no civil rights legislation. Many blacks complained that the New Deal was just the "old raw deal" they had been receiving for years.

Despite its poor civil rights record, the Roosevelt administration was popular with black voters. They credited the president with providing them with some economic relief during the desperate times of the Depression. Harry Hopkins, director of the Works Progress Administration, maintained a color-blind hiring policy that provided over one million blacks with work. Blacks also appreciated several incidents of a more symbolic nature. While attending a conference in Birmingham, Alabama, in 1938, First Lady Eleanor Roosevelt shocked southerners when she refused to comply with a Jim Crow law that segregated audiences. She and Secretary of the Interior Harold Ickes helped organize a free concert featuring black singer Marian Anderson and held on the steps of the Lincoln Memorial, which was attended by over 75,000 people. Black voters supported the Democratic party because of the economic relief provided by the New Deal and the symbolic gestures that recognized the value of black Americans.

While politicians in Washington did little to advance the cause of civil rights, attorneys for the National Association for the Advancement of

Colored People (NAACP) began implementing a long-term legal strategy. Special Counsel Charles Houston believed that blacks could never achieve equality in the United States if they received an inferior education. The segregated school systems of the South were a permanent barrier to racial justice. Houston decided to attack the issue in the nation's courts and establish a series of precedents that would eventually overturn *Plessy* v. *Ferguson* and end legal segregation.

Attorney Thurgood Marshall discovered a case that fit the NAACP strategy perfectly. Donald Gaines Murray had been denied admission to the University of Maryland law school because he was black. The state of Maryland did not maintain a black law school, but did offer out-of-state scholarships to black students who wished to study law. Murray believed his rights had been violated and filed a lawsuit. The case of *Murray* v. *Maryland* was heard in June 1935. Marshall argued that the university had an obligation to provide Murray with an education equal to that offered to white students. The scholarships were merely a means of avoiding that obligation. As there was no separate black school, Marshall continued, the only way Murray could receive an equal education was to attend the white school. The judge agreed and ordered the law school to admit Murray as a student. The Supreme Court heard a similar case, *Missouri ex rel. Gaines* v. *Canada,* in 1938, and also ordered the black student admitted to the University of Missouri law school. Blacks celebrated the decisions, but Charles Houston realized that these victories were merely the beginning of a long battle to achieve equality.

World War II signaled a change in the struggle for civil rights. Although Adolf Hitler's virulent racism appalled Americans and ended "scientific" assertions of black inferiority, black Americans still suffered from prejudice. President Roosevelt refused to integrate the nation's armed forces, and blacks who served their country in uniform were segregated from white soldiers. Blacks attempting to find work in wartime industries faced discrimination, and lynchings and beatings continued in the South. Racial tensions grew in the North too, as several cities experienced race riots.

Several positive developments occurred during the war years. The NAACP continued its legal battles, attacking the segregated primary elections in Texas and poll taxes across the South. In Chicago, the Congress of Racial Equality (CORE) experimented with nonviolent protest in order to desegregate restaurants and movie theaters. Blacks also discovered that they could use political pressure to their advantage. In 1941, labor leader A. Philip Randolph threatened a mass march on Washington if President Roosevelt did not end employment discrimination in companies holding government contracts. Worried that such a march would reflect poorly on the United States in the eyes of its wartime allies, Roosevelt created the Fair Employment Practice Committee (FEPC) to oversee hiring practices. Black civil rights leaders were beginning to use public opinion and political muscle to achieve their goals.

Black veterans returning home at war's end were no longer willing to comply with the South's Jim Crow laws. They began to demand their right to vote, often at the risk of a beating or worse. Whites continued to thwart blacks who tried to register, so the number of actual black voters grew slowly in the South. Although the gains made at this time were limited, a new era in the struggle for civil rights had begun. Black Americans had turned to active protest, a method that would grow increasingly popular and effective in the coming years.

After the war, civil rights became a national issue. Northerners could no longer consider race a "southern problem" because millions of blacks lived in northern cities. Increasingly reliant upon the votes of northern blacks, the Democratic party slowly responded to their concerns. President Harry S Truman, whose Senate record on civil rights was lukewarm, recognized the value of black votes. Truman was also horrified by the lynchings of black servicemen in the South. In 1946 he established the President's Committee on Civil Rights, and he included many of this committee's recommendations in his 1948 civil rights message to Congress. In that message, Truman asked for a federal anti-lynching law, the creation of a permanent Fair Employment Practices Committee, protection of voter rights, and an end to the poll tax. However, Congress was not responsive. A powerful coalition of Republicans and conservative Southern Democrats allied to block the civil rights legislation. Acting on his own, Truman issued an executive order that ended segregation in the nation's armed forces. While the achievements of the Truman administration were limited, they signaled a commitment on the part of the Democratic party to the cause of civil rights. Blacks continued to favor Democrats when they went to the polls, playing an important role in Truman's election in 1948.

While black citizens turned to activism and the federal government grappled with the issue of civil rights, Thurgood Marshall and the attorneys of the NAACP pursued the legal strategy they had developed in the 1930s. Two important cases, *Sweatt* v. *Painter* and *McLaurin* v. *Oklahoma*, appeared before the U.S. Supreme Court in 1950. The law school at the University of Texas had denied Sweatt admission, instead opening a "law school" for blacks in a downtown basement. A court order had instructed the University of Oklahoma to admit George McLaurin as a graduate student. The university complied, but forced McLaurin to sit in assigned classroom seats and use the cafeteria at odd hours, which in effect segregated him within the graduate school. Both men sued. Marshall argued that the act of segregation itself made the experiences of the students unequal to that of whites. The Court agreed that both students were receiving inferior educations and ordered Texas to admit Sweatt to the law school and Oklahoma to end its restrictions on McLaurin. Although the Court refused to acknowledge that segregation always resulted in unequal treatment and segregation remained legal, these two cases established important precedents that undermined the *Plessy* ruling.

In 1953, the Supreme Court heard the case of *Brown* v. *Board of Education of Topeka*. In actuality five separate cases regarding school segregation, *Brown* remains one of the most important Supreme Court cases in American history. Marshall and the NAACP attorneys maintained that segregation psychologically damaged black schoolchildren. The attorneys presented as evidence sociological studies that proved black children in segregated schools believed that black skin color indicated inferiority. The doctrine of "separate but equal" was not only undesirable but unattainable—the very act of segregating children led to differences in self-esteem and education.

Chief Justice Earl Warren spent several months trying to persuade his fellow justices to render a unanimous opinion on *Brown*. He presented the Court's opinion in May 1954. The Court ruled that separate educational facilities were inherently unequal and that, in the area of education, segregation laws violated the Fourteenth Amendment. The NAACP strategy of combatting segregation through lawsuits had resulted in a major victory. Civil rights advocates across the nation cheered the Court's decision. However, not all Americans lauded the ruling. The majority of white southerners viewed *Brown* as an attack on their way of life. President Dwight D. Eisenhower refused to endorse the Court's decision. He believed that gradual change through education was the best way to cure the nation's racial problems. In the president's mind, using the legal authority of the federal government to ensure racial equality would inevitably lead to conflict.

Conflicts did occur because many white southerners defied the *Brown* ruling. In 1955, the Court ordered integration to begin "with all deliberate speed," a vague phrase that segregationists interpreted to mean "as slowly as possible." Southern legislators passed laws intended to thwart school integration. Angry whites formed citizens' groups to harass and intimidate blacks who demanded their rights. In 1957, President Eisenhower sent troops to Little Rock, Arkansas, to enforce a court order demanding integration of Central High School. Troopers escorted nine black children past jeering mobs and up the schoolhouse steps. The soldiers remained at Central High for several months. Although the *Brown* ruling was a victory, the struggle for racial justice would be won, not by attorneys in the nation's courthouses, but by brave men, women, and children who would risk their safety to win their rights.

Activism became the most effective weapon in the battle for civil rights. In 1955, Rosa Parks, a black seamstress in Montgomery, Alabama, refused to give up her bus seat for a white passenger. When Parks was arrested for violating the city's segregated bus laws, the city's black leaders organized a boycott of the bus line. At a mass meeting held later that week, a young minister named Martin Luther King, Jr. urged the boycotters to avoid violence. Montgomery's black citizens endured the harassment of whites and the inconvenience of carpooling for over a year. The boycott, which made both national and international news, ended in 1956 when the Supreme Court declared the segregated bus laws unconstitutional.

Southern blacks found Reverend King's nonviolent protest methods effective. In 1960, four black students in Greensboro, North Carolina, ordered coffee at a whites-only lunch counter. When they were refused service because of their color, they remained at the counter. Students across the South adopted this "sit-in" strategy, while northern students organized support rallies. The Student Nonviolent Coordinating Committee (SNCC) was established in April 1960 to coordinate protests and share information. Democratic presidential candidate John F. Kennedy praised the students for their courage.

While Kennedy offered only cautious support for civil rights during the campaign, his candidacy still held promise. Under President Eisenhower the federal government had moved too slowly. The passage of civil rights acts in 1957 and 1960 was symbolically important, but neither act led to significant changes in the lives of black Americans. Civil rights advocates lauded Kennedy's promise to end housing segregation. When Kennedy personally assisted Martin Luther King in gaining release from an Atlanta jail, he gained the votes of blacks across the nation.

Once in office, however, Kennedy worried that a strong civil rights stand might drive southern white voters away from the Democratic party. He also feared alienating powerful southern senators whose support he needed on other issues. Kennedy offered no civil rights legislation to Congress. When pressed to end housing discrimination by executive order, the president stalled. However, Kennedy quickly learned that the activist nature of the civil rights movement would make it impossible to ignore. Within months of taking office he faced a crisis that demanded his attention.

In 1960, the Supreme Court had banned segregation in bus and train facilities that serviced interstate travel. James Farmer, national director of the Congress of Racial Equality (CORE), wanted the federal government to enforce the Court's decision. Volunteers known as Freedom Riders received training in nonviolent protest strategies and began traveling through the South. Mobs of angry whites attacked the Freedom Riders, both white and black, while local police merely watched. The violence made headlines and news broadcasts around the world. Dismayed by the tarnishing of America's international prestige, President Kennedy wanted the Freedom Riders to abandon their campaign, but they refused. The Freedom Rides ended in late 1961, when the Interstate Commerce Commission prohibited the segregated facilities. Civil rights advocates learned that the president would respond only in times of crisis. The strategy of nonviolent protest continued in the South. The hatred of white racists would provide the conditions requiring federal intervention.

Kennedy hoped to channel the civil rights protestors into less confrontational activities. Administration officials made it clear that they would support and protect voter registration drives in the South. After vigorous debate, the members of SNCC began several registration projects. The idea was a failure. Volunteers were harassed, arrested, beaten, and, in several instances, murdered. The Justice Department failed to intercede and stop the violence. The student volunteers grew increasingly bitter toward the federal government, an attitude that would significantly alter the movement in coming years.

The violence in the South continued. In 1962, a federal judge ordered the all-white University of Mississippi to admit James Meredith. Kennedy had to send in federal marshals and the National Guard to enforce the court order. Mob violence left two dead and hundreds injured, but Meredith did enroll and later graduated. Since the president only reacted when violence threatened, Martin Luther King decided that a continued strategy of confrontation was the most effective means of pressuring Kennedy. King and other civil rights leaders planned a protest that they knew would provoke a violent response from whites. Known as "Project C," with the "C" standing for confrontation, the plan would leave the president no option but to support the civil rights struggle.

They chose the city of Birmingham, Alabama, notorious for its commitment to segregation and bloodletting. King's plan included an economic boycott and active demonstrations. The protests began in early April 1963, when blacks picketed local department stores. City police promptly arrested everyone involved. A protest march the following week also ended with mass arrests. Birmingham became the focus of national attention. On May 2, hundreds of schoolchildren joined the protest. Police arrested and jailed them. The following day, police used fire hoses and attack dogs on the demonstrators, many of whom were children. The violence escalated throughout the week. Americans saw it all on television and were horrified. Kennedy threatened the use of federal troops and urged the city to negotiate with the civil rights leaders. The protests ended with a settlement that desegregated lunch counters and promised blacks jobs in local industries.

Project C was successful. The president feared that the nation was becoming racially divided and that the violence would soon become uncontrollable. He also worried that America's image would become soiled, thus aiding the spread of communism. On the evening of June 11, Kennedy appeared on national television. He declared racial justice to be a moral issue that America had to face and announced that he would send a civil rights bill to Congress. The bill sent to Congress the following week included a ban on segregation in public facilities.

To ensure that the bill would not disappear in Congress, civil rights leaders organized a march on Washington in August. The march would keep civil rights in the public eye and show the country that the struggle for justice could be peaceful and bring Americans together. President Kennedy feared that violence would mar the event and asked that it be cancelled, but the organizers refused. The president's concerns were unfounded. The march on Washington was one of the high points of the civil rights movement, drawing over a quarter million Americans of all races together for a day of peaceful celebration. That afternoon King delivered his most famous speech, declaring to Americans, "I have a dream." The march on Washington confirmed that King's dream might one day become reality.

President Kennedy did not live to see his civil rights bill become law. Many blacks feared that his successor, the Texan Lyndon Johnson, might not support their cause. In fact, Johnson included civil rights among his administration's highest priorities. Johnson used his considerable legislative skills to push the bill through Congress. The Civil Rights Act of 1964 outlawed discrimination in the use of public facilities. The courage of America's civil rights activists had ended the long reign of Jim Crow in the South.

These successes inspired other Americans to press for their rights. Increasingly discontented with their role as housewives, women began to question their place in American society. They faced limited employment opportunities and received less pay than men. Title VII of the newly passed Civil Rights Act included a provision banning discrimination on the basis of sex. This provision would prove to be important as women used the nation's courts to end discrimination in the workplace.

Southern blacks still faced discrimination when registering to vote. Students—both black and white—organized a registration drive in the summer of 1964. Angry whites harassed the "Freedom Summer" volunteers. Three men working on the project were murdered in Mississippi, which again drew the nation's attention toward the South. In 1965, King began demonstrations protesting black disenfranchisement in Selma, Alabama. On March 7, police used whips, chains, and tear gas to end a protest march; the brutal attack on the peaceful demonstrators made national news. Eight days later President Johnson submitted a voting rights bill to Congress. Signed into law that August, the Voting Rights Act of 1965 ended literacy tests and allowed the federal government to intervene in areas where voter registration was unusually low.

At the moment of its greatest triumphs, however, the civil rights movement was fragmenting. Many volunteers never forgot the federal government's failure to protect students who worked on voter registration projects. The strategy of nonviolent confrontation had been useful, but years of harassment and abuse had taken their toll. Moreover, the end to legal discrimination did little to raise blacks out of poverty. A more radical vision began to take root among many blacks seeking justice. Malcolm X rejected nonviolence and advocated black nationalism. Stokely Carmichael, a SNCC veteran, raised the cry of Black Power. The Black Power movement emphasized self-reliance and racial unity instead of integration. Some militant civil rights leaders questioned the viability of American democracy and capitalism. The call for civil rights took on an increasingly radical cast that alienated many white supporters.

The situation worsened in the mid-1960s as riots swept through the nation's urban centers. Inner-city blacks discovered that the end to discrimination did not ensure equality of economic opportunity. With rioting in Watts (Los Angeles) in 1965, Newark and Detroit in 1967, the nation seemed gripped by violence that was tearing it apart. After the assassination of Martin Luther King in April 1968, riots rocked over 125 cities, including the nation's capital. Many American whites believed that the civil rights movement had gone far enough. President Johnson found limited congressional support for his civil rights initiatives. A bill banning housing discrimination failed in 1966 and 1967, finally passing in 1968.

Race became an important issue in the 1968 presidential election. Republican nominee Richard M. Nixon correctly sensed that most Americans no longer supported the civil rights struggle. During the campaign, he ignored the black vote, hoping instead to capture the votes of white southern conservatives alienated from the Democratic party. He opposed busing as a means to desegregate schools and called for "law and order," a catch phrase with racist overtones in the South. In office, Nixon attempted to weaken the enforcement provisions of the Voting Rights Act and continued to oppose busing. He nominated several conservative southerners to serve on the Supreme Court. While Congress, the courts, and the federal bureaucracy often frustrated Nixon's attempts to slow the civil rights struggle, the era of federal activism had clearly ended.

While the movement for racial justice fragmented and faltered, women worked to overcome internal differences in their movement. Radical feminists engaged in a larger critique of American life. They used demonstrations and "speakouts" to bring attention to issues such as abortion and rape. Other women, such as the members of the National Organization of Women (NOW), emphasized legal and economic equality. Though these groups articulated different concerns, they all supported the Equal Rights Amendment (ERA). Although some women feared that the ERA would destroy the traditional "protected" status of women in American society, many women of different backgrounds united to support its passage.

Concerted opposition prevented the ratification of the ERA, but women's rights activists scored strong gains in the 1970s. Several court rulings undermined discrimination against women. In 1971, the Supreme Court struck down an Idaho law that preferred the use of men over women as estate administrators. The Court deemed the law to be an arbitrary distinction between the sexes and thus unreasonable. In 1973, the Court ruled that the U.S. military had to provide the same benefits to women that they offered men. In a case settled out of court in 1973, government attorneys filed a sex discrimination suit against AT&T, one of the nation's largest corporations. While not admitting guilt, AT&T agreed to reimburse millions in back pay to women and minority workers in its employ. While all these cases advanced the cause of women's equality in society and the workplace, none was as important or as controversial as the 1973 Supreme Court decision in *Roe* v. *Wade*, which recognized the legal right to abortion. While this ruling stimulated a powerful conservative response to women's issues, the Court had affirmed a woman's right to control her body and her privacy. *Roe* v. *Wade* remains an important landmark in the struggle for women's rights.

While women fared well in the 1970s, advocates of racial justice tried to hold their ground. In 1978, the Supreme Court heard the case of Alan Bakke. Bakke claimed that he had been denied admission to a California medical school because he was white and was, therefore, a victim of reverse discrimination. His suit was an attack on affirmative action programs, which had been instituted to give minorities employment and educational opportunities. The Court's ruling in Bakke's favor was a serious blow to affirmative action. The 1980s were little better. The executive branch of the government under presidents Ronald Reagan and George Bush did little for civil rights. Black leaders worried about the growing black underclass and a disturbing new racism on the nation's campuses. Women found themselves under attack from conservatives who saw their movement as destructive of family values.

Some black Americans did make significant gains during those years. The size of the black middle class grew, and the number of black officials elected to public office mushroomed. Americans willingly accepted black athletes and entertainers, as evidenced by the popularity of Michael Jordan and Bill Cosby. However, poor blacks suffered. The inner cities became battlegrounds, avoided by whites and ignored by politicians. Criminals, gangs, and drug dealers controlled the streets. The gains of the civil rights movement meant little to people who feared leaving their homes and apartments.

Civil rights remain a national concern. African Americans still combat racism and poverty. Hispanic Americans and Native Americans have launched significant movements to improve their economic and social status. Gay rights activists have effectively used the courts, political pressure, and protest to make their cause known; the AIDS epidemic has done much to legitimize their movement. Advocates of children's rights have made use of the courts. Women continue to press for economic opportunity and changes in the workplace and to preserve abortion rights. The bloody Los Angeles riots of 1992 revealed the risk the country takes when it ignores the disadvantaged. Seeing no hope for economic advancement and no justice, inner-city poor of all races turned to burning and looting their own neighborhoods. Perhaps these people will turn to more productive forms of protest, using the strategies that were successful during the earlier struggles for equality in the United States.

Although the 1970s and 1980s were a difficult time for civil rights advocates, the triumphs of the movement during the 1960s remain a source of pride for the United States. Four important factors explain civil rights successes during that decade: timing, leadership, federal assistance, and the involvement of average Americans in the cause. The time was right for Americans to respond to the civil rights message. After World War II, the United States was the most powerful nation in the world. Americans believed that their nation's commitment to democracy served as an example to other countries. Discrimination and racism had no place in a nation dedicated to the ideals of freedom and liberty, and when American minorities protested the violations of their rights, many Americans agreed that a great wrong needed to be corrected.

Credit must be given to the leaders of the civil rights movement, who developed strategies, organized protests, and motivated activists. Gifted attorneys such as Charles Houston and Thurgood Marshall capably presented their arguments in the nation's courts. The brilliant speeches of Martin Luther King, Jr. moved Americans, both black and white, to rally to the cause. Malcolm X offered a vision of black nationalism that emphasized the talents and skills of the black community. Civil rights leaders never gave up, even when they faced threats and violence. Their courage served as an example and an inspiration to supporters.

The role of the federal government cannot be downplayed when considering the successes of the movement. Federal court decisions that ended discrimination against blacks and women were important tools in the fight for equal rights. The Justice Department and the FBI investigated cases of discrimination and violence when state officials refused to do so. Finally, presidents Kennedy and Johnson placed the power of the White House behind the cause of civil rights. While the federal government was often slow and reluctant to aid the movement, the civil rights movement needed federal assistance to overcome racism at the state and local levels.

However, the true heroes of the civil rights movement were not the dynamic leaders nor the judges nor the politicians. The heroes of the movement were the thousands of Americans, black and white, who risked their jobs, their safety and even their lives to advance their cause.

Rosa Parks risked jail to defend her right to sit on a bus. The school-children of Little Rock walked past crowds screaming threats at them. Southern blacks who registered to vote lost their jobs and often feared for their lives. Student volunteers were beaten, shot at, and in some cases murdered, as they encouraged southern blacks to vote. The citizens of Birmingham were attacked by dogs and knocked down in the streets when they protested segregation. Had these Americans changed their minds and backed down when confronted with hatred and violence, the civil rights movement would have collapsed. Instead, they bravely continued, confident that their cause was right. Their idealism and courage serve as reminders that, in the future, the advancement of civil rights in the United States will depend upon the support of all Americans.

SELECTED BIBLIOGRAPHY

Acuña, Rodolfo. *Occupied America: A History of Chicanos.* 3d ed. New York: Harper & Row, 1988. The final chapters of this historical survey deal with the role of Mexican Americans in the civil rights movement.

Branch, Taylor. *Parting the Waters: America in the King Years, 1954–1963.* New York: Simon and Schuster, 1988. This Pulitzer Prize-winning book examines King's rise to national prominence.

Brauer, Carl M. *John F. Kennedy and the Second Reconstruction.* New York: Columbia University Press, 1977. Lauds Kennedy's role in responding to the civil rights movement.

Burk, Robert Fredrick. *The Eisenhower Administration and Black Civil Rights.* Knoxville: University of Tennessee Press, 1984. A study of the executive branch and civil rights in the 1950s.

Davis, Michael D., and Hunter R. Clark. *Thurgood Marshall: Warrior at the Bar, Rebel on the Bench.* New York: Birch Lane Press, 1992. An accessible biography of a key figure in the legal struggle for justice.

Deloria, Vine, Jr. *Behind the Trail of Broken Treaties: An Indian Declaration of Independence.* Austin: University of Texas Press, 1985. Includes a useful chapter on Native American activism.

Ellison, Ralph. *Invisible Man.* New York: Random House, 1952. This important novel portrays the life of a young black man as he discovers his identity in postwar America.

Evans, Sara. *Personal Politics: The Roots of the Women's Liberation Movement and the New Left.* New York: Alfred A. Knopf, 1979. Examines the roots of the women's movement in the civil rights movement of the 1960s.

Fine, Sidney. *Violence in the Model City: The Cavanagh Administration, Race Relations, and the Detroit Riot of 1967.* Ann Arbor: University of Michigan Press, 1989. A detailed study of one of America's worst urban riots.

Faludi, Susan. *Backlash: The Undeclared War against American Women.* New York:

Crown Publishers, 1991. Discusses the backlash against women's rights in the 1980s.

Garrow, David J. *Bearing the Cross: Martin Luther King, Jr., and the Southern Christian Leadership Conference.* New York: William Morrow, 1986. Analyzes King's role as a civil rights leader.

Gould, Lewis L. *1968: The Election that Changed America.* Chicago: Ivan R. Dee, 1993. Examines race as an election issue in 1968.

Graham, Hugh Davis. *Civil Rights and the Presidency: Race and Gender in American Politics, 1960–1972.* New York: Oxford University Press, 1992. Looks at the presidencies of Kennedy, Johnson, and Nixon.

Hampton, Henry and Steven Fayer. *Voices of Freedom: An Oral History of the Civil Rights Movement from the 1950s through the 1980s.* New York: Bantam Books, 1990. A collection of interviews of participants in the civil rights movement.

Harvey, James C. *Black Civil Rights during the Johnson Administration.* Jackson: University and College Press of Mississippi, 1973. Examines the civil rights movement during the crucial years of Johnson's presidency.

Lawson, Steven F. *Running for Freedom: Civil Rights and Black Politics in America since 1941.* Philadelphia: Temple University Press, 1991. Discusses the importance of enfranchisement and black politics.

Lemann, Nicholas. *The Promised Land: The Great Black Migration and How It Changed America.* New York: Alfred A. Knopf, 1991. An account of several families who moved from Mississippi to Chicago and federal policies that influenced their lives.

Lukas, J. Anthony. *Common Ground: A Turbulent Decade in the Lives of Three American Families.* New York: Alfred A. Knopf, 1986. Black and white families experience turmoil in 1970s Boston.

Marable, Manning. *Race, Reform, and Rebellion: The Second Reconstruction in Black America, 1945–1990.* Rev. ed. Jackson and London: University Press of Mississippi, 1991. A provocative assessment of the civil rights years.

Matusow, Allen J. *The Unraveling of America: A History of Liberalism in the 1960s.* New York: Harper & Row, 1984. A critical evaluation of liberalism, with emphasis on federal policy and black power.

Moody, Anne. *Coming of Age in Mississippi.* New York: Dell, 1970. The life of a Mississippi woman and her experiences during the Freedom Summer.

Norrell, Robert J. *Reaping the Whirlwind: The Civil Rights Movement in Tuskegee.* New York: Vintage Books, 1985. The tale of one town and its century-long struggle for black rights.

Sitkoff, Harvard. *A New Deal for Blacks: The Emergence of Civil Rights as a National Issue.* New York: Oxford University Press, 1978. Assesses the role of the Roosevelt administration in attaining civil rights.

———. *The Struggle for Black Equality, 1954–1992.* Rev. ed. New York: Hill and Wang, 1993. Provides a useful overview of the civil rights movement.

Wilkinson, J. Harvie III. *From Brown to Bakke: The Supreme Court and School Integration, 1954–1978.* New York: Oxford University Press, 1979. Examines the important Supreme Court cases concerning education.

Woodward, C. Vann. *The Strange Career of Jim Crow.* Rev. 3d ed. New York: Oxford University Press, 1974. The classic study of the rise and fall of segregation.

X, Malcolm, and Alex Haley. *The Autobiography of Malcolm X.* New York: Ballantine Books, 1977. The fascinating life story of the controversial black leader.

9

The Vietnam War, c. 1950–1975

INTRODUCTION

Vietnam, which along with Laos and Cambodia, comprised the colony of French Indochina, first came to the attention of U.S. policymakers in 1950, after the focus of the Cold War had shifted to the Far East with the "loss" of China to the forces of Mao Zedong. Since 1946, France had been trying to reestablish colonial dominance in Vietnam in a struggle with the Democratic Republic of Vietnam, a nationalist movement led from the northern city of Hanoi by Ho Chi Minh, a charismatic leader who had spent many years in both Paris and Moscow. In the Cold War context of the day, this civil war was seen as yet another contest of the forces of freedom against communism; and, in early 1950, the United States committed itself to the French cause by recognizing the government of Bao Dai, which the French had set up in the southern city of Saigon as a rival Vietnamese government to that of Ho Chi Minh. In June 1950, after the Korean War broke out, the United States began to send military assistance to the French forces in Vietnam. Meanwhile, both the Soviet Union and the People's Republic of China (PRC) recognized and were aiding the government of Ho Chi Minh.

Although the United States provided some $1.2 billion in aid to the French between 1950 and 1954 and sent several hundred technicians and

General William Westmoreland, commander of U.S. forces in Vietnam, greets arriving troops in 1967. (Reproduced from the Collections of the Library of Congress)

advisers to Vietnam, the French were unable to win. In 1954, Ho Chi Minh's forces besieged the French army at the remote town of Dien Bien Phu for nearly two months, forcing its surrender on May 7. The Eisenhower administration fiercely debated the wisdom of intervening to try and save the French military, in the midst of which the president outlined the famous Domino Theory in support of intervention, asserting that if Vietnam fell to the Communists, it would be like the first in a row of dominoes: just as the whole row of dominoes would topple, so, too, would all the rest of the countries in Southeast Asia fall to communism. But the French surrender came before a decision about intervention could be reached in Washington.

Meanwhile, between April and July 1954, representatives from France, Great Britain, the United States, Laos, Cambodia, and the PRC, as well as the Democratic Republic of Vietnam, met in Geneva, Switzerland, to negotiate an end to the problems of former French Indochina. In July, the Geneva Accords, as the two agreements were called, were signed. One simply ended the fighting in Vietnam, while the other attempted to bring about a political settlement there by temporarily dividing the country at the 17th parallel until reunification elections could be held, sometime within two years. Ho Chi Minh was to control the territory north of the dividing line, while all French forces were to move south. The elections were never held, and this division became the border between the two ostensibly independent nations of North Vietnam and South Vietnam.

Significantly, the United States chose not to sign the Geneva Accords, as doing so would create the appearance that the Communists had devoured yet another piece of the world, a situation that would cause domestic political problems for the Republican Eisenhower administration. Instead, the United States moved quickly to replace the French as the anti-Communist force in Vietnam. Shortly after the conclusion of the Geneva conference, Ngo Dinh Diem had, with Washington's blessing, become the prime minister of South Vietnam; in October 1955, he ousted Bao Dai in a national referendum to become president. One of his first acts was to announce that no national election would be held, as his government had not been a party to the accords. The Eisenhower administration, knowing that Ho Chi Minh would easily win such an election, supported Diem.

The refusal of Diem to hold this election led to the beginnings of Viet Cong terrorism in South Vietnam. The Viet Cong, supporters of Ho Chi Minh who lived in the south, gradually increased the level of violence until a full-scale civil revolt was underway by the time John F. Kennedy entered the White House in 1961. Efforts to persuade Diem to build up his popularity and political base so as to be able to resist the Viet Cong more effectively had proven futile; and by mid-1961, there was concern in Washington for the survival of South Vietnam.

President Kennedy sent Vice-President Lyndon Johnson to Vietnam in the summer of 1961 to assay the situation; Johnson returned with a glowing public appraisal of Diem and an analysis of the situation based on the Domino Theory. Later in 1961, a fact-finding mission headed by national security adviser Walt W. Rostow and White House military adviser Maxwell Taylor went to Vietnam. Among other things, the Taylor-Rostow mission recommended the sending of up to 10,000 combat troops who could be rapidly deployed if the situation warranted; Kennedy, however, was not ready to escalate American involvement to that degree.

In 1963, the situation in Vietnam began to deteriorate. Viet Cong forces (now aided by infiltrating North Vietnamese) were making headway against Diem's troops, and public opposition to the war was building in the south, highlighted by the public self-immolations of protesting Buddhist monks. Kennedy sent Henry Cabot Lodge, a tough diplomat, to Saigon to tell Diem to shore up his political and military base, but this effort was to no avail. In early November, Diem was deposed and murdered in a coup d'etat led by some of his generals. Three weeks later, President Kennedy was assassinated.

The new American president, Lyndon Johnson, inherited a very unstable situation in South Vietnam. Frequent political changes in Saigon and the increasing likelihood of a Communist victory caused the president to begin planning for greater U.S. involvement. Contingency plans were drawn up for American action against North Vietnam, and lists of bombing targets for a future air war were compiled. McGeorge Bundy, the new national security adviser, wrote a resolution authorizing the president to intervene militarily in Vietnam; the resolution would be sent to Congress in the wake of a suitably hostile incident on the part of North Vietnam.

In August 1964, it was reported that on two separate occasions, North Vietnamese patrol boats had attacked U.S. destroyers in the Tonkin Gulf off the coast of Vietnam. Though no one was killed nor was any significant damage inflicted, the administration felt that the incident was dramatic enough to warrant sending the resolution to Congress. In the excitement of the moment, both houses of Congress approved it by nearly unanimous votes. The Tonkin Gulf Resolution, as it was called, authorized the president to repel any armed attack against the United States and to take any and all necessary measures to prevent further aggression.

The election campaign of 1964 prevented Johnson from escalating the war immediately; but in February 1965, the Viet Cong attacked a military base near Pleiku, killing eight, wounding more than a hundred, and destroying several planes. Johnson seized on this incident to launch a bombing campaign against the north and to order 3,500 marines into combat. By the end of the year, American troop strength in Vietnam would reach 180,000.

Despite the intensive and protracted bombing campaign and the steady increase in the number of troops in Vietnam, the military situation was stalemated throughout 1966 and 1967. What did change was the public attitude about the war in the United States. By 1967, a divisive public debate over the war had spread to most areas of the country and was particularly heated on college campuses, where activist students and faculty held "teach-ins" and sponsored protest rallies. Those who opposed the war, called "doves," were not effective in bringing about policy changes because they lacked unity; but they did incur the wrath of the "hawks," who supported the war and felt that most doves were, at worst, traitors, and, at best, naive individuals who were by their actions lending support to the enemy. A complicating factor was television coverage of the war; many people began to sense by what they saw on television that the administration was not telling the public the truth about the course of the war.

One of the most important events of the war was the Tet Offensive in January 1968. This was a coordinated attack on twenty-six South Vietnamese cities during the Vietnamese New Year (Tet) by combined Viet Cong and North Vietnamese forces. Although U.S. and South Vietnamese troops recaptured control of all the cities within a few days, the American public was shocked when, after months of optimistic statements about the war, they saw what the enemy seemed capable of doing. Polls showed that a "credibility gap" existed; a majority of Americans no longer believed what the Johnson administration was saying about the war.

President Johnson, shaken by the turn of events, found his political support waning and surprised the nation by announcing in March 1968 that he would not seek reelection later that year, but would instead seek an end to the war. War protests continued during the year; they were especially violent in Chicago at the time of the Democratic national convention, and it was clear that Richard M. Nixon, the Republican victor in November, would have to steer the nation on a different course in Vietnam. By the time of Nixon's inauguration in January 1969, some 530,000 U.S. troops were fighting in Vietnam, and over 35,000 combat deaths had been recorded.

Nixon's new direction was called Vietnamization, a plan to withdraw American troops gradually while training South Vietnamese troops to take their place in combat zones and continuing to provide supplies and air support. By the end of 1969, slightly over 100,000 Americans had been withdrawn, with a corresponding drop in the casualty rate, and the public debate over the war had lessened. In April 1970, however, the president authorized an incursion, or limited invasion, into Cambodia, ostensibly to capture an enemy headquarters and supply depot. The incursion was launched without consulting Congress and sparked a firestorm of protest among Americans who felt that the administration was widening the war. Tragically, six college students, four at Kent State University and two at Jackson State University, were killed by National Guard troops during antiwar rallies. In February 1971, another incursion was made into Laos, but this time, South Vietnamese troops were used, and there was considerably less public protest.

Meanwhile, secret negotiations had begun in 1969 between Henry Kissinger, President Nixon's national security adviser, and Le Duc Tho, a North Vietnamese diplomat. These talks became more frequent in 1972, particularly after the president had gone to the PRC, North Vietnam's principal ally, and initiated the process of normalizing diplomatic relations. A peace settlement appeared to be at hand in October 1972, but new complications arose, and the final document was not signed until January 1973.

The terms of the Paris Peace Agreement included the withdrawal of the remaining U.S. troops from Vietnam, along with the dismantling of U.S. bases and the removal of U.S.-laid mines in North Vietnamese harbors. An international truce team was to supervise a cease-fire, and all U.S. prisoners of war were to be returned. The political future of Vietnam was to be decided by a council of representatives from the governments of both North and South Vietnam as well as the Viet Cong, which was to plan and conduct national elections.

U.S. involvement in Vietnam continued after the 1973 agreement in the form of substantial numbers of advisers, diplomatic officials, and technicians, all there to maximize the chances for success of the Saigon government and army. In addition, Congress appropriated, after much debate, millions of dollars of additional aid for South Vietnam. But the process of Vietnamization had not produced a very good Army of the Republic of Vietnam (ARVN), and its performance was further compromised by a mutual lack of cultural understanding between the American advisers and the Vietnamese soldiers. Moreover, the ARVN was mired deeply in a system that fostered corruption, low morale, and a high desertion rate. Many of these problems were largely hidden from Washington by the optimistic reports of the American ambassador, Graham Martin.

Between 1973 and 1975, Vietnam attracted little attention in the United States because U.S. troops were no longer fighting and dying. The Nixon administration was disintegrating over the Watergate scandal, and the turmoil in the Middle East had led to the Arab oil embargo, which was creating serious economic repercussions for the United States.

North Vietnamese leaders, aware of the distractions in the United States, escalated their military activity in South Vietnam, and, when there was no response from Washington, they moved their armies forward on several fronts. A congressional fact-finding delegation visited Vietnam in February, found Ambassador Martin as optimistic as ever, and recommended no change in American policy. In March, the North Vietnamese began their final offensive, moving toward Saigon with little resistance. The South Vietnamese government surrendered on April 30, as the remaining Americans and a few fortunate Vietnamese were airlifted to safety from the roof of the U.S. embassy.

Since 1975, Vietnam has been unified under a totalitarian government centered in Hanoi. The bloodbath of South Vietnamese loyal to the United States that many had predicted did not occur, although many were deprived of their property and sent to harsh "re-education" camps. Saigon was renamed Ho Chi Minh City, and the country suffered extreme poverty, although in the 1980s, a number of industrialized countries began to invest in development projects in Vietnam. But because many Americans believe that U.S. prisoners of war are still being held captive in Vietnam, it was not until February 1994 that the United States lifted its trade embargo against Vietnam. In July 1995, the United States and Vietnam established full diplomatic relations, marking a formal end to the war.

INTERPRETIVE ESSAY
Jerry A. Pattengale

During the late 1960s and early 1970s, the United States found itself in social and political turmoil. In 1968, the political fallout from the Tet offensive and the growing antiwar movement convinced President Lyndon Johnson that the White House could no longer command the necessary respect for implementing its policies. Many historians assume that American public disapproval of the Vietnam War was a factor in bringing about the gradual withdrawal of American troops during the first term of President Richard M. Nixon, although it is questionable to what degree public sentiment was responsible for the ultimate humiliating defeat of America's client, South Vietnam, in 1975.

However, the interpretive war over the meaning of Vietnam continues. While there is general consensus that keeping troops in Vietnam into the 1970s was a mistake measured in staggering human proportions, the 1995 publication of Robert S. McNamara's *In Retrospect: The Tragedy and Lessons of Vietnam* launched a fury of journalistic jabs. McNamara, who served as secretary of defense under Presidents Kennedy and Johnson and had been a key player in developing policies for the war, had remained silent for twenty-seven years; and predictably, his book served as a barometer for writers and interpreters of the history of the war. McNamara asserts that the respective administrations "acted according to what we thought were the principles and traditions of this nation. We made our decisions in light of those values. Yet we were wrong, terribly wrong" (p. xvi). Some might argue that the altruistic reasons of the United States for entering the conflict should have led to our withdrawal after the coup that resulted in the death of Premier Ngo Dinh Diem in November 1963, and some insiders maintain that Kennedy would have done so after his reelection that following year. McNamara expressed his concern with the direction of U.S. policy when he resigned in 1967, yet the war wound down for eight more years.

McNamara's book did serve to reopen some old wounds from the days of the antiwar movement. After its publication, a respected journalist for *The New Republic*, Mickey Kaus, surmised, "Has any single American of this century done more harm than Robert McNamara?" The April 16,

1995, *Los Angeles Times* ran a venomous "Column Left" by Robert Sheer, entitled "Sorry, Mac-You're Not Forgiven: Those Who Protested the Vietnam War Remain the Heroes, McNamara the Fraud." An April 12 *New York Times* editorial mocked McNamara's "stale tears" and encouraged readers to invoke a "lasting moral condemnation." Ironically, the *Times* and many other major papers had unabashedly endorsed the war at one time.

But the arguments over McNamara's confession in *In Retrospect* deal only with the responsibility of one individual and whether his belated admission was anything more than self-serving. What is more important to remember about the war in Vietnam is the legacy that it left for the foreign and domestic policies of the United States.

Indeed, one of the first "results" of the war came even before the war officially ended in 1975. In 1970, Nixon ordered an incursion into neighboring Cambodia, ostensibly to capture an enemy command post and supply depot and thus make more secure the gradual withdrawal of American troops then underway. This incursion touched off a civil war within Cambodia won by Communist forces known as the Khmer Rouge. After U.S. withdrawal from Indochina, the Khmer Rouge renamed Cambodia as Kampuchea and proceeded to execute 40 percent of the population. By 1979, perhaps as many as two million people had died at the hands of the fanatical Communist Pol Pot, the kind of genocidal horror that some U.S. politicians in the 1950s thought all Communists were capable of. But most Americans and many members of Congress were far less concerned with what was going on in Cambodia than they were with what was going on in the White House. Resenting the secret way in which Nixon had "widened" the war, Congress passed the War Powers Resolution in 1973, requiring the president to report to Congress any deployment of armed forces abroad and to withdraw them within sixty days unless Congress approved their continued utilization. While Nixon and all succeeding presidents have opposed this resolution and declared it to be an unconstitutional restraint of their power as commander-in-chief of the armed forces, they have usually paid attention to its provisions.

Another result of the unhappy Vietnam experience has been a greater reluctance to commit conventional forces to action in various trouble spots. Here one can cite several examples. In late 1975, a civil war broke out in newly independent Angola, a former Portuguese colony. Secretary of State Henry Kissinger worried that the Soviet-and Cuban-supported leftist side would prevail without large amounts of U.S. military aid and the possible deployment of U.S. troops. Congress, fearful of a Vietnam-style escalation, voted to stop all military aid to Angola, asserting that no vital U.S. interests were at stake in that distant African nation.

In 1981, the Ronald Reagan administration came into office amidst the rhetoric of renewed Cold War hostility. The Soviet Union was dubbed an "evil empire," and some of its imperial outreach projects were close by, in Cuba and Central America, the "backyard" of the United States. Reagan, who liked to refer to Vietnam as a "noble cause," had no qualms about using U.S. forces in the struggle against communism. Over the next few years, his administration worked hard to root communism out of places like Nicaragua and El Salvador by outfitting a rebel army, called the Contras, to try to overthrow the Nicaraguan government and sending U.S. military advisers to assist the El Salvador army in putting down a Communist-led insurgency. Rhetorically, the administration applied the Domino Theory to the Central American situation, noting ominously that if the United States failed to stop the Communists in El Salvador, it would have to deal either with them or with millions of refugees fleeing from them on the Texas-Mexico border.

From the beginning of U.S. involvement in Central America, some administration critics likened the situation to that of Vietnam in the 1950s, when only a handful of U.S. military advisers were in Vietnam. It was easy to imagine a scenario where, in a few years, many thousands of U.S. combat troops would be engaged in hand-to-hand combat with Communists in the Central American jungles. But the criticism was tempered by the fact that Central America is much closer to the United States than Vietnam, and its proximity suggested that important national interests were involved. As a consequence, Congress provided limited funding for a few years, but when it appeared that the Nicaraguan rebels were getting nowhere and diplomacy might work to bring peace in El Salvador, Congress pulled the money plug. Undeterred, staff members in the president's National Security Council continued our involvement in Central America by secretly (and illegally) selling arms to Iran and sending the profits to friendly forces on the isthmus. When discovered, the Iran-Contra affair, as it came to be known, proved a major embarrassment to the Reagan administration and further undercut the confidence of many Americans in their government.

Even as late as 1991, the Persian Gulf War showed that the shadow of Vietnam still remained. After Iraq seized Kuwait in August 1990, the administration of President George Bush gathered some allies and, in January 1991, launched an air and ground war to liberate Kuwait. Although Kuwait was quickly freed from Iraqi domination and American missiles did considerable damage to military installations and government buildings in Iraq, the Bush administration, fearful of the conflict turning into another Vietnam, quickly withdrew U.S. forces, leaving the Iraqi government of Saddam Hussein essentially intact and seething with resentment.

On the other hand, there have been occasions, particularly during the Reagan and Bush administrations, in which the president, wanting to "make America stand tall again" after the defeat in Vietnam, has ordered a large-scale military operation against a hapless foe in order to score an easy win. In 1983, President Reagan sent a large contingent of troops to the Caribbean island of Grenada, ostensibly to protect American medical students studying there, but in reality to topple an unfriendly leftist government. Despite the fact that some U.S. military blunders occurred, the local defense forces were no match for the Americans; and within a short time, the Grenadan government has been replaced, the medical students "rescued," and the flag appropriately waved.

Similarly, in 1989, the Bush administration sent several thousand troops into Panama in order to bring to justice Manuel Noriega, the country's leader and a former CIA operative, who had fallen out of favor because of his alleged involvement with Latin American drug trafficking. Although a few hundred Panamanians were killed and a good deal of property was destroyed, Noriega was corralled and brought to Miami for eventual trial. More importantly, perhaps, American might had been demonstrated.

With respect to domestic affairs, the Vietnam War had a profound impact on the U.S. economy. During his tenure in the White House, Lyndon Johnson developed a creative domestic program known as the Great Society, based on the idea of using New Deal-style programs to help those individuals and communities that were not able to enjoy an era of general prosperity. Many of the Great Society programs were designed to help the poor of America's cities, while others focussed on such matters as education and medical care. All were expensive and represented a further expansion of the federal bureaucracy, but Johnson, who had come to political maturity during the Depression, believed wholeheartedly in their worth and successfully used his political skills to drive them through Congress in the mid-1960s.

The Vietnam War, however, was a very expensive proposition itself. By 1966, the United States was spending more than $20 billion a year on the war; in 1967, Congress passed a ten percent surcharge on personal and corporate income taxes to help pay for the war. It was not enough. Inevitably, Congress had to scale back funding for the Great Society programs in order to finance the war. Federal deficits rose substantially during the late 1960s and set the stage for major economic difficulties, including double-digit inflation, in the early 1970s. It can be argued that the $167 billion total cost of the Vietnam War contributed significantly to the continuing growth of the federal deficit and the budgetary problems the United States faced in the 1990s.

Another domestic issue that is a residue of the Vietnam experience concerns veterans of the war. Altogether, some 2.15 million Americans served in Vietnam. A disproportionate number of them were poorly educated, or members of a minority race, or both. College students found deferments relatively easy to obtain during most of the war years; others joined the National Guard in order to avoid having to go to Vietnam. By those means, such prominent American politicians of the 1990s as President Bill Clinton, Vice-President Dan Quayle, and Senator Phil Gramm never served in the war. Those who did serve, however, frequently came home with serious physical or mental problems, made worse by the fact that the war's unpopularity transferred to them personally and made them literally unwelcome in their own country.

Although more than 58,000 Americans died in the war, and some 300,000 were wounded (including 10,000 who became paraplegics), a longer-term problem has been the damage caused to many returning veterans by Agent Orange, a chemical defoliant that was used from 1962 on to kill jungle plants and expose enemy positions. During the war, some 12 million gallons of Agent Orange defoliated much of the South Vietnamese countryside, often in areas close to American combat units.

At the time, no one thought Agent Orange was in any way dangerous to humans, but by 1979, the Veterans Administration (VA) had had requests for medical attention from hundreds of veterans complaining of various problems ranging from cancer to birth defects in their children to lesser kinds of aches and pains. All had one thing in common: they had been exposed during the war to Agent Orange. At first, the VA would treat only cases of chloracne, a skin rash associated with exposure to chlorinated compounds like Agent Orange. If a veteran had any other medical problem in conjunction with chloracne, he could be treated; if there was no chloracne present, then the VA concluded that Agent Orange was not the culprit.

Later experiments proved that a chemical called dioxin was also a dangerous constituent of Agent Orange. The VA responded that it could treat Agent Orange victims only if it could be proven that the government knew that the dioxin in Agent Orange caused certain symptoms, knowledge that was available only through extensive research that had never been done at the time Agent Orange was developed as a defoliant.

In 1979, the public knew very little about Agent Orange, although there had been a Chicago-produced documentary film in 1977, *Agent Orange—Vietnam's Deadly Fog,* and Dr. Barry Commoner, an environmental activist, had declared that Agent Orange contained chemicals that might be stored in the body and cause illness years later. The VA said it would look into the question but generally relied on "experts" who worked for the military or the chemical companies that made Agent Orange.

Late that year, a class action lawsuit was brought against five chemical manufacturers of Agent Orange, including Dow Chemical, an industry leader. The government, immune to suits, continued to deny culpability, although in 1980, Ronald Reagan campaigned for treatment of Agent Orange victims. Once in office, however, Reagan was apprised of the potential cost of treating thousands of victims, and his campaign promise was quietly forgotten. When the issue was raised, the administration criticized the media for exaggerating the problem and attacked veterans for attempting to profit during economic bad times. Sympathizers in Congress tried to pass a bill compensating Agent Orange victims, but it failed in the face of VA claims that there was no absolute proof that the defoliant was the cause of the problem. Meanwhile, the class action suit against the chemical companies was settled out of court in 1984 for $180 million. Later in the 1980s, further studies were conducted that showed, for example, that Vietnam veterans were dying at a rate 45 percent higher than those who served in the military at the same time but did not go to Vietnam. The VA itself ran a study that revealed that marine ground troops (the individuals most likely to have been exposed to Agent Orange) had a much higher incidence of lung and lymphatic cancer and even admitted that Agent Orange "may be suspected." But in general, the VA continued to downplay the significance of the problem.

Another problem concerning veterans related to their psychological adjustment upon returning to the United States. This, of course, is not a problem confined to the Vietnam War, but rather one that has affected veterans coming home from every war. In World War I, the term "shell-shocked" was used to describe soldiers who became psychologically disturbed during the war; and at the end of World War II, there were widespread fears that the intensity of combat would turn soldiers into maniacal rapists and murderers when they returned. With Vietnam, however, the situation seemed different; there were an unusually high number of returning veterans with psychological adjustment problems. Some have suggested that the difference is that after World Wars I and II, soldiers returned home to an appreciative civilian population, while after Vietnam, they returned home to a public that had grown bitter and cynical about the war and transferred that bitterness to the veterans, letting them know in various ways that they were not heroes and their efforts in Southeast Asia were not appreciated. With the revelation of wartime atrocities such as My Lai (1968), moreover, the antiwar movement attacked returning veterans as "babykillers" or worse.

Some of the signs of psychological breakdown among troops were evident even before they came home. After the beginning of Vietnamization in 1969, American troops became increasingly frustrated and saw their main goal as survival; human rights atrocities rose significantly, and a popular T-shirt among American soldiers read, "KILL THEM ALL! LET GOD SORT THEM OUT!" Instances of violence by enlisted men against their own officers and noncommissioned officers, including "fragging" or assassination, became more common, and drug use among troops was widespread. The number of army desertions increased substantially; by the war's end, nearly half a million Americans who served in Vietnam had received less-than-honorable discharges. In 1971, John Kerry, a Vietnam veteran and later a U.S. senator from Massachusetts, testified before Congress that, from his seasoned jungle perspective, the war was "the height of criminal hypocrisy." Clearly, many other soldiers shared his opinion about the war.

Thus, bitter, frustrated soldiers, many with a drug dependency, came home to an American public that was at best indifferent; at worst, overtly hostile. It should not be surprising that many developed a condition termed "postwar trauma," characterized by feelings of deep depression often alternating with uncontrollable rage, intolerable flashbacks, or severe insomnia. Psychiatrists renamed the condition "post-traumatic stress disorder" and likened it to similar feelings experienced by people who had survived an earthquake or other natural disaster. The VA estimated that as many as 700,000 veterans (one-third of the total number who served in Vietnam) suffered some degree of post-traumatic stress disorder; nearly all had either served in combat or had participated in or witnessed wartime atrocities against civilians or enemy troops. What this has meant for many of these veterans is the inability to hold a job, alienation from family and friends, homelessness, and in many cases, suicide. Marilyn B. Young, in *The Vietnam Wars, 1945–1990* (1991), notes that more Vietnam veterans have committed suicide since the war than died in it.

A final legacy of the war related to veterans is the long-standing prisoner of war-missing in action (POW-MIA) controversy. Although North Vietnam returned about eight hundred POWs in compliance with the terms of the 1973 Paris Peace Agreement, a number of veterans' groups (and some politicians) maintained that there were still hundreds, if not thousands, of Americans in North Vietnamese prison camps and that it was the obligation of the federal government to obtain the release of these men, or if they were dead, to bring home their bodies. This emotionally-charged issue proved politically popular and blocked serious negotiations concerning the normalization of relations with Vietnam for many years. Occasionally, a few bodies would be returned, but numerous "fact-finding" trips to Vietnam have not turned up the anticipated large numbers of missing Americans. Indeed, the percentage of Americans unaccounted for in the Vietnam War is considerably less than that for either World War II or the Korean War.

The war in Vietnam lingers on as historians and military experts try to analyze what happened and why. Gradually, after the end of the American involvement in Vietnam, three schools of thought evolved, ably articulated by George C. Herring in an article, "American Strategy in Vietnam: the Postwar Debate," published in *Military Affairs* (April 1982). Herring describes the "hawks" as those individuals, many of them military officers, who believed that U.S. forces could have won the war had they been allowed to win the war. Their view is that politicians in Washington, fearful of widening the war and involving the People's Republic of China or the Soviet Union, placed restrictions on what the military could do, and in so doing, they prevented the victory that everyone sought.

Another school of thought, which Herring describes as the "counterinsurgency school," puts the blame on the military for not utilizing the right strategy and tactics. For example, the military placed too much reliance on the effectiveness of the air war, which could not and did not stop the North Vietnamese and, indeed, probably gave them a psychological boost. The ground strategy of "search and destroy," designed to bring about a victory through attrition by killing as many of the enemy as possible, failed because no one understood that North Vietnam could replace their fallen troops just as fast as they fell. As a result, search and destroy ruined the countryside, created a huge refugee problem, and cost a great deal of money, all for no lasting results.

A third school of thought, which Herring calls the "impossible war," argues that the United States failed in Vietnam because there was no way not to fail. The United States did not have enough of a stake in the war to warrant widening it to the degree necessary to achieve a military victory, given the risks involved in widening the conflict. And even if the United States had been able to win a military victory, it almost certainly would have been a Pyrrhic one, since South Vietnam did not have the history, traditions, or the governmental institutions to survive as an independent nation without the constant supervision of the United States. Vietnam was simply not susceptible to our will.

Another way to look at the war is to consider it in terms of the Just War theory of St. Augustine, presented in his fifth-century magnum opus, *The City of God.* While our two-party system will continue to vacillate on foreign policy, overall, Vietnam has helped emblazon the essence of St. Augustine's principles in the American mindset. Augustine argues that, in order to engage in any war, one should have a just cause, one's intentions should be just, and troops should be dispatched only as a last resort. When all diplomatic attempts to obtain peace have failed, then one should designate only the proportionate means to secure peace. These resources should be committed to limited objectives, and one should make every effort to avoid killing noncombatants.

Was the Vietnam conflict a just cause, a crisis worthy of outside intervention for resolution? True, peace in Vietnam appeared unattainable without U.S. intervention, and the perils of Communist rule were undesirable. By the 1970s, however, any consensus on how to achieve peace had long since disappeared, and the "doves" and the "hawks" had opposing views for achieving it. The administration's concerns of the early 1960s had come under serious attack. Distance had clouded interpretation, and many highly critical books and movies further confused the issue.

The Just War question was indelibly linked to the Domino Theory, the rationale of which was not as far-fetched as some liberal scholars argue. As mentioned above, many who later became critics had initially supported the war. Given the realistic fears of the early Cold War years, the intentions of the Soviet Union and the People's Republic of China loomed large in the minds of policymakers and much of the American public. The imposing threat of China's Mao Zedong, allied with Ho Chi

Minh, was serious. In light of the waves of Chinese troops Mao had thrown at American forces in Korea in 1950 and 1951, President Johnson and the South Vietnamese seemed to have been justified in proactive policies. Furthermore, most U.S. government analysts contend that Moscow expended $5 billion in Vietnam during the war, which was 65 percent of the total aid received by North Vietnam between 1965 and 1975. In 1968 alone, the USSR's contributions to North Vietnam exceeded its total support to the Communist side throughout the entire Korean War. Although this amount was a mere pittance compared with what the United States spent in Vietnam, it may help answer the question: Was U.S. intervention the "last resort," and if so, "against what?"

Probably the most sensitive issue with regard to the war was that of direct American involvement—the sending of troops. Was the deployment of troops to Vietnam our last resort in securing peace? In 1954, President Dwight D. Eisenhower had warned that a unilateral U.S. military presence in Asia would provoke charges of imperialism, or, at best, paternalism. McNamara, in *In Retrospect,* admits that the Johnson administration "did not hold to the principle that U.S. military action— other than in response to direct threats to our own security—should be carried out only in conjunction with multinational forces supported fully (and not merely cosmetically) by the international community." Furthermore, the administration "failed to recognize the limitations of modern, high-technology military equipment, forces, and doctrine in confronting unconventional, highly motivated people's movements" (pp. 322–23).

Military intervention had been carried out, in part, on the assumption that Southeast Asians could not successfully resist Communist-backed advances. History proves this erroneous. The Communists were not unified in their ideology and frequently quarreled among themselves. Until President Nixon's recognition (and exploitation) of the widening Sino-Soviet split, Washington had operated under the premise that communism was a monolithic force. By 1969, the rift between China and the USSR was pronounced (reflected by military clashes at their mutual border) and this prompted Nixon's 1972 visit to China. By this time, the theory of monolithic communism was dead. After the United States began air raids against North Vietnam in 1965, the Soviets and Chinese showered Hanoi with competitive bids for influence over North Vietnam's leadership. The North Vietnamese, however, wanted independence more than communism or democracy. Their frustration with French and then American "colonialism" took an ironic turn after 1975.

In time, the Vietnamese would perceive the Soviets and the Chinese as the last colonial powers in Southeast Asia and would themselves act for a while as an imperial power in Cambodia.

American policymakers simply could not conceive of any Third World country, especially one allied to the Soviet Union or China, staving off their imperialistic designs. They were all too familiar with the picture of Mao Zedong standing alongside Nikita Khrushchev in Red Square in 1957 at the fortieth anniversary of the Bolshevik Revolution. The nationalist spirit, however, was what drove these newly independent countries. Their struggles were for independence, economic development, and regional security in Southeast Asia. What had begun in 1967 as a loose association among Singapore, Indonesia, Malaysia, Thailand, and the Philippines has become one of the most successful regional groupings in the Third World—the Association of Southeast Asian Nations (ASEAN)—and all without any significant assistance from the United States.

Did the United States designate proportionate means and pursue limited objectives in Vietnam? Considering that McNamara himself thinks not, the answer is a resounding negative. For example, the entire air war, designed to bring Hanoi to its knees pleading for negotiations, produced the opposite effects. As late as 1972, when American involvement was nearly over, President Nixon unleashed a massive bombing campaign to teach his adversaries a lesson. Not unlike the Nazi bombing of Britain, Nixon attempted to break the will of North Vietnam through mass destruction. He promised that "the bastards [who had just launched successful offensives throughout Cambodia and South Vietnam] have never been bombed like they are going to be bombed this time" (quoted in Olson and Roberts 1991, 248).

The carpet bombing, wartime atrocities, and growing disillusionment among American troops helped sour the American perception of war itself. Augustine's charge not to kill civilians was grossly violated. As the twentieth century closes, Americans are rejecting this type of behavior, choosing to adopt, though largely unknowingly, tenets of the Just War theory. The United States, it might be argued, will never again allow its forces to be party to rapacious and unconscionable acts. During the Persian Gulf War, acted out before the international media, the Bush administration painstakingly detailed its attempts to strike only military targets and confine its military activity to carefully defined and limited goals.

Perhaps it was the dedication of the Vietnam War Memorial in Washington in 1982 that marked a turning point in American attitudes toward the war. While President Ronald Reagan trumpeted his belief that the war had been a "noble cause," validating the traditional American commitment to freedom and democracy, others launched initiatives to help rectify the wrongs dealt veterans. Through aggressive bargaining, the political commitment to honor the families of prisoners of war became more public and gained support within the Reagan and Bush administrations. Popular culture lent its support through a number of Rambotype movies, and the harsh criticism of the war and those who made it seemed to soften.

Robert McNamara ends his book with the following tribute:

> In the end, we must confront the fate of those Americans who served in Vietnam and never returned. Does the unwisdom of our intervention nullify their effort and their loss? I think not. They did not make the decisions. They answered their nation's call to service. They went in harm's way on its behalf. And they gave their lives for their country and its ideals. That our effort in Vietnam proved unwise does not make their sacrifice less noble. It endures for all to see. Let us learn from their sacrifice and, by doing so, validate and honor it. (pp. 334–35)

Their sacrifice was noble. The United States has learned. Although the U.S. military budget equals that of the rest of the world, it will not likely be used for conventional war in the near future. And any deployment of troops will be well calculated, carefully justified, and done with popular support. The era of the Great Power rivalry is gone for now, and smaller conflicts are being treated with more caution and with greater interest. The war in Vietnam helped bring the United States to this point.

SELECTED BIBLIOGRAPHY

Berman, Larry. *Lyndon Johnson's War: The Road to Stalemate in Vietnam.* New York: W.W. Norton, 1989. A good account of the Johnson administration's escalation of the war.

Clodfelter, Mark. *The Limits of Air Power: The American Bombing of North Vietnam.* New York: Free Press, 1989. A critical account of the air war in Vietnam.

Cooper, Chester. *The Lost Crusade: America in Vietnam.* New York: Dodd, Mead, 1970. An insider's account of the war from the 1954 Geneva Conference until 1970.

Halberstam, David. *The Best and the Brightest.* New York: Random House, 1972.

A well-written examination of policy development with respect to Vietnam during the Kennedy and Johnson years, with emphasis on the individuals who made the policy.

Herring, George C. *America's Longest War: The United States and Vietnam, 1950–1975.* New York: Alfred A. Knopf, 1979. Probably the best general treatment of the long American involvement in Vietnam.

———. *LBJ and Vietnam: A Different Kind of War.* Austin: University of Texas Press, 1994. A study of policymaking within the Johnson administration.

Hersh, Seymour M. *The Price of Power: Kissinger in the Nixon White House.* New York: Summit, 1983. A very critical analysis of Nixon-Kissinger foreign policy, including that pertaining to Vietnam.

Hilsman, Roger. *To Move a Nation: The Politics of Foreign Policy in the Administration of John F. Kennedy.* Garden City, NY: Doubleday, 1967. A detailed account reflecting Hilsman's perspective as a State Department officer during the Kennedy years.

Hoopes, Townsend. *The Limits of Intervention: An Inside Account of How the Johnson Policy of Escalation in Vietnam Was Reversed.* New York: McKay, 1969. Details the growing doubts within the Johnson administration about its war policy.

Karnow, Stanley. *Vietnam: A History.* 2d ed. New York: Viking, 1991. A general and anecdotal account of the war that formed the basis for an excellent television documentary.

Kearns, Doris. *Lyndon Johnson and the American Dream.* New York: Signet, 1976. An insightful analysis of the president who brought the United States all the way into the war, by a historian who was very close to him.

Kissinger, Henry. *White House Years.* Boston: Little, Brown, 1979. Kissinger's memoirs provide insight into Nixon era foreign policy and the author's secret negotiations with Le Duc Tho.

Lewy, Guenter. *American in Vietnam.* New York: Oxford University Press, 1978. Lewy emphasizes the military history of the war, casting the role of U.S. forces in a favorable light.

McNamara, Robert S. *In Retrospect: The Tragedy and Lessons of Vietnam.* New York: Random House, 1995. The belated admission that the war was a mistake, by the secretary of defense under Kennedy and Johnson.

Oberdorfer, Don. *Tet!: The Turning Point in the Vietnam War.* Garden City, NY: Doubleday, 1971. The best account of the event that was, as the title suggests, the turning point of the entire war.

Olson, James S., and Randy Roberts. *Where the Domino Fell: America and Vietnam, 1945 to 1990.* New York: St. Martin's Press, 1991. General treatment of the war with a good chapter on its influence on popular culture.

The Pentagon Papers: The Defense Department History of United States Decisionmaking on Vietnam. The Senator [Mike] Gravel Edition. 4 vols. Boston: Beacon Press, 1971. Generally considered to be the most detailed of the several editions of these documents.

Pike, Douglas. *Vietnam and the Soviet Union: Anatomy of an Alliance.* London: Westview Press, 1987. A study of the role of Soviet foreign policy toward North Vietnam.

Porter, Gareth. *A Peace Denied: The United States, Vietnam, and the Paris Agreements.* Bloomington: Indiana University Press, 1975. A detailed account of the 1973 Paris Peace Agreement and its aftermath.

Rostow, W. W. *The Diffusion of Power: An Essay in Recent History.* New York: Macmillan, 1972. Rostow was Kennedy's national security adviser and a stalwart defender of U.S. policy in Vietnam.

Shawcross, William. *Sideshow: Kissinger, Nixon, and the Destruction of Cambodia.* New York: Simon and Schuster, 1979. A critical account of how U.S. policy led to civil war and genocide in Cambodia.

Sheehan, Neil. *A Bright Shining Lie: John Paul Vann and America in Vietnam.* New York: Random House, 1988. A long, detailed, and highly critical account of the war.

Snepp, Frank. *Decent Interval: An Insider's Account of Saigon's Indecent End.* New York: Random House, 1977. The best account of the last two years of the Vietnam War; highly critical of U.S. Ambassador Graham Martin.

Young, Marilyn B. *The Vietnam Wars, 1945–1990.* New York: HarperCollins, 1991. Another good survey of the whole U.S. experience in Vietnam.

President Ronald Reagan, shown here at a press conference, was known as the "Great Communicator" for his relaxed and articulate manner of public speaking. (Reproduced from the Collections of the Library of Congress)

10

The Reagan Revolution, 1981–1989

INTRODUCTION

The term "Reagan Revolution" does not refer to a revolution in the commonly accepted sense of the word, in which a government is overthrown, usually by military force, and replaced with a new and quite different government. Rather, the Reagan Revolution reflects the perception that the presidency of Ronald Reagan (1981–1989) represented a significant change in the philosophy that governed federal policymaking and in the style of the presidency itself.

By the time of the election of 1980, Democrat Jimmy Carter's administration had accumulated a vast array of political problems, both domestic and foreign. The domestic economy was in shambles, plagued by an inflation rate exceeding 10 percent, an unemployment rate approaching 7 percent, federal budget deficits soaring past $40 billion annually, and worsening trade deficits. Moreover, the Carter administration appeared to have no coherent plan to restore health to the economy, and a petulant President Carter blamed the problems on a "national malaise" that had somehow struck the population.

If Carter's domestic problems were daunting, his foreign problems were, in a word, insoluble. In 1980, the administration had to cope with both the Iranian hostage crisis, in which Iranian militants held captive some fifty-three American citizens who had been seized at the U.S. embassy, and the Soviet invasion of Afghanistan, an apparent act of aggression that reminded Americans of the tension-filled years of the early Cold War. Although the Carter administration tried to rescue the hostages by means of a military mission and tried to pressure the Soviet Union with a cessation of grain sales and a boycott of the 1980 Moscow Olympics, its efforts proved futile; and the president launched his reelection campaign with many blots on his record.

In 1980, Ronald Reagan easily captured the Republican nomination for president. The affable and articulate former actor, known as the "Gipper" from one of his film roles, had nearly won the nomination in 1976 and had kept his name in the news by leading an unsuccessful campaign against the ratification of the Panama Canal Treaties (1977). An independent candidate, John Anderson, a congressman from Illinois, also ran, hoping to attract the votes of those who disliked both Carter and Reagan.

The Republicans criticized Carter's record as president and offered, through Reagan, a vision of a strong and proud America under his leadership. Although the Democrats tried to persuade voters that Reagan was a militaristic individual who would lead America into war, voters liked his comfortable style and pleasant homilies and elected him by a margin of 51 percent to 41 percent for Carter, with 7 percent going to Anderson.

After Reagan's inauguration in January 1981, his administration began to reshape the country's domestic and foreign policy agendas. The president's plan for dealing with the multiplicity of economic problems inherited from Carter was based on the theory of "supply-side" economics developed by Arthur Laffer, a California economist. The basis of this theory, which the media dubbed "Reaganomics," was that current tax rates were so high that investments, savings, and even work were discouraged, which reduced the supply of goods and brought about inflation, or an unhealthy rise in prices. To deal with this problem, the government had to make major reductions in the tax rates, so that people would have more incentive to invest, save, and work harder. Thus, the supply of goods would increase, prices would level off, and the rate of inflation would fall. More people would be working and paying taxes, and this would offset the loss of tax revenue occasioned by reducing the tax rates. In addition, Laffer's theory called for reductions in government spending and tight control over the money supply, which would reduce federal deficits and help lower the rate of inflation.

After a sharp partisan debate, Congress passed a tax cut, lowering income taxes by 25 percent over three years. Although Republicans had captured control of the Senate in the 1980 election, it was significant that a sizable number of conservative Democrats voted with the Republican minority in the House of Representatives to pass the act.

In practice, Reaganomics had mixed results for the American economy. The administration's policies helped lower the inflation rate to between 4 and 5 percent and brought about a general economic recovery, with most sectors reporting increased production and sales. However, the unemployment rate rose to nearly 11 percent before slowly returning to the 6 to 7 percent level; and, because of that, as well as increased defense spending, federal deficits climbed to new record highs.

With regard to social issues, the Reagan administration offered rhetorical support to organizations seeking to restrict the availability of abortions, eliminate school busing for racial balance, and defeat the Equal Rights Amendment (ERA). In addition, the administration did little to promote civil rights enforcement or environmental protection regulations. During his administration, the president had the opportunity to appoint three new justices to the Supreme Court; each of them, Sandra Day O'Connor, Antonin Scalia, and Anthony M. Kennedy, brought solid conservative credentials to the bench. The president also promoted conservative associate justice William Rehnquist to the post of chief justice in 1986, following the retirement of Warren E. Burger.

During the 1980 campaign, Reagan had sharply criticized Carter's weak and bumbling foreign policy and promised to repair America's damaged reputation as a global leader. Although the Iranian hostages had been released at the time of Reagan's inauguration, the Soviet invasion of Afghanistan continued, and the president, whose strong anti-Communist views dated back to the late 1940s, adopted a strident anti-Soviet foreign policy in which he characterized Moscow as an "evil empire."

The administration first attacked communism in Central America where, because of its proximity to the United States, Soviet response would necessarily be limited. In Nicaragua, a leftist movement, the Sandinistas, had toppled the brutal but anti-Communist Somoza dictatorship in 1979 and had established close ties with the Soviet Union and Cuba. In nearby El Salvador, a Communist insurgency was threatening the stability of the anti-Communist central government, and the Reagan administration claimed that the insurgents were receiving arms from the Sandinistas. Ostensibly to interrupt this arms traffic, the administration authorized the Central Intelligence Agency (CIA) to organize and train

an army of former Somoza supporters and other opponents of the Sandinista regime. This army, which became known as the "Contras,"
trained and operated out of bases along the border between Honduras
and Nicaragua and gradually grew to some 12,000 troops. Congress supported the Contras with periodic appropriations until 1985, although
there was considerable concern that the real objective of the rebel army
was to overthrow the Sandinista government, something Congress forbade in a measure called the Boland amendment. In El Salvador, U.S.
military and economic aid and some fifty-five military advisors helped
the government keep the insurgency at bay; here the concern was over
the blatant disregard for human rights on the part of a paramilitary organization with ties to the Salvadoran army. U.S. protests had only minimal effect in reducing the number of killings attributed to the "death
squads," as they were called.

   In the Middle East, the administration confronted dangerous situations
in both the Persian Gulf area, where Iran and Iraq were engaged in a
bloody war, and in the eastern Mediterranean area, where chronic hostility between Israel and its Arab neighbors constantly threatened war.
In June 1982, an Israeli invasion into southern Lebanon, culminating in
the expulsion of a large number of Palestinians to Tunisia, escalated tensions and brought to Lebanon a United Nations peacekeeping team that
included a contingent of U.S. marines. While efforts to bring about a
political settlement in Lebanon were unsuccessful, the marines were increasingly harrassed by Muslim extremists, who felt that the American
troops were allied with their Christian adversaries. This harrassment
reached a tragic climax in October 1983 when a suicide truck-bomber
drove into the marine barracks at the Beirut airport; the explosion de-
molished the building and killed 241 American troops. Within a few
months, the remainder of the troops were withdrawn.

   Meanwhile, in the mid-1980s, clandestine efforts were undertaken to
sell arms to the Iranians, who were still locked in a war with Iraq (whom
the United States had also aided). There were perhaps three objectives
at work here: to maintain a relative balance in the Iran-Iraq war so neither side could score a decisive victory; to bring about the release of
several hostages being held in Lebanon and thought to be subject to
Iranian control; and to make contact with Iranian moderates, who might
some day attain political power. Congress, however, had forbidden arms
sales to Iran in the wake of the hostage crisis and, in 1985, had cut off
aid to the Nicaraguan Contras.

   Out of this set of circumstances developed the Iran-Contra scandal.

Inspired by an Israeli suggestion that arms sales to Iran would be useful, this deal was perpetrated by the National Security Council (NSC) under Robert McFarlane and John Poindexter, with the active assistance of Colonel Oliver North, a particular friend of the Contras. Between January and October 1986, a number of arms sales were made to Iran, generating substantial profits, which were diverted to the Contras. Although exact figures are unknown, it is estimated that between $10 million and $30 million went to Central America as a result of arms sales to Iran. The scandal broke in November 1986 in an obscure Lebanese newspaper and quickly became a major problem for the Reagan administration. A congressional investigation, headed by Republican senator John Tower of Texas, looked into the affair, as did a team led by special prosecutor Lawrence Walsh. Eventually, Poindexter, North, and two arms dealers were convicted on charges of perjury and obstruction of justice but saw their convictions overturned on appeal. In 1992, former defense secretary Caspar Weinberger was indicted on perjury charges but was pardoned by President George Bush before his trial. As for President Reagan, no credible evidence linked him directly to the Iran-Contra scandal, but the special prosecutor's final report concluded that, in a broad way, the president had "set the stage" for the activities of those implicated in the scandal.

The Reagan administration had entered office in 1981 on a wave of anti-Communist rhetoric; it left office in 1989 with U.S.-Soviet relations at their closest since World War II. The adaptation of the Reagan administration to sea changes in the Soviet Union during the 1980s represents almost a revolution within the Reagan revolution.

During the first Reagan administration, Soviet leadership was in constant turmoil: Leonid Brezhnev died in 1982; then Yuri Andropov and Konstantin Chernenko, Brezhnev's successors, each died after only a year or so in power. During this time, the Reagan administration continued to characterize Moscow as a threat to world peace, to build up America's defense establishment, and to install more nuclear weapons in Europe. In 1983, Reagan introduced a space-based defensive system, the Strategic Defensive Initiative (SDI), in which powerful laser beams would shoot down enemy missiles heading for North America. Although "Star Wars," as SDI became popularly known, was enormously expensive and thought to be little more than science fiction fantasy by many physicists, the administration pursued it with great enthusiasm for several years as a defense against a perceived Soviet threat.

In early 1985, Mikhail Gorbachev emerged as the new Soviet premier.

Much younger and more energetic than his septuagenarian predecessors, Gorbachev sensed that radical changes were necessary to salvage the crippled economy of the Soviet Union; one of these changes was the improvement of relations with the United States. Perhaps stung by Democratic charges in the 1984 campaign that he was the first president since Calvin Coolidge not to have met with a Soviet leader, Reagan was receptive to Gorbachev's approaches, and the two met in summit conferences on five occasions between November 1985 and December 1988. Out of these summits came a renewal of arms reduction negotiations, which bore fruit in 1987 with the signing of the Intermediate Nuclear Force (INF) treaty.

The INF treaty broke new ground in arms negotiations in several ways. First, it brought about an actual reduction in the number of nuclear weapons maintained by each side by mandating the destruction of all intermediate-range (300 to 3000 miles) missiles placed by each superpower in Europe. Second, it marked the first time the principle of asymetrical arms reduction had worked, because in order to achieve the goals of the treaty, the Soviets had to destroy four times as many missiles as the United States. Finally, the INF treaty included the most intrusive verification procedures ever agreed upon, with teams of inspectors from each nation allowed to watch the destruction of the other's missiles. In addition to the INF treaty, some progress was made on the reduction of long-range missiles and on the number of conventional forces in Europe. Finally, the improved climate between the United States and the Soviet Union was partially responsible for an agreement bringing about the gradual withdrawal of Soviet troops from Afghanistan. By the end of Reagan's second term, some people, including British prime minister Margaret Thatcher, had declared that the Cold War was over.

In November 1988, the Reagan Revolution was passed on to George Bush, Reagan's vice president, who won an easy election victory over the hapless Democratic candidate, Governor Michael Dukakis of Massachusetts. Although Bush generally carried on Reagan's economic policies, except for a tax increase in 1990, and oversaw the breakup of the Soviet Union into its constituent republics, marking the real end of the Cold War, he did not have the charisma that carried Reagan to such heights of popularity. As a consequence, Bush failed in his bid for reelection in 1992, losing to Bill Clinton, the governor of Arkansas. After twelve years, the Reagan Revolution was over.

INTERPRETIVE ESSAY
John Robson

While in office, Ronald Reagan towered over the political landscape the way Franklin Roosevelt had two generations earlier. It seemed that his legacy would be a reorientation of American policy and political life comparable to that of FDR, though in the opposite direction. Politically, he was unbeatable; in a telling "Bloom County" cartoon from 1984, a Mondale/Ferraro delegate wandered into the Meadow Party convention, found that its candidate against Reagan was a dead cat, and decided that this offered a better chance of unseating the Gipper than the Democratic ticket. And indeed it did.

Yet within five years of his departure from the presidency, it was already difficult to recall that Reagan had been president, let alone why. His political coalition, such as it was, had shattered; and if the core "conservative" position is a strong national defense, free market economics, and traditional social values, then his policy achievements were both limited and transient. Reagan talked like a conservative, governed like a neoconservative, and left the liberal movement in America as strong as, or stronger than, when he challenged its dominance in 1980. When the charismatic former actor left the White House, Americans began to question the damage done to their country.

This outcome had two main causes, one political and the other intellectual. In political terms, it simply turned out that the social-service needs of the economy demanded fairly high taxation. In intellectual terms, Reagan's own inconsistencies were dreadfully amplified by his aides. In fact, Reagan was, in large measure, a neoconservative himself—like so many of them he had been a liberal Democrat in his youth—and he was surrounded by neoconservatives who sought to use his charisma, the popular appeal of authentic conservatism, and the undoubted tactical effectiveness of conservative policies to advance what were essentially liberal goals.

The political dimension is ominous enough to warrant some discussion. But in the end, as John Maynard Keynes had said, in other circumstances, it is ideas that matter; and the core of the Reagan failure was that the president was neither clear enough himself on what he was fundamentally trying to do, nor could he find enough talented advisers who held truly conservative ideas, to prevent administration initiatives from being sidetracked into essentially harmful policies. The aides bear much of the blame, as do Republican politicians who were actually what Harry Truman had said they were long ago: "me too" Democrats with a "yes but" platform.

But Ronald Reagan himself was the man in charge, and, in the end, blame for his policy failures must lie, in large part, with him. Maybe reversing the trend toward bigger government could not have been done, and he did make a valiant effort. But he could have done more, better, on more crucial issues. The most important distinction he failed to draw was between those who thought big government was doing the wrong things and those who thought big government was inherently bad. Reagan said that government, far from being the solution to Americans' problems, actually was the problem. If that is true, then Reagan too, far from being the solution to Americans' problems, actually was the problem.

The ongoing influence of the New Deal on American politics can be dealt with briefly in print, but could not be dealt with at all in politics under Reagan. Between the inauguration of FDR and 1995, the Democratic party controlled the U.S. House of Representatives for all but four years (1947–1949 and 1953–1955) and the Senate for all but ten (those four plus 1981–1987). The problem is a classic public choice trap: while it is in principle desirable to cut back on the growth of Leviathan, it remains true that if one elects a representative or senator who refrains from the politics of plunder, the rest of them keep one's taxes high and hand over the loot to their constituents. The worst example of this, or at least the most brazen, occurred when William F. Buckley, Jr.'s brother, James Buckley, was a senator from New York for one term in the 1970s. When a "Christmas tree" bill came to the floor with fifty clauses, each providing benefits for a particular state, Buckley proposed fifty amendments, each one to strike one of the clauses. The Senate voted down forty-nine of them, but passed that for Buckley's home state of New York. *The New York Times* rewarded Buckley's interesting manipulation of the political system with a headline "Isn't It Time We Got Ourselves a Real Senator?"

The problem is not that the *Times* was being irrational, but that it was being rational.

In a politicized economy where one's wealth depends on one's skill at political plunder rather than one's usefulness to one's fellow citizens, it makes sense to behave in this way. To accomplish this, American government since the New Deal has had to sweep aside many constitutional restrictions on government (especially the Fifth and Fourteenth Amendment protection of property); and as Rexford Guy Tugwell admitted many years later, it did so deliberately. Again, the result is a "public choice" trap in which behavior that is bad for the community is good for the individual.

This is not, in its essence, the fault of Ronald Reagan. The American people preferred to think that the cost of government was largely due to other peoples' benefits, not their own, when the reverse is true: middle-class entitlements are the core of the problem.

Moreover, to be fair, the political risks in attacking the system were enormous, as the Reagan administration discovered when they made an infamous budget deal in 1982 that enabled the Democrats to castigate them in the 1982 midterm elections for attacking the elderly, which resulted in the Republicans losing several Senate seats. After this debacle, the Reaganites accepted that the basic structure of American politics involved bribing citizens with their own money, and then taking the bribe, because the only alternative was to have other people's politicians bribe them with their own money. The last serious attempt to break this cycle came in 1982, when the president asked for a balanced budget amendment from Congress; the Republican Senate gave it to him, but the Democratic speaker of the House, Thomas P. (Tip) O'Neill, used his procedural mastery to keep it from coming to a vote.

Thus, the first obstacle to meaningful reform under Reagan was the"public choice" trap of the modern welfare state, in which the entire wealth of the nation is expected to succor the poor and disadvantaged. But the Reagan Revolution was fatally undercut intellectually as well by the presence of so many neoconservatives within the inner circle. These people truly believed in the power of government to improve people's lives, provided it were done sensibly; and they liked nothing better than to assure welfare activists that they shared their goals but questioned their means. Ronald Reagan could not find enough political allies or policymakers with the beliefs of a Calvin Coolidge or a Barry Goldwater to make a significant challenge, operationally or rhetorically, to the idea that government is a powerful force for good in a society beyond the traditional function of protecting the lives and liberties of citizens. So Americans got neoconservatives like Jack Kemp instead, and then George Bush, both of whom sought to use big government to "empower" people (a term which implies passive receipt of benefits from government even on the part of the person acquiring power), instead of a John Calhoun, who would have had people reacquire the power that is legitimately theirs by restricting government to its proper functions of protecting the lives, liberties, and property of citizens.

Admittedly this was not all the president's fault; politicians generally get more credit than they deserve for good things, at the cost of getting more blame than they deserve for bad ones. On economic as on other issues, Ronald Reagan was often deserted by "moderate" Republicans, who, in the words of generally hard-line conservative Strom Thurmond, "headed for the tall grass" on too many key issues. The political realities were unfavorable.

But Reagan lacked the stamina, apparently, to stay the course on this as on many other issues; and the fact is that his administration did not submit balanced budgets to Congress, presumably on "pragmatic" grounds, although the Reagan budgets were pronounced "dead on arrival" by Capitol Hill Democrats anyway, so the practical gains were nonexistent. When politicians talk of balanced budgets but write ones with huge deficits, it is an inescapable conclusion that they are deceiving themselves, the voters, or both about their real, gut-level philosophy. It will not do for a president to ask for a balanced budget amendment to the Constitution if he not only fails to veto the big-spending bills that Congress sends for his signature, but also cannot write his own balanced budgets because in fact he believes in the various programs on which such huge amounts are spent. Reagan himself claimed that the problem was that he did not possess a line-item veto, enabling him to reject specific spending items. But President Franklin Pierce once vetoed a bill establishing an asylum for the indigent insane on the grounds that, if Congress could do that, it could establish one for the nonindigent also, and the Constitution forbade such actions. Ronald Reagan never tried to do anything similar; but since he was denied a line-item veto, why did he not veto the entire bill and explain which clauses must be removed to secure his signature?

So on economic issues Reagan was paralyzed intellectually as well as politically. And, in the end, the former mattered more. Thus, despite a lot of rhetoric both from the administration and from its critics, domestic spending under Reagan went up; the share of Gross National Product (GNP) taken by the federal government went up; the deficit went up; entitlements expanded. Regulation decreased somewhat; but, for the most part, the growth of the welfare state proceeded as though Jimmy Carter were still in office. And on a more minor but important issue, when Reagan came into office, one-eighth of U.S. imports were subject to restraints, often with the insincere label "voluntary"; by the time he left, the figure was more like one-fourth. Readers may be surprised to hear this with respect to economic and social policy, because commentators generally described and condemned the wholesale dismantling of the welfare state under Reagan even though this was not happening; a typical cartoon showed George Bush saying "Read my lips" and a kid replying "I can't, you guys cut funding for education"—which is very funny, except that federal education funding went up substantially, not down, under Reagan.

The only bright spots in the economic picture were the reduction in regulations (promptly undone by George Bush) and the fact that Reagan appointed hundreds of lower court judges during his time in office. The last may be the great "sleeper" achievement of the Reagan Revolution: the greater economic sophistication of these new judges and their corresponding tendency to rule in favor of property rights, against the state, and against entitlements, may, over time, produce a subtle but very important reduction in the arbitrary power of government.

But on policy and legislative questions, the Reagan Revolution saw the state intervening ever more deeply into the economy, and the Gipper's rhetoric was not matched by an aggressive and aggressively pushed legislative program. That battle was lost and, in the end, as much by default as anything else.

Both the political and intellectual problems were, if anything, worse regarding social policy. Ever since Daniel Patrick Moynihan got shredded in the 1960s for pointing to the breakdown of the black family as a major cause of social pathology and of black poverty, misery, and despair in America, the topic has been taboo. To be accepted in polite company, it has been important to advocate big government in the economy, but vital to demonstrate one's commitment to the viability of "alternative lifestyles." Reagan himself, admittedly, was a divorcee whose family was not, in the minds of some, strictly wholesome. But the current argument about what constitutes a respectable and viable American family, has meant that no government has tried to muster support for the traditional nuclear family. Actually, to assume that government can restore respect for traditional family values because it has neglected them is contrary to real conservatism; however, Reagan was unable to achieve even the lesser and proper task of getting government to stop destroying the family.

Likewise Reagan professed Christianity and ended his speeches with

"God bless you," but he, and his party, regarded the evangelicals as embarrassing country cousins. And on the key issue of abortion—key not for voters, but for organizers—Reagan could not appoint judges to the Supreme Court who would try to overturn *Roe* v. *Wade* without more effort than he himself was willing to exert. Of course, his liberal critics in the Senate made the universal availability of safe abortion the litmus test for Supreme Court nominees. (It should be observed that Supreme Court appointees often disappoint those who appoint them, particularly if those who appoint them are Republicans; in the classic phrase, they "surprise friend and foe alike" by following their own consciences.)

On the social issues, which do reach the heart of ordinary voters in middle America, Reagan found himself unable to do much because he could not muster support among the intellectual community. His own commitment to the concept of limiting government interference in people's lives was itself suspect; his major domestic crusade, a war on drugs, was a true conservative's nightmare, bolstering the power of the state to meddle in the private lives of citizens in a way that, among other things, pushed violent criminals out of jails and back onto the street. But to the extent that he was sincere, he was virtually alone, even within his party.

This was reflected above all in the 1992 Republican convention, when the "divisive" talk about these matters produced the one surge of popular support for George Bush that occurred in the whole campaign but was promptly condemned by the media and disavowed by Bush and his handlers. Seeking to scoop up left-of-center voters at the expense of their core constituency and the public generally, they proceeded to erect a politically correct big tent that was empty on election day.

In the mid-1990s, the national debate turns on how, not whether, the government should run health care; how, not whether, it should run welfare; and how, not whether, it should intervene in the lives of families. Thus, the social policy battle was lost, and perhaps it could not be otherwise; perhaps Daniel Patrick Moynihan was right in saying that deviant behavior is now so widespread that American society cannot afford to recognize it as deviant. But whether or not this battle could have been won, it was lost, and as much by default as anything else.

The one sphere in which Reagan was, at least superficially, highly successful was with respect to foreign policy. There the Reagan policies had the full and enthusiastic support of neoconservatives, both within the administration and among the American public. They had seen the folly and futility of Vietnam, but they had also seen the folly and futility of Jimmy Carter, whose big smile and pious wishes produced disaster abroad. By 1980 the neoconservatives believed that what had been wrong in Vietnam was not too much force but too little, not too long an involvement but too short; they knew what happened in Cambodia under the Khmer Rouge and how it made a mockery of the peace movement's self-proclaimed moral superiority.

The neoconservatives also believed that the Soviet Union really was what Reagan had called it, an "evil empire." They knew this even though many of them previously had insisted that it was not, that the United States and the USSR were morally equivalent, particularly in foreign policy, and that a more trusting, less militaristic policy toward them would melt Cold War tensions. But they had seen that when Carter had attempted such an approach, the rapprochement that had taken place under Nixon was replaced by ferocious hostility. And so they were convinced that "peace through strength" worked.

Despite much liberal protest, Reagan greatly increased military spending, raising through the Strategic Defense Initiative the specter of a technological race that the decrepit and backward, if heavily armed, USSR could not possibly participate in. And on this issue, Reagan's neoconservative allies stood firm. They knew enough of the history of U.S.-Soviet relations to think that strength and resolve worked, and mush and good intentions did not. And so the USSR pitched forward, stone dead.

It should be mentioned that on one critical issue, the Central American conflict, in which the administration believed that the leftist Sandinista government of Nicaragua was spreading subversion to its neighbors and formed a client military force, the Contras, to overthrow the government, Reagan sidestepped a potentially defining battle with Congress. Rather than accepting congressionally imposed limits on his powers and telling the American people whom to blame, he allowed his National Security Council (NSC) to stage the egregious Iran-Contra affair that in the classic phrase was "worse than a crime, it was a blunder." The president should have accepted the rule of law and let the American people judge the outcome. In the end, Reagan's reputation was saved by Colonel Oliver North, an NSC operative, who turned the public relations tables on the Congressional committee investigating the affair.

But in foreign policy too, the enduring legacy is most disappointing. George Bush came into office speaking about a New World Order, and everyone believed it, including the neoconservatives. The reason is that, like liberals, neoconservatives think morality is central to diplomacy, regard all setbacks as temporary delays on the road to the New Jerusalem, and are sure that there is some way to ensure lasting peace. And so the idea that Peace Through Superior Firepower had worked under Nixon and Reagan, and might have prevented World War I and World War II, as well as Korea, Vietnam and most of the Cold War, struck them as an interesting reflection on the past, not a permanent lesson about an imperfect world. Times have changed, they declared, and now we will have a U.N.-led, moral, nation-rebuilding force that will quash Saddam Hussein's invasion of Kuwait but not strike at him, and that will bring peace and plenty, and social justice to other global trouble spots. Yet here, too, Reagan must bear some of the blame. To paraphrase Lincoln, the neo-conservatives were not so much with him as he was with them. For Reagan believed in an almost Wilsonian crusade to spread democracy; he was just clearer than Woodrow Wilson on the need to use force to do it.

Here the truly conservative policy was not that of Reagan, even rhetorically, but of Richard Nixon, who agreed that the Soviets were evil but insisted that this was irrelevant. Perfect peace, Nixon told us, is found only at the typewriter and in the grave; elsewhere a messy, bloody perpetual chaos prevails, in which the interests of nations objectively understood really are in conflict, disputes can only be managed, not solved, and one must have a sense of the limits of the possible. And in this view, the job of the president of the United States is to use a judicious blend of sticks and carrots to protect his country's national interest, not to play Boy Scout or Caped Crusader. Reagan never sold his Cold War this way (nor did Nixon succeed in selling his, despite his best efforts and the proof of his stunning successes). And for this Reagan bears some blame, since in misadventures like that in Lebanon in 1982, when he fell for the idea that sending a bunch of underarmed and improperly commanded marines into a millennia-long battle will produce peace. By the same token, the Reaganites portrayed the alternative in Nicaragua as communism versus democracy, when the situation was really much more complicated. Reagan did not accept the limits of U.S. power even in Central America and believed the U.S. government could transform lives and societies abroad, when all it can really do is defend the national interest. But, again, one must also blame those people who actually think government is the key to happiness and stumble around brandishing it and looking for the lock. So this battle was lost too, and, indeed, the fortress of pragmatic policymaking was not stormed by liberals but abandoned by conservatives. In the end this, too, was a loss by default.

In the hothouse intellectual atmosphere of the late 1970s, the election of Ronald Reagan seemed about as likely, and about as desirable, as a T. Rex dropping by for dinner. And by the terms of that debate, Reagan while in office starved the poor, ate black single moms, and killed us all in a nuclear war, or would have done all these things if it weren't for Mikhail Gorbachev.

In reality, Reagan's presidency represented a rhetorical vacillation between smaller government and better government, with a policy emphasis on the latter. He failed to disentangle the state from the economy as he had intended. He faced many political obstacles along the way, but the absence of a legacy is more the product of lack of resolve and conviction than it is of political difficulties. In the broader sense he did not reverse a nation in decline. Despite the alarmed rhetoric of modern liberals, he did not bring conservatism to Washington even temporarily. He talked like a conservative, governed like a neoconservative, and left liberalism in America as strong as or stronger than it had been in 1981.

The great fear of the Founding Fathers had been of liberty lost to a gilded cage, self-reliance undermined for luxury, the state buying the freedom of the people with their own money. A true conservative regards this process as well-advanced in the United States, and its undoing as crucial to the nation's future. Reagan did nothing effective to stop it, partly for political and partly for intellectual reasons, and most of his policies would have horrified the "radical" Thomas Jefferson almost as much as the conservative George Washington. Under Ronald Reagan the "managerial state" turned back a largely rhetorical assault and prevented a true conservative revolution from taking place. Progressive values triumphed in the 1992 election, and they did so because they continued to triumph among the electorate.

SELECTED BIBLIOGRAPHY

Anderson, Martin. *Revolution.* New York: Harcourt Brace Jovanovich, 1988. A very favorable account of the Reagan administration and of Reagan himself.
Barnet, Richard J. *Real Security: Restoring American Power in a Dangerous Decade.* New York: Touchstone, 1981. A superb, but totally wrong, New Left account of American diplomacy.
Carter, Jimmy. *Keeping Faith: Memoirs of a President.* New York: Bantam Books, 1982. Carter's account of his own presidency, showing his episodic rather than patterned perception of international affairs.
Divine, Robert. *Since 1945: Politics and Diplomacy in Recent American History.* 3d.

edition. New York: Alfred A. Knopf, 1985. The best brief introduction to the period, with an interpretation that is sensible, but not intrusive.

Friedman, Milton, and Rose Friedman. *Free to Choose.* New York: Avon Books, 1981. The authors are as responsible as anyone for rehabilitating *laissez faire* economics in the United States.

Frum, David. *Dead Right.* New York: New Republic Books, 1994. Devastating critique of conservatism in the Reagan period.

Gaddis, John Lewis. *Strategies of Containment: A Critical Appraisal of Postwar American National Security Policy.* New York: Oxford University Press, 1982. Demonstrates, among other things, the differences between Democratic and Republican foreign policy.

Galbraith, John Kenneth. *American Capitalism: The Concept of Countervailing Power.* Boston: Houghton Mifflin, 1952. Best book by the most influential liberal postwar theorist of why *laissez faire* was obsolete.

Gilder, George. *Wealth and Poverty.* New York: Bantam Books, 1982. Brilliant supply-side economic analysis of how and why big social programs cause economic and social disaster, especially for those they try to help.

Goldwater, Barry. *The Conscience of a Conservative.* New York: Hillman Books, 1960. An authentic conservative vision by the most conservative candidate to run for president since Calvin Coolidge and the individual who drew Reagan into elective politics.

Harrington, Michael. *The Other America: Poverty in the United States.* New York: Macmillan, 1994. Originally published in 1971, this book presents the intellectual foundations for the welfare state; good for background on the pre-Reagan era and for understanding the concept of the welfare state.

Hartz, Louis. *The Liberal Tradition in America: An Interpretation of American Political Thought since the Revolution.* New York: Harcourt Brace Jovanovich, 1955. Classic argument as to why there is no real conservatism in America, only classical liberalism.

Higgs, Robert. *Crisis and Leviathan: Critical Episodes in the Growth of American Government.* New York: Oxford University Press, 1987. Higgs argues that government gets bigger in every crisis and never gets smaller again. The Reagan presidency fits this pattern.

Matusow, Allen J. *The Unraveling of America: A History of Liberalism in the 1960s.* New York: Harper & Row, 1984. Excellent history of how, where, and why liberal ideas failed the test of practicality, as the "revolution" of the 1960s produced the opposite of what it had promised.

Mayer, Jane, and Doyle McManus. *Landslide: The Unmaking of the President, 1984–1988.* Boston: Houghton Mifflin, 1988. Study of Reagan's second term, with an extensive discussion of the Iran-Contra scandal.

Murray, Charles. *Losing Ground: American Social Policy, 1950–1980.* New York: Basic Books, 1984. A decisive intellectual and empirical refutation of the ideas behind the welfare state.

Rydenfelt, Sven. *A Pattern for Failure: Socialist Economies in Crisis.* San Diego, CA: Harcourt Brace Jovanovich, 1984. A Swedish economist argues that free market economies work better than socialism even in developing countries.

Schweizer, Peter. *Victory: The Reagan Administration's Secret Strategy that Hastened the Collapse of the Soviet Union.* New York: Atlantic Monthly Press, 1994. Highly favorable view of Reagan's diplomacy, showing it to be more complex, thorough, and sophisticated than most contemporary observers believed.

Tsongas, Paul. *The Road from Here: Liberalism and Realities in the 1980s.* New York: Vintage Books, 1982. Practical analysis of where liberalism should go in the 1980s, which was ignored by liberal politicians.

Tucker, William. *Vigilante: The Backlash against Crime in America.* New York: Stein & Day, 1985. Emphasizes the importance of crime as a contemporary political issue in America.

Vanderbilt Agrarians. *I'll Take My Stand: The South and the Agrarian Tradition.* Baton Rouge: Louisiana State University Press, 1977. Originally published in 1930, this book demonstrates that only in the South was there ever a truly conservative society.

Wanniski, Jude. *The Way the World Works.* New York: Simon and Schuster, 1983. A thorough presentation of the key economic theory behind the Reagan tax cuts.

Wills, Garry. *Reagan's America: Innocents at Home.* Garden City, NY: Doubleday, 1987. Comprehensive and critical view of Reagan and his presidency.

Appendix A

Glossary

Acheson, Dean (1893–1971). Secretary of State (1949–1953) under President Harry S Truman, Acheson was particularly influential in the formulation of policy during the height of Cold War tensions. He helped establish NATO and took much of the political blame for the "loss" of China to the Communists in 1949.

Arab Oil Embargo (1973–1974). The work of the Organization of Petroleum Exporting Countries (OPEC), this embargo was instituted in 1973 as a way of protesting Western support for Israel in the continuing Arab-Israeli dispute. When the embargo was lifted in 1974, Western nations found themselves paying much more for imported oil.

"Bloom County." A popular comic strip of the 1980s that frequently lampooned contemporary political personalities and issues.

Bohlen, Charles E. (1904–1974). A prominent Cold War-era diplomat, Bohlen helped develop the Marshall Plan and was ambassador to the Soviet Union from 1953 to 1957.

Bolsheviks. Followers of Lenin within the Russian Social Democratic party, the Bolsheviks captured control of Russia in November 1917 and created the Soviet Union.

Buckley, William F., Jr. (b. 1926). A prominent conservative spokesman, Buckley is the founder and publisher of *National Review*, an influential political magazine.

Calhoun, John C. (1782–1850). Calhoun, from South Carolina, was at various times a U.S. representative, a U.S. senator, secretary of state, and vice president. He was best known for his avid support of states' rights, an important issue in the South before the Civil War.

Casus Belli. From the Latin, this phrase means "occasion of war" and refers to an act or event that brings on a war.

Comintern. A Bolshevik organization, formally known as the Third Communist International, that was created in 1919. The Comintern was, among other things, a vehicle for the spread of communism to other parts of the world. It was dissolved in 1943.

Communist Manifesto *(1848).* Written by Karl Marx (1818–1883) and Friedrich Engels (1820–1895), this document introduced the idea of "scientific socialism," but it had less influence on the Communist movement than did Marx's *Das Kapital.*

Cordon Sanitaire. A buffer zone of friendly nations protecting another nation from potential enemies. The phrase is sometimes used to describe the east central European nations separating the Soviet Union from western Europe during the Cold War.

Declaration on Liberated Europe (1945). A statement signed by the United States, Great Britain, and the Soviet Union at the Yalta Conference in early 1945 in which they agreed to work together to help those nations liberated from Nazi occupation become politically stable, presumably with some kind of representative government in power.

Du Bois, W.E.B. (1868–1963). One of the greatest civil rights leaders in the United States, Du Bois was instrumental in the founding of the National Association for the Advancement of Colored People (NAACP) in 1909. He took a more activist approach toward civil rights than his contemporary, Booker T. Washington, and wrote a number of important historical and sociological studies.

Equal Rights Amendment (ERA). A proposed constitutional amendment that would have guaranteed gender equality in all aspects of American life. Passed by Congress and sent to the states for ratification in 1972, the ERA failed to win acceptance in enough states to be added to the Constitution.

Evangelicals. A term used to describe believers in any of a number of Protestant denominations that accept the literal truth of the Bible. In recent years, the term has been applied to people who support the notion that religion should play a greater role in American political life.

Goldwater, Barry (b. 1909). A U.S. Senator from Arizona, Goldwater was the Republican candidate for president in 1964. He is best known for his unabashed conservative views in support of free enterprise, a strong military establishment, and vigilant anticommunism.

Gross National Product (GNP). A figure representing the total value of all goods and services a nation produces in a year.

Haymarket Riot (1886). At a labor rally in Haymarket Square, Chicago, on May 4, 1886, a bomb exploded, provoking a panic in which seven policemen were killed and many people were injured. Eight rioters were convicted of murder, and the labor movement was severely discredited.

Homestead Strike (1892). This strike at the Carnegie Steel Company in Homestead, Pennsylvania, resulted in a number of deaths when strikers and Pinkerton detectives, hired by management, battled each other until state militia troops restored order and broke the strike.

Hopkins, Harry (1890–1946). One of Franklin D. Roosevelt's most important advisers, Hopkins directed the huge Works Progress Administration (1935–1938) and served as secretary of commerce (1938–1941). During World War II, he directed Lend-Lease and assisted Roosevelt at wartime diplomatic meetings.

Houston, Charles (1895–1950). After serving as dean of Howard University Law School, Houston became chief counsel for the NAACP and, with Thurgood Marshall, brought suit against a number of segregated law and other professional schools in the 1930s and 1940s. These cases were important forerunners to *Brown* v. *Board of Education of Topeka* (1954).

Hungarian Revolution (1956). In October 1956, anti-Communist groups in Hungary demanded the removal of a Stalinist president and Soviet troops. Although the Soviets initially complied, they soon changed their minds and sent the troops back into Hungary, brutally crushing the revolt. Western powers, then involved in the Suez crisis, could do nothing to help the Hungarians.

Hussein, Saddam (b. 1935). The military dictator of Iraq, whose occupation of Kuwait in August 1990 provoked the Persian Gulf War the following year.

If Christ Came to Chicago *(1893).* In this book, William T. Stead, an Englishman, described the sinful condition of Chicago in the 1890s; the book's popularity led to the formation of the Civic Federation, which worked to clean up the city.

Kemp, Jack (b. 1935). As a young man, Kemp was a professional football quarterback. In 1970, he was elected to Congress as a Republican from New York; in the 1980s, he served as secretary of housing and urban development and achieved prominence as a moderate Republican.

Keynes, John Maynard (1883–1946). A British economist and Labour party politician who believed that state spending on such things as public works could revive a depressed economy. Keynesian economics were influential in the New Deal.

Khmer Rouge. A Communist faction in Cambodia which came to power in 1975 after a five-year civil war against the pro-U.S. government of Lon Nol. In power, the Khmer Rouge were brutal and oppressive, killing a substantial portion of the population before they were overthrown by Vietnamese forces in 1979.

Khrushchev, Nikita S. (1894–1971). As first secretary of the Communist party, Khrushchev was the leader of the Soviet Union from 1954 until 1964. Generally, he pursued a policy of peaceful coexistence with the West and was more flexible in domestic policy than Stalin had been.

Knowland, William (1908–1974). A U.S. senator from California (1945–1958) and publisher of the *Oakland Tribune* (1965–1974), Knowland led Senate Republicans in denouncing the Truman administration for "losing" China in 1949 and for following a weak policy with respect to international communism.

League of Nations (1920–1946). This international organization, a forerunner of the United Nations, was created in the Treaty of Versailles (1919). Functioning in between the two World Wars, the League of Nations accomplished very little of a lasting nature and was useless in preventing the onset of World War II.

Lippmann, Walter (1889–1974). Lippman was one of America's most prominent journalists and political commentators for more than forty years. Over the years, he became more conservative and less optimistic, but he was always thoughtful and articulate in expressing his views.

Marshall, Thurgood (1908–1992). An associate justice of the U.S. Supreme Court from 1967 to 1991, Marshall first achieved prominence as a lawyer for the NAACP, arguing such cases as *Brown* v. *Board of Education of Topeka* (1954), which advanced the cause of equal rights for black people. On the Supreme Court, he continued to press for the protection of individual rights.

Morgenthau, Hans J. (1904–1980). A noted political scientist, Morgenthau espoused the "realist" approach to foreign policy, arguing that nations acted according to their self-interest in international affairs. Morgenthau, who emigrated to the United States from Germany in 1937, was a strong opponent of U.S. involvement in Vietnam.

Moynihan, Daniel Patrick (b. 1927). Moynihan achieved a certain notoriety in the 1960s for advocating "benign neglect" with respect to racial and urban problems. He served as ambassador to India and to the United Nations before his election as a Democratic Senator from New York in 1976.

My Lai (1968). The name of the Vietnamese hamlet where, in March 1968, the most publicized U.S. atrocity of the Vietnam War took place. Under the command of Lieutenant William Calley, U.S. troops killed more than two hundred unarmed civilians, including many women and children.

National Association for the Advancement of Colored People (NAACP). Organized in 1910, the NAACP was for many years the most prominent civil rights organization, attempting to win equal rights for blacks through education, lobbying activities, and court cases.

Nazi-Soviet Nonaggression Pact (1939). This treaty between Germany and the Soviet Union pledged each country to remain neutral in a conflict involving the other. The treaty also provided for a division of Poland if war did come. The German invasion of the Soviet Union in June 1941 effectively nullified the treaty.

Niagara Movement (1905). Under the leadership of W.E.B. Du Bois, a group of blacks interested in securing equal rights met in 1905 at Niagara Falls, Canada. They incorporated themselves as the Niagara Movement and met annually at different locations until they were merged into the NAACP in 1910.

Niebuhr, Reinhold (1892–1971). A leading American Protestant thinker with an international reputation for ecumenical dialogue, Niebuhr also spoke out frequently on political issues, denouncing Nazism and U.S. isolationism in the 1930s and communism after World War II.

Nixon Doctrine (1969). Pronounced by President Richard M. Nixon in 1969, this held that while the United States would continue to provide nuclear protection and military assistance to Asia, U.S. ground troops would not be used in any future Asian war, unless existing treaty obligations mandated their use. In 1971, the doctrine was extended to Iran.

Office of Economic Stabilization. This federal agency was created in 1942 to stabilize wages and control the cost of living in the United States during World War II. Its first director was James F. Byrnes.

Office of Price Administration (OPA). Created in 1941, this federal agency handled price controls, rent controls, and rationing of a number of basic commodities in the United States during World War II.

O'Neill, Thomas P. (TIP) (1912–1994). A U.S. representative from Massachusetts from 1953 to 1987, O'Neill capped his career as Speaker of the House from 1977 to 1987. He was known as a consummate politician with a vast knowledge of congressional procedure.

Open Door Policy (1899–1900). Strictly speaking, this was a diplomatic policy, developed by Secretary of State John Hay, designed to protect Chinese territorial integrity and access to trade in China. Since 1900, the phrase has occasionally been used to describe the U.S. desire to have trade access anywhere in the world.

Panama Canal Treaties (1977). These two treaties between the United States and Panama provided for Panama to assume full control of canal operations by the year 2000 and for the canal to be permanently neutral. The United States agreed to help Panama defend the canal's neutrality. The U.S. Senate ratified the treaties in 1978 after a long and contentious debate.

Plessy *v.* Ferguson *(1896).* A U.S. Supreme Court decision that established the legality of the principle that public facilities, such as schools, could be segregated, as long as the separate facilities were equal.

Populism. An agrarian-based reform movement of the 1890s that grew out of farmers' discontent with discriminatory railroad practices, among other things. The Populist party ran a candidate for president in 1892 but joined with the Democrats in 1896 and never regained its independent identity. Many of its ideas, however, found new life in the Progressive movement.

Potsdam Conference (1945). Conference held near Berlin shortly after the German surrender ending World War II in Europe. President Harry S Truman, Premier Joseph Stalin, and Prime Minister Winston Churchill (replaced in mid-conference by Clement Attlee) discussed reparations and German occupation issues.

Progress and Poverty *(1879).* Written by Henry George (1839–1897), this best-selling book set forth the argument that since increases in land values were not the result of work by landlords, this "wealth" should be taxed. A "single tax" on land would allow for the elimination of all other taxes. George's ideas were popular and influential at the end of the nineteenth century.

Pullman Strike (1894). This bloody strike began after George Pullman, owner of the Pullman Sleeping Car Company, lowered wages during the depression of the 1890s. The American Railway Union supported the strike, which spread across the nation and was broken only by the use of federal troops.

Red Scare (1919–1920). Concern about the spread of the Bolshevik Revolution through the many immigrants of radical political beliefs led to a national fear of communism soon after World War I. The attorney general, A. Mitchell Palmer, attempted to exploit this fear for political purposes by rounding up and trying to deport suspected radical aliens. Renewed fear of communism after World War II culminated in the movement known as McCarthyism.

Roe *v.* Wade *(1973).* This Supreme Court decision legalizing most abortions has led to a sustained political controversy pitting the right of a woman to choose whether to bear a child against the right of the unborn to be born.

Salt I (1972). SALT stands for Strategic Arms Limitation Talks. This treaty between the United States and the Soviet Union was intended to limit the growth of nuclear arms and diminish the tensions of the Cold War.

Salt II (1979). This treaty, which built upon the arms limitation provisions of SALT I, was signed by representatives of the United States and the USSR, but was never ratified by the U.S. Senate in the wake of the Soviet invasion of Afghanistan in December 1979.

Suez Crisis (1956). Following the Egyptian nationalization of the Suez Canal, Israel, Great Britain, and France schemed to instigate a military operation that would bring the canal back to British and French management. United Nations intervention, with the support of the United States and the Soviet Union, doomed the plan and cost the perpetrators much influence in the region.

Taft, Robert A. (1889–1953). The son of President William Howard Taft, Robert Taft was a U.S. senator from Ohio (1938–1953) and a longtime Republican party leader, earning the nickname "Mr. Republican." On most issues he was staunchly conservative, although he favored international initiatives such as the Marshall Plan after World War II.

Third World. A term referring to those countries classified as developing or undeveloped. Many are former colonies, are nonwhite, and are located in the southern hemisphere.

T. Rex. Short for *tyrannosaurus rex,* a large and socially unacceptable dinosaur prominently featured in the movie *Jurassic Park.*

Trotsky, Leon (1879–1940). Lenin's partner in the successful Bolshevik revolution of 1917 and the creation of the USSR, Trotsky later fell out of favor with Stalin and lived in exile in Mexico until one of Stalin's agents assassinated him.

Tugwell, Rexford Guy (1891–1979). An original member of President Franklin D. Roosevelt's inner circle of advisers, known as the "brain trust," Tugwell was influential in formulating New Deal agricultural policy. Later, he was head of the New York City Planning Commission and governor of Puerto Rico.

United Nations Charter. The "constitution" of the United Nations, created at the end of World War II.

V-E Day (1945). The name given to the day (May 7) that Germany surrendered to Allied forces, marking the end of the war in Europe.

Victorian Era. A term referring to the years of the reign of Britain's Queen Victoria (1837–1901), when, on the surface at least, attitudes of high moral virtue prevailed.

Victory Program. A term referring to the program of military production that the Roosevelt administration proposed in January 1942, involving the building of thousands of planes, tanks, ships, and anti-aircraft guns.

Wallace, Henry A. (1888–1965). Henry Wallace was a key political figure in the 1930s and 1940s, serving as secretary of agriculture (1933–1940) and vice president (1941–1945). Very liberal in his views, he broke with the Democratic party in 1948 and ran for president on the Progressive party ticket, advocating a much more conciliatory policy toward the Soviet Union.

Warren, Earl (1891–1974). Chief justice of the U.S. Supreme Court from 1953 until 1969, Warren headed a court that broke new ground in the area of individual rights. *Brown* v. *Board of Education of Topeka* (1954) overturned *Plessy* v. *Ferguson* (1896) and may be said to have begun the civil rights movement, while other important decisions dealt with voting rights and criminal suspect rights.

Washington, Booker T. (1856–1915). The most prominent black American of the turn-of-the-century period, Washington headed the Tuskegee Institute, a black school in Alabama, for many years. He argued that blacks would be better off striving for economic gains rather than political or social equality, a viewpoint which many whites accepted but which other black leaders, such as W.E.B. Du Bois, rejected.

Watergate (1972–1974). A political scandal during the presidency of Richard M. Nixon, which broke when burglars were caught in Democratic party headquarters located in the Watergate apartment complex in Washington D.C. After more than two years of congressional and criminal investigation, many of Nixon's associates had been convicted of various crimes and Nixon himself was forced to resign from the presidency.

Xenophobia. A word that means hatred of strangers or (especially) foreigners, most particularly those who look different or hold different political or cultural views.

Appendix B

Timeline

1900	Carrie Nation begins raiding saloons
	Boxer rebellion in China threatens foreigners
1901	President McKinley assassinated
	Hay-Pauncefote Treaty clears way for United States to build Panama Canal
1903	Wright brothers make first powered flight
	Panama Canal Treaty signed with newly independent Panama
	Wisconsin initiates first direct primary voting system
1904	Roosevelt Corollary authorizes United States intervention in Latin America
	Ida Tarbell publishes *History of the Standard Oil Company*
1906	Roosevelt signs Pure Food and Drug Act
	San Francisco earthquake and fire
1907	Great White Fleet leaves on round-the-world cruise
1908	Henry Ford introduces Model T car
1909	Peary reaches North Pole
1911	Supreme Court dissolves Standard Oil Company

1912	Arizona and New Mexico become states
	Titanic sinks
1913	Federal Reserve System authorized
	First income tax imposed as part of Underwood Tariff Act
1914	Archduke Franz Ferdinand assassinated; World War I begins
	Panama Canal finished
1915	*Lusitania* sunk by German torpedo; 128 Americans killed
	Panama-Pacific International Exposition in San Francisco
1916	Montana voters send first woman to U.S. House of Representatives
1917	Zimmermann telegram fosters anti-German feelings in United States
	United States enters World War I
	Bolsheviks come to power in new Soviet Union
1918	Fourteen Points presented by Wilson as guideline for peace
	Armistice ends fighting in World War I
1919	Eighteenth Amendment (Prohibition) ratified
	Treaty of Versailles formally ends World War I
1920	Nineteenth Amendment (Woman Suffrage) ratified
	Senate defeats League of Nations membership
	First commercial radio broadcast
	Black Sox scandal revealed
1921	Emergency Quota Act, limiting immigration, passed
1922	Washington Naval Arms Conference
1923	Equal Rights Amendment first introduced in Congress
1924	Teapot Dome scandal revealed
1925	John Scopes found guilty of teaching evolution
	Rudolph Valentino dies suddenly
1926	Florida land boom collapses
	United States celebrates its sesquicentennial
1927	Sacco and Vanzetti executed
	Lindbergh flies solo across Atlantic

1928	Kellogg-Briand Pact outlaws war as an instrument of national policy
1929	Stock market crash; Great Depression begins
1930	Smoot-Hawley Tariff Act raises tariff levels
1931	Manchurian crisis threatens Asian peace
1932	Bonus Army marches on Washington
1933	FDR's New Deal begins
	Good Neighbor Policy initiated with Latin America
	Hitler comes to power in Germany
	Twenty-first Amendment ends Prohibition
	United States goes off gold standard
	A Century of Progress Exposition held in Chicago
1934	Federal Communications Act passed to regulate radio
	Nye Committee studies reasons for U.S. entry in World War I
1935	Social Security Act
	Wagner Act gives organized labor new rights
	Congress of Industrial Organizations (CIO) established
	First Neutrality Act attempts to keep United States out of international crises
1936	Spanish Civil War begins
	Edward VIII abdicates British crown
1937	Major flooding along Ohio River
	FDR attempts to pack Supreme Court
	Neutrality Act extended and broadened
	World War II begins in Asia
1938	Fair Labor Standards Law sets twenty-five cents per hour minimum wage
1939	World War II begins in Europe
	First commercial television broadcast in United States
	New York World's Fair celebrates technology and the future
1940	France falls to Nazi forces
	Congress approves first peacetime draft
1941	Lend-Lease Act provides war supplies to allies

Germany invades the USSR

Pearl Harbor attacked

United States enters World War II

1942   Civilian auto production ceases

Rationing of gasoline and other commodities begins

Battle of Midway blunts Japanese naval offensive

1943   Teheran Conference brings allied leaders together

War contractors barred from racial discrimination

1944   G.I. Bill of Rights provides education benefits to veterans

D-Day marks beginning of allied offensive in France

Bretton Woods Conference plans postwar economic
        reconstruction

1945   Yalta Conference deals with postwar political questions

Atomic bombs dropped on Japan

World War II ends

United Nations Charter approved; UN begins operations

Chicago Cubs win their last National League pennant

1946   Churchill speaks of "Iron Curtain"

Philippines given independence

Atomic Energy Commission established

1947   Taft-Hartley Act restricts certain labor activities

Truman Doctrine extends aid to Greece and Turkey

Marshall Plan proposed to aid European reconstruction

Jackie Robinson breaks major league baseball's color line

1948   Berlin blockade and airlift

United Nations creates independent state of Israel

Organization of American States (OAS) established

1949   North Atlantic Treaty Organization (NATO) formed

China falls to Communists

1950   Korean War begins; command given to General Douglas
        MacArthur

"McCarthyism," or anti-Communist movement in United
        States, begins

U.S. involvement in Vietnam begins

1951	President Truman fires General MacArthur for insubordination
1952	United States detonates first H-Bomb
	More than six million television sets produced
1953	Truce ends Korean War
	Ethel and Julius Rosenberg executed as atomic spies
1954	Joseph McCarthy censured by Senate
	Atomic Energy Act passed
	Rock 'n' roll music introduced on radio
	Brown v. *Board of Education of Topeka* decision launches modern civil rights movement
	Southeast Asia Treaty Organization (SEATO) created
	Domino Theory spelled out by President Eisenhower
1955	AFL and CIO merge
	Warsaw Pact formed as eastern bloc counter to NATO
	Rosa Parks begins Montgomery bus boycott
1956	Suez Crisis aids nationalistic movements in Middle East
	Hungarian revolt tests Communist solidarity
1957	Little Rock Central High School incident
	Sputnik flight begins space age
1958	John Birch Society founded
1959	Fidel Castro comes to power in Cuba
	Mercury Seven astronauts selected
	Television quiz shows investigated
1960	U-2 incident damages U.S.-Soviet relations
	OPEC formed to control international sale of petroleum
	Lunch counter sit-ins begin in the South
	First televised presidential campaign debates
1961	United States sends first American into space
	Berlin Wall constructed
	Bay of Pigs invasion in Cuba pushes Castro toward Moscow
	McDonald's restaurant chain established
1962	Cuban Missile Crisis

Century 21 International Exposition in Seattle

1963   March on Washington highlights civil rights movement

Betty Friedan publishes *The Feminine Mystique*

John F. Kennedy assassinated

Partial Nuclear Test Ban Treaty signed

First commercial nuclear reactor becomes operational

Satellite television transmission begins

1964   Civil Rights Act desegregates public accommodations

Tonkin Gulf Resolution authorizes U.S. combat in Vietnam

Beatles make first U.S. appearance

1965   U.S. combat role begins in Vietnam

Medicare provides health care assistance for elderly

Voting Rights Act

1966   National Organization of Women (NOW) formed

1967   Six-Day War in Middle East

Thurgood Marshall becomes first black Supreme Court justice

1968   Tet offensive marks turning point in Vietnam War

Martin Luther King, Jr., assassinated

Robert Kennedy assassinated

Nuclear Non-Proliferation Treaty approved by UN

1969   United States lands men on the moon

United States begins gradual withdrawal of troops from Vietnam

1970   Cambodian incursion

Beginning of detente, a friendlier relationship with the Soviet Union

First Earth Day celebration

1971   Laos incursion

Pentagon Papers, detailing early Vietnam policy, published

Cigarette advertising banned from television

1972   SALT I Treaty signed with Soviet Union

Nixon goes to China

Massacre of Israeli athletes at Munich Olympics

	Congress passes Equal Rights Amendment
1973	Paris Peace Agreement ends U.S. involvement in Vietnam
	Yom Kippur War between Israel and Arab neighbors
	Vice President Spiro T. Agnew forced to resign
	Arab oil embargo
	Roe v. *Wade* decision legalizes most abortions
1974	Nixon resigns
1975	Fall of Saigon marks end of Vietnam War
	Apollo-Soyuz joint US-USSR space mission
	Videocassette recorders (VCRs) introduced in U.S. market
1976	United States celebrates its bicentennial
	Viking I unmanned spacecraft lands on Mars
1977	Carter pardons draft evaders
	Elvis Presley dies
1978	Camp David accords between Egypt and Israel
	Panama Canal treaties ratified
1979	Beginning of Iranian hostage crisis
	Soviet invasion of Afghanistan ends detente
	SALT II signed
	Three Mile Island nuclear plant accident
1980	Iran-Iraq War begins
	Solidarity movement begins in Poland
1981	Iran frees American hostages
	Intermediate Nuclear Force (INF) talks start in Geneva
	Sandra Day O'Connor becomes first female Supreme Court justice
	Congress approves major tax cut
	U.S. intervention in Nicaragua and El Salvador
1982	Falkland Islands War between Great Britain and Argentina
	START talks begin in Geneva
	Knoxville [Tenn.] World's Fair
1983	USSR shoots down Korean jetliner
	Truck bomb kills 241 Americans in Beirut, Lebanon
	U.S. invades Grenada

1984	U.S. withdraws troops from Lebanon
1985	*Achille Lauro* hijacked by Arab terrorists
	Mikhail Gorbachev becomes leader of Soviet Union
1986	U.S. bombs Libya
	Reagan-Gorbachev summit in Reykjavik
	Challenger space shuttle disaster
	Iran-Contra affair revealed
1987	Intermediate Nuclear Force (INF) treaty signed
1988	Reagan-Gorbachev summit in Moscow
	U.S. cruiser *Vincennes* shoots down Iranian airliner
1989	Berlin Wall falls
	Exxon Valdez causes largest oil spill in U.S. history
	U.S. intervenes in Panama to apprehend Manuel Noriega on drug trafficking charges
1990	Germany reunified
	Congress passes Americans with Disabilities Act
1991	Persian Gulf War liberates Kuwait
	USSR collapses
1992	European Community achieves full economic integration
1993	Apartheid in South Africa ends
	Israeli-Palestinian peace accords
	North American Free Trade Agreement (NAFTA) signed
	World Trade Center [New York] bombed
1994	Jean-Bertrand Aristide returned to Haitian presidency
	Israel-Jordan peace accord
	World Series cancelled due to baseball strike
	Republicans capture control of both houses of Congress
1995	Federal building in Oklahoma City bombed

Appendix C

Presidents, Vice Presidents, and Secretaries of State in the Twentieth Century

President	Vice President	Secretary of State
Theodore Roosevelt (1901–1909)	Charles Fairbanks (1901–1909)	John Hay (1901–1905)
		Elihu Root (1905–1909)
		Robert Bacon (1909)
William Howard Taft (1909–1913)	James S. Sherman (1909–1913)	Philander C. Knox (1909–1913)
Woodrow Wilson (1913–1921)	Thomas R. Marshall (1913–1921)	William Jennings Bryan (1913–1915)
		Robert Lansing (1915–1920)
		Bainbridge Colby (1920–1921)
Warren G. Harding (1921–1923)	Calvin Coolidge (1921–1923)	Charles E. Hughes (1921–1923)
Calvin Coolidge (1923–1929)	Charles G. Dawes (1925–1929)	Charles E. Hughes (1923–1925)
		Frank B. Kellogg (1925–1929)
Herbert C. Hoover (1929–1933)	Charles Curtis (1929–1933)	Henry L. Stimson (1929–1933)
Franklin D. Roosevelt (1933–1945)	John Nance Garner (1933–1941)	Cordell Hull (1933–1944)
	Henry A. Wallace (1941–1945)	Edward R. Stettinius, Jr. (1944–1945)

President	Vice President	Secretary of State
	Harry S Truman (1945)	
Harry S Truman (1945–1953)	Alben W. Barkley (1949–1953)	Edward R. Stettinius, Jr. (1944–1945)
		James F. Byrnes (1945–1947)
		George C. Marshall (1947–1949)
		Dean G. Acheson (1949–1953)
Dwight D. Eisenhower (1953–1961)	Richard M. Nixon (1953–1961)	John Foster Dulles (1953–1959)
		Christian A. Herter (1959–1961)
John F. Kennedy (1961–1963)	Lyndon B. Johnson (1961–1963)	Dean Rusk (1961–1969)
Lyndon B. Johnson (1963–1969)	Hubert H. Humphrey (1965–1969)	Dean Rusk (1961–1969)
Richard M. Nixon (1969–1974)	Spiro T. Agnew (1969–1973)	William P. Rogers (1969–1973)
	Gerald R. Ford (1973–1974)	Henry Kissinger (1973–1977)
Gerald R. Ford (1974–1977)	Nelson A. Rockefeller (1974–1977)	Henry Kissinger (1973–1977)
James E. Carter (1977–1981)	Walter Mondale (1977–1981)	Cyrus A. Vance (1977–1980)
		Edmund S. Muskie (1980–1981)
Ronald W. Reagan (1981–1989)	George H.W. Bush (1981–1989)	Alexander M. Haig, Jr. (1981–1982)
		George P. Shultz (1982–1989)
George H.W. Bush (1989–1993)	J. Danforth Quayle (1989–1993)	James A. Baker, 3d (1989–1992)
		Lawrence Eagleburger (1992–1993)
William J. Clinton (1993–)	Albert Gore (1993–)	Warren M. Christopher (1993–)

Index

About the Editors and Contributors

THOMAS CLARKIN is completing his dissertation on civil rights during the Lyndon Johnson presidency at the University of Texas and has also written on the Bakke case.

JOHN E. FINDLING is professor of history at Indiana University Southeast. He received his Ph.D. in history from the University of Texas and is the author of *Dictionary of American Diplomatic History* (1980, 1989), *Close Neighbors, Distant Friends: United States–Central American Relations* (1987), and *Chicago's Great World's Fairs* (1994). With Kimberly D. Pelle, he edited *Historical Dictionary of World's Fairs and Expositions, 1851–1988* (1990) and *Historical Dictionary of the Modern Olympic Movement* (1996); and, with Frank W. Thackeray, he edited *Statesmen Who Changed the World* (1993) and *Events That Changed the World in the Twentieth Century* (1995).

ANDERS GREENSPAN received his Ph.D. from Indiana University. His dissertation dealt with the restoration of Colonial Williamsburg, and he has written several papers on the Great Depression. Teaching posts have included Indiana University, Anderson College, Franklin College, and Bowling Green State University.

LAURA HAGUE is a doctoral student at the University of Texas, working on the conservation policies of the Lyndon Johnson administration and the history of conservation in general.

JAMES W. KUNETKA is a professional writer and educational consultant residing in Austin, Texas. He is the author of *City of Fire: Los Alamos and the Atomic Age, 1943–1945* (1978) and *Oppenheimer: The Years of Risk* (1982) and the coauthor of a novel, *WarDay* (1985).

DAVID MAYERS is associate professor of history and political science at Boston University. He is the author of *Cracking the Monolith: U.S. Policy against the Sino-Soviet Alliance, 1949–1955* (1986) and *George Kennan and the Dilemmas of U.S. Foreign Policy* (1988).

JERRY A. PATTENGALE is associate director of the Scriptorium Center for Christian Antiquities in Grand Haven, Michigan. He contributed to the *Historical Dictionary of the Modern Olympic Movement* (1996) and formerly taught at Azusa Pacific University.

JOHN ROBSON, a native of Canada, earned his Ph.D. at the University of Texas and is a policy analyst for the Fraser Institute in Vancouver, British Columbia. He is the editor of *The NAFTA Network* (1993) and other studies for the Fraser Institute.

JAMES E. ST. CLAIR is assistant professor of journalism at Indiana University Southeast. A former newspaper editor, he is the coauthor of a forthcoming biography of former Supreme Court Justice Sherman Minton.

FRANK W. THACKERAY is professor of history at Indiana University Southeast. He received his Ph.D. from Temple University and was a Fulbright scholar in Poland. The author of *Antecedents of Revolution: Alexander I and the Polish Congress Kingdom* (1980), he also published several articles on Russian-Polish relations in the nineteenth century and Polish-American relations in the twentieth century. With John E. Findling, he edited *Statesmen Who Changed the World* (1993) and *Events That Changed the World in the Twentieth Century* (1995).

LARRY THORNTON is associate professor of history at Hanover College. He received his Ph.D. from the University of Illinois and is the author of articles on human rights and a contributor to *Events That Changed the World in the Twentieth Century* (1995).

JACOB VANDER MEULEN is assistant professor of history at Dalhousie University in Halifax, Nova Scotia. He received his Ph.D. from the University of Toronto and is the author of *The Politics of Aircraft: Building an American Military Industry* (1991) and *Who Built the B-29?* (1995).